ICE STORM

The Rise and Fall

of the Greatest

Vancouver Canucks

Team Ever

ICE STORM

BRUCE DOWBIGGIN

GREYSTONE BOOKS

Vancouver/Berkeley

Greystone Books Ltd.
www.greystonebooks.com
Cataloguing data available from Library and Archives Canada
ISBN 978-1-77164-131-9 (pbk.)
ISBN 978-1-77164-132-6 (ebook)

Copy editing by Lloyd David
Cover design by Peter Cocking
Text design by Nayeli Jimenez
Cover photograph by John Sherlock
Cover model: Peter Cocking
Printed and bound in Canada by Friesens
Distributed in the U.S. by Publishers Group West

We gratefully acknowledge the financial support of the Canada
Council for the Arts, the British Columbia Arts Council, the
Province of British Columbia through the Book Publishing Tax
Credit, and the Government of Canada through the Canada Book
Fund for our publishing activities.

Greystone Books is committed to reducing the consumption
of old-growth forests in the books it publishes.
This book is one step towards that goal.

CONTENTS

I know you've taken it in the teeth out there, but the first guy through the wall ... It always gets bloody, always. It's the threat, and not just the way of doing business, but in their minds it's threatening the game. But really what it's threatening is their livelihoods, it's threatening their jobs, it's threatening the way that they do things.

BOSTON RED SOX OWNER JOHN HENRY, as portrayed by Arliss Howard in the movie *Moneyball*

INTRODUCTION

Canucktivity

THE HALLWAY OUTSIDE the visitors' dressing room at Rogers Arena in Vancouver can accommodate, at best, two hockey players passing each other. "Snug" might best describe the cramped space. Between the first and second periods on the night of January 18, 2014, the narrow passageway looked like the scene of an attempt to see how many hockey people could be stuffed into a very tiny space. A television camera mounted in the ceiling caught the riotous scene as Vancouver Canucks coach John Tortorella paid an unexpected call to the Calgary Flames dressing room. It was not a cordial visit. Tortorella sizzled with rage. The sudden appearance of a rival coach drew many of the Flames players and personnel into the hallway. There were also a few more Canucks coaches, arena workers, and (maybe) one Vancouver player jammed into the melee. Experienced hockey viewers couldn't remember this much hallway chaos since the day New Jersey Devils coach Jim Schoenfeld accosted NHL referee Don Koharski during a 1988 playoff game with the immortal phrase, "You fat pig! Have another doughnut!"

Tortorella's impromptu visit was provoked by the starting lineup iced that night by Calgary coach Bob Hartley, a longtime Torts nemesis. Hartley had opened with his heavy cannons— Brian McGrattan, Kevin Westgarth, and Blair Jones—causing Tortorella to fight fire with fire, starting his own fourth line. The line matching produced a throwback brawl just two seconds into the game. Eight of the players on the ice were ejected from the game, including huge Vancouver rookie Kellan Lain, whose NHL debut lasted all of two seconds. At the Vancouver bench, Tortorella kept up a steady rant against Hartley, punctuated with finger-pointing and facial contortions. Hartley stood impassively behind the Calgary bench. The chippiness of the remaining nineteen minutes and fifty-eight seconds of the first period did little to calm down the voluble Canucks coach. So as the period ended, Tortorella made a beeline underneath the stands to the hallway outside the Flames dressing room, promising retribution (if he could get his hands on Hartley). A phalanx of Flames prevented Torts from advancing, leaving him like the kid in the lunchroom fight, struggling to land punches over a wall of humanity.

The scene went viral on the web. Media that never talked about hockey couldn't say enough about the donnybrook. Seattle Seahawk Richard Sherman, seeking to downplay his own verbal outburst at the end of the 2014 National Football Conference championship game, pointed out, "I saw a hockey game where they threw the puck aside and just started fighting. And I'm like, 'I'm the thug? Really?' "

To those familiar with Tortorella's act in his previous stops around the league, the outburst came as little surprise to opponents or media members. He'd been challenged under hockey's code, which demands an eye for an eye and a punch for a punch. And Torts is nothing if not a disciple of The Code. Adding to Tortorella's frustration, his team had been pounded 9-1 a few nights before in Anaheim, part of an epic losing streak that would eventually see the Canucks collapse from third place in

2

the Western Conference to playoff also-rans. His stewardship of the team that had been the league's best just two seasons before was failing. Injuries were racking the team. Torts's response: an outburst that he'd promised, upon being hired the previous summer, wouldn't happen.

Vancouver general manager Mike Gillis, himself a former NHL player who did any raging in private, understood Torts's motivation, if not his method. "Absolutely, I understand," Gillis told the Vancouver radio station The Team 1040. "He's an emotional guy who wears his heart on his sleeve. He was trying to right a wrong. You can't do that, but he was so angry with the situation we were faced with." The NHL took a dim view of Torts's frontal assault, summoning him across the continent on the red-eye to receive a fifteen-day suspension. At just the point when the faltering team needed its coach, the Canucks would have to play six games without him.

Torts's blowup also left many in the hockey world scratching their heads about the Canucks. The team that, under Gillis, had striven to be known for cool cunning was suddenly being compared to the Broad Street Bullies, the brawling Philadelphia teams of the 1970s. In 2013–14, the Canucks were at the top of the league in fights and feuding—just like a throwback NHL club. Where were the science and analytics that had characterized the Canucks' management since 2008? Where was the hip Left Coast attitude? Where was Gillis's quiet hockey revolution that seemed unstoppable in the 2011 playoffs?

Where indeed? Within two months of the Calgary carnage, Tortorella's actions would help precipitate a stunning collapse, consigning the team's unparalleled success over the previous five years to the rubbish bin of team history. A city that had twice rioted over its team losing the Stanley Cup would suffer another fainting spell over the club's dispiriting demise in 2014. The Canucks' owners would be so alarmed by what a "lynch mob" mentality was doing to their brand that they fired the most

3

successful GM in club history and sought out the most popular former player, one with no hockey executive experience, to calm what was described as "a toxic waste spill," leaving Mike Gillis's once-celebrated Canucktivity experiment as collateral damage.

MY FIRST EXPOSURE to Mike Gillis came in a Toronto courtroom, where I stared at the back of his head for about six weeks in 1996. I had been tipped off that someone might finally get Gillis's former agent and union leader, Alan Eagleson, to testify under oath about his controversial activities as executive director of the National Hockey League Players' Association and director of international play for Hockey Canada for the previous quarter-century. So I left the radio studios of The Fan 590, where I was doing a show each morning with Steve Paikin, to hustle down to the University Avenue courtroom to watch the proceedings. Gillis was suing his former agent and friend for stealing $41,250 of his NHL disability insurance when he was forced into retirement by a badly broken leg. Eagleson had then countersued Gillis for $244,000.

Eagleson sat in his finely tailored suit that morning, his Order of Canada pin on his lapel, a faint smile playing across his lips, looking like a man who was sure he couldn't lose. And why not? He was a smooth operator who travelled first class (at others' expense). He had the ease of a man comfortable in his own skin—even though he was a fugitive from the U.S. justice system at that moment. "Who is Mike Gillis to challenge this icon?" his smirk seemed to say as he looked across the courtroom at his former client.

For the moment, Gillis was a struggling prospective lawyer living in Kingston, Ontario, locked in a grim struggle with the man he once considered a surrogate father after his own father, Patrick, passed away. Were Gillis to lose, he'd be in serious debt—and, perhaps worse, discredited as he launched his own post-playing career. In the incestuous, clannish world of the NHL, which believes it has little to learn from other sports, it was not a done thing for a player of modest accomplishments to take down the mighty Eagleson, whose best pals included John Ziegler, former president of the NHL; Chicago owner Bill Wirtz, chairman of the NHL's board of governors; John Turner, former prime minister; and John Sopinka, a justice of the Supreme Court of Canada. Launching a lawsuit of this type was tantamount to writing a suicide note in the hockey industry. That's why so many players who'd been ripped off by Eagleson chose silence.

Gillis had decided to fight. Then as now, he valued his independence and privacy. He and his wife, Diane, who had known each other since teenage years, were not showy people, preferring their family to the glitz and fortunes of a multibillion-dollar business such as the NHL. As it later became clear to the media and fans who follow the Canucks, he was not comfortable in the media spotlight. He didn't seek out the attention I was giving his case on my radio show and in my job at CBC Television. Years later, as he made his way through a Vancouver market or sat in one of the city's restaurants, he was unfailingly polite to well-wishers, even if their unbridled passion sometimes startled him. For Gillis, winning is important, but for the victory-starved Canuck fans, it is a religious experience, a burning desire to bring the city its first Stanley Cup championship since 1915.

This is my second book in which Gillis has been a central character. (The first was *Money Players,* a study of the 2004–05 NHL lockout.) His odyssey, from the obscurity of the Toronto courtroom in 1996 to the seventh game of the 2011 Stanley Cup final to the melodrama involving goalie Roberto Luongo, has been a compelling journey. That's because Gillis, like Oakland A's GM Billy Beane in *Moneyball,* constantly re-evaluated the state of play in his sport and business, asking, "Can we do better?" Even when his critics in the Vancouver and Toronto media mocked him for exploring new concepts, he put his faith in the unconventional concept called Canucktivity. "The one thing that Mike Gillis brings is

5

a real progressive outlook," former NHL coach Craig MacTavish told Edmonton's CHED radio. "He's looking for new and creative and innovative ways to give [himself] a competitive advantage."

The Canucks' owner, Francesco Aquilini, was of a similar mind, if not always a similar disposition, when they met in 2008. Aquilini is passionate where Gillis is cool. After the near-miss in the 2011 final, they did not always agree on philosophy. But Aquilini, too, seeks the same competitive edge. Many teams rolling in money would grow complacent, but Gillis and Aquilini took the opposite approach, hoping to blow open a gap between themselves and the competition if they could find unique methods of acquiring, signing, or drafting players. Their willingness to open new windows in a dark room made them a big target. Ironically, it was the mundane business of NHL contracts and soothing egos that later led to their schism.

Gillis's confidence and the Canucks' financial advantages were often misunderstood. The sangfroid was much praised when Gillis got the Canucks back to the playoffs and within one win of the Stanley Cup in 2011. At the same time, that ironclad confidence was mocked when Gillis refused to trade star goalie Luongo for less than market value. Many saw the self-assurance as arrogance, too much swagger. After the Canucks, who had finished first overall in the NHL in the regular season, were easily dispatched from the 2012 playoffs by the Los Angeles Kings, the eighth seed in the Western Conference, an anonymous Kings employee used the team's Twitter account to razz their opponents: "To everyone in Canada outside of BC, you're welcome."

"Same ol' Canucks. Divers and fakers. Why rest of country hates 'em," tweeted Damien Cox of the *Toronto Star,* whose column ran under the headline VANCOUVER CANUCKS COULD BE NHL'S MOST DESPISED TEAM. On the *Toronto Sun*'s website, it was the same: EVERYONE LOVES TO HATE THE CANUCKS.

There were no neutral viewpoints about Canucktivity. Here is why.

6

1

"The Most Arrogant Team"

"They've got a bunch of idiots over there."

DETROIT RED WINGS GOALIE JIMMY HOWARD

AN OLD CLICHÉ, sometimes attributed to Napoleon, says that history is written by the winners. In hockey terms, this maxim has no finer example than the 2011 Stanley Cup final, one of the meanest, nastiest final series in recent memory. The two teams, Vancouver and Boston, represented distinct philosophies of how the game should be played: "classic" versus "modern." The Bruins were a classic hockey team, a blend of skill and menace, proud successors to a Boston tradition that dated back almost a century to Eddie Shore. This included the presence of a player to police those opponents who might choose to take liberties against the Bruins' skill players.

The Canucks, however, were "neo" in all their functions— a highly skilled team that was long on agitation but eschewed goonery. Vancouver conspicuously lacked a policeman to intervene in matters of The Code, the unofficial system of NHL justice that functions in the manner that the Sopranos did in the eponymous TV show. They put their faith in the referees to call the games. To help in that process, they sometimes made a point of falling down when punched or reacting when otherwise abused—a cardinal sin against The Code. In a copycat league, the winner of the series would likely influence how the sport would be played thereafter.

The historical hinge came late in Game 6 of the 2011 Stanley Cup final. To the delight of ecstatic Boston fans at the TD Garden, the hometown Bruins were closing out the hated Canucks 5–2 to force a seventh game in Vancouver. Bruins fans hate all their team's opponents with a ferocious zeal, but they had reserved a special place for the Canucks after the first two games in Vancouver featured biting and taunting and resulted in a 2–0 series lead for the Canucks. A town that advertises its lunch-pail values, Boston found the Canucks a tad effete.

At 18:29 of the third period, after another close call in the Vancouver crease, the players began to jostle and shove. To the side of the net, Vancouver's Daniel Sedin, the NHL's scoring leader and one of the top half-dozen players in the league, was grabbed by pugnacious Boston rookie Brad Marchand, who had been a thorn in Vancouver's side the entire series. With the referees off in the corner breaking up another altercation, Marchand's left hand grabbed Sedin's collar. That allowed the Bruin to easily land a gloved punch to the right side of the Canuck star's face. It wasn't enough to injure Sedin; more like a rabbit punch, a rude jab to his pride. There was no reply from Sedin. Quickly, Marchand repeated the punch. Again, Sedin turned his head to absorb the blow. Seeing no resistance to his attack, Marchand landed another four blows in rapid succession, all without pushback.

It was a stunning act of disrespect for one of the stars of the NHL. A shocked Pierre McGuire of NBC, broadcasting from between the two teams' benches, didn't know how to describe this naked aggression. "You understand what he's doing, but for a guy who's got a reputation, that's not wise," said McGuire. What many, McGuire included, didn't know was that the Canucks had been told by management not to post-whistle scrums. Sedin was simply following or let the fireplug Marchand use his head as a speed bag. none of the punches was damaging, the cumulative effect left Sedin stunned and the TD Garden fans thrilled. After Marchand landed half a dozen punches, referee Kelly Sutherland finally took note and intervened. Canuck fans expected the veteran referee to talk sternly to rookie Marchand, who was taking advantage of Vancouver's lost-cause game to "send a message."

Instead, Sutherland had an animated conversation with Sedin. ("I asked him why he didn't call the penalty," Sedin told reporters in the subdued Vancouver dressing room. "He said he was going to.") Finally, the linesmen arrived to separate the pair; Sutherland issued a minor penalty to Marchand, a wrist tap in a game out of reach for the Canucks. Afterward, Marchand was asked why he abused the gentlemanly Sedin. "Because I felt like it," an insouciant Marchand replied. Why shouldn't he smile? He used garbage time in a game to get away with intimidating a star player. There was no supplemental discipline for Marchand, who took full advantage of his reprieve to score two goals in the Bruins' Cup-clinching triumph in Game 7.

The 2011 final had its defining image: a player with fewer than a hundred NHL games under his belt brazenly punching an unresisting superstar of the sport, the man who would barely miss out on the Hart Trophy as the MVP of the league. Imagine the reaction if an NFL rookie had used Tom Brady's head as a speed bag after a whistle or a role player had repeatedly punched NBA star Steve Nash as he headed to the bench. Likely, the impertinent young player would get a suspension, maybe as long as ten games by NBA standards. But in the NHL? Marchand was not suspended, and Sedin's Canucks were widely ridiculed for turning the other cheek, not dispensing instant justice to Marchand. Former player (and current Sportsnet TV analyst) Nick Kypreos summed up the hockey culture about the Swedish

9

twins. "If the Sedins would just push back, the referees would cut [them] a little slack," Kypreos told listeners, employing the pretzel logic that governs hockey justice. The Sedins, along with Toronto's Phil Kessel, were voted the "most easily intimidated" players in a *Sports Illustrated* poll.

The Canucks were certainly no angels, playing with a mouthy edge. Defenceman Aaron Rome's late check on Nathan Horton of the Bruins in Game 3 earned him a four-game suspension. But divine retribution? The Canucks' loss in seven games to Boston, said *Toronto Star* columnist Damien Cox, was an "admonishment from the hockey gods that if you don't play the game the right way, you may not get the ending you desire. That would be the story of the 2010-11 Vancouver Canucks, the team that looked poised to go wire-to-wire as the best squad in the sport but instead tried to dive and connive its way to a championship and choked on its own bile."

This biblical interpretation airbrushed a few inconvenient facts about the Bruins. There was Marchand's speed-bagging an opponent's head and Patrice Bergeron sticking his fingers into an opponent's mouth after a whistle, or Adam McQuaid pile-driving Mason Raymond into the boards till the Canuck forward's back broke. In Cox's interpretation, apparently, that was "playing the game the right way."

Cox had company. Some Canucks fans felt their club needed to push back hard when Daniel Sedin was boxed by Marchand. "I'd like to see the Canucks—and the Sedins—play it the way the Sabres did [against Boston]," said one frustrated poster to ProHockeyTalk.com in 2012. "Come out with an edge, play a spirited game, and let the physical game out to play. Hit Bruins, get in the corners, play their game a little. It can't hurt to show that side of your game sometimes, right?"

Daniel Sedin had heard it all before. In a radio appearance on The Team 1040 in Vancouver, he later explained the price of pushing back. "I've [hit back] before, and all of a sudden we're frustrated. For me and Henrik, it's a no-win situation. Whatever we do is going to be the wrong thing, so we're not too worried about that." (To emphasize his point, in March of 2012, just moments after Sedin checked Brent Seabrook into the glass behind the Chicago net, he sustained a severe concussion when Seabrook's teammate Duncan Keith delivered a retaliatory elbow. Sedin slumped to the ice and was helped off. Keith received a two-minute penalty for the hit and later was suspended five games by the NHL. Sedin missed the nine remaining games of the regular season and three crucial playoff games in the Canucks' loss to Los Angeles. The physical effects lingered into Sedin's next season.)

Not everyone placed the blame for the Marchand moment on the Canucks, however. "I broke with the sport that year," says *New Yorker* writer and hockey fan Adam Gopnik. "With the Marchand–Sedin incident in the playoffs, I felt physically, truly physically ill when I watched that... The response of the hockey community in a sense was 'Ah, that'll teach him, he's like a girl, he let somebody hit him around the head.' When I heard the response... I felt for the first time in my forty years as a hockey lover, I felt this is wrong, this game is out of control, this is not the game I want to love."

Musician and hockey fan Dave Bidini wonders how much of the subsequent Vancouver riot was spawned by the Marchand incident and others like it in the final. "Let's ask this question," says the author of several excellent hockey books. "Does that riot happen if the Bruins win by purely athletic play? Let's face it, the Bruins manhandled the Canucks. I wonder whether that might have caused resentment, beaten into the ground, that last game in Boston. If a beautiful goal wins in overtime and it's a peaceful series, I wonder if the spike is as sharp?"

As Game 7 dawned two days after the Sedin–Marchand incident, it would have been safe to say that neither style had yet triumphed. The fact that the series was now tied was largely a

11

function of the goaltending each side had received. In Boston's case, thirty-seven-year-old Tim Thomas had been brilliant, while Vancouver's Roberto Luongo had been inconsistent. Boston was also the healthier team heading into Game 7, with Vancouver missing four regulars while three others were hampered by injuries. Either team could make an argument for winning the pivotal contest at Rogers Arena. It was now in the hands of the gods.

Or in the hands of Tim Thomas. Backed by their eccentric goalie, Boston won 4–0. While not a sieve, Luongo was again outperformed by Thomas, and the Bruins lifted the Cup before disconsolate Vancouver fans (some of whom later rioted). But in the eyes of many, Boston's win was more than a simple Stanley Cup. There is a Cup winner every year, but the Bruins' win proved, at least to those inclined towards the Don Cherry perspective, that Vancouver's eggheaded approach could not win. Forget that the Canucks had gone from missing the playoffs in 2008 to within a game of the Stanley Cup championship three years later. Forget that they had been the NHL's best team in 2010–11 and had won three previous playoff series—one over the defending Stanley Cup champion Chicago Blackhawks. The Game 7 showdown in which Thomas's goaltending crushed the Canucks' power play proved that the celebrated new approach taken by Vancouver GM Mike Gillis and head coach Alain Vigneault was a failure. They would seemingly have to conform or face more defeats in the future.

CONTROVERSY WAS A lifestyle choice with the Canucks, ever since Mike Gillis's hiring to manage the club in 2008. By doing things differently, the Canucks became a boon to journalists looking for a story. When they adopted a sleep consultant, hockey laughed. When they experimented with yoga, diet plans, and endorphins, hockey chuckled behind its glove. When Gillis announced that Vancouver would become a destination for hockey players choosing a team, hockey yawned.

And when the Canucks stumbled, many in the hockey culture took pleasure in Vancouver's pain. The denunciation of the Canucks' methodology was reminiscent of how the Oakland Athletics' theories were trashed by traditionalists when the team failed to win in the playoffs between 2000 and 2003—a key ingredient in the landmark book *Moneyball*. "If we don't win the last game of the series, they'll dismiss us," says Billy Beane in the movie based on the book. "I know these guys. I know the way they think, and they will erase us. And everything we've done here, none of it will matter. Any other team wins the World Series, good for them. They're drinking champagne, they'll get a ring. But if we win . . . we'll change the game."

The Canucks didn't win that one game. It can be fairly suggested that their attempt to reimagine what works in the NHL was largely dismissed because they lost a single contest in an otherwise superb season. Making it sweeter for the traditionalists was to see Vancouver's swagger reduced. General manager Gillis and coach Alain Vigneault had worn it well. When the series was over, Bruins veteran Mark Recchi made plain what he thought of the Canucks' pest control. "In [twenty-two] years they are the most arrogant team I played against and the most hated team I've ever played against. I couldn't believe their antics, their falling and diving." Ryan Whitney of the Edmonton Oilers declared the Canucks "so easy to hate it's unbelievable." Mike Duco, then of the Florida Panthers, chimed in on Twitter, "Sick of watching the Sedins dive and lay on the ice." (Duco briefly became a Canuck later, prompting a follow-up: "Lesson learned, I'll keep my comments on the ice.")

"Honestly, I think most of the backlash against the Canucks has had more to do with the abrasive on-ice personalities of guys like Kesler, Burrows, [and] Bieksa than Gillis per se," says TSN broadcaster Bob McKenzie, the dean of hockey panelists. "But there's no question that, from the time Gillis took over, there was very much a fox-in-the-henhouse mentality or skepticism of him as the new GM on the block."

13

Nothing epitomized the Canucks' edge like the post-whistle episode in Game 1, when Boston's Patrice Bergeron stuck his fingers into the mouth of the Canucks winger Alex Burrows, who promptly bit Bergeron's finger. While the NHL vindicated Burrows for dining out on his fellow Quebecer's digit, the bite ignited a series-long theme. Maxim Lapierre later dangled his fingers in Bergeron's face. Despite Boston coach Claude Julien's claim that the Bruins "were not that kind of team," Boston's Milan Lucic did the same finger jab on Burrows. Even a year later, Recchi was still spitting vituperation. "It was very frustrating," he said, "but at the same time, as the series wore on we knew we were getting to them."

Recchi wasn't alone in his disdain for Vancouver. In the NHL's macho culture, the Canucks were seen as outliers, trying to have it both ways. Before the uncivil war with the Bruins, the Sedins and the Canucks had engaged in three bitter playoff series with the Chicago Blackhawks between 2009 and 2011. The Blackhawks established a template for how to bully, batter, and bruise the Canucks as they won consecutive six-game series in 2009 and 2010—the second after Vancouver had jumped out to a 2-0 lead in games. Chicago's bruising forwards and defencemen schooled the Canucks to the tune of the Fratellis' "Chelsea Dagger," the team's theme song at the United Center.

When the clubs met yet again in 2011, Vancouver grabbed a lead once more—in this case, three games to none. The defending Stanley Cup champs then roared back with three convincing wins to force a seventh game in Vancouver. The final game, which the Canucks played under suffocating pressure, mirrored the series. Vancouver established a 1-0 lead in the first period which they hung on to until Chicago's Jonathan Toews tied the game with a shorthanded goal just a minute from full time. This time, however, Vancouver found a winner from Burrows in overtime to move on to Round 2 and slough off the Chicago jinx.

That loss didn't humble the Hawks' Dave Bolland, who took to Chicago's WGN radio in the fall of 2011 to dis the Canucks' image. "There's a lot of weirdos there," said Bolland of Vancouver. "You don't want to be out there too long."

A young fan in the audience asked Bolland, "Do you hate everyone on the Canucks, or just a lot of them?"

"I hate all of them," said the Blackhawks forward.

Co-host Andrea Darlas asked, "If the Sedins become Hawks, will they still be sisters?" After a pause to let the Chicago laughter die down, Bolland quipped, "Well, they'll never become Hawks. I don't think we'd let them on our team. That'd probably be one thing. We'd be sure not to let them on our team. And, yeah, they probably still would be sisters. I think they might sleep in, like, bunk beds. The older one has the bottom one, the younger one's got the top."

There was similar friction with Detroit, the skilled team upon which Gillis had modelled his own club. "They've got a bunch of idiots over there," said Detroit goalie Jimmy Howard.

HOW DID THE Canucks become such a lightning rod? Hockey's culture, like that in other sports, is protective of its traditions and assumptions about the sport. The Canucks seemed too clever by half. In leaving no stone unturned, they joined other rebels who sought to move the needle by questioning those assumptions—men such as Father David Bauer, who ran Canada's national team in the 1960s. Father Bauer believed in self-discipline and skill in defeating the Soviets, Czechs, and other teams then dominating international play. Father Bauer "had the quaint (for hockey) notion that a player could be rugged without being dirty," wrote Scott Young in 1976, "and that mental discipline and development of the mind were as important as physical development and hockey skills. Even more galling to old-style hockey men was that much of the time his teams could beat their teams."

15

Since the mid-1990s, the Detroit Red Wings have been the NHL's predominant team by defying convention themselves. After stumbling for the two decades following Gordie Howe's retirement, the Red Wings overhauled their organization by emphasizing skill and incorporating Europeans in significant numbers into their roster. Detroit defied the notion, perpetuated by the Don Cherry brigade, that you couldn't win in the playoffs with too many Europeans. This bias was fed when, after dominant regular seasons in the mid-nineties, Detroit stumbled and failed to win a Cup. It was whispered that Detroit would only win a Cup by conforming to conventional wisdom.

General manager Jimmy Devellano and his successor, Ken Holland, stuck with their blueprint. The back-to-back Stanley Cup champions of 1997 and '98 employed as many as five Russians on the ice at a time, and a third of their roster was European. (Undaunted, Cherry whined that Detroit ticket buyers were nonetheless put off by all the "foreigners" on the championship team.)

Despite four Stanley Cup titles and another two trips to the final in the years since 1995, the Red Wings' model has been treated as an outlier as teams remained wedded to the belief in intimidation and effort as keys to winning. The NHL itself did little to promote the Wings' skill, sticking to its rock-'em, sock-'em narrative to sell the game. Nothing in the sacred canon of old-time hockey is more venerated than toughness. Yet Detroit (and later Pittsburgh) got by without goons. Perhaps nothing speaks to the notion of the Red-Wings-as-outliers better than the case of Swedish defenceman Nicklas Lidstrom. Despite the fact that Lidstrom's lack of thundering bodychecks and fights won him seven Norris Trophies, his style was rarely in vogue on "Coach's Corner" on *Hockey Night in Canada*. Despite being arguably the greatest defenceman of all time outside of Bobby Orr, Lidstrom was overshadowed by the rugged Scott Stevens model of punishing checks and intimidation.

One person who did think the Detroit template worth emulating was player agent Mike Gillis, who also represented skilled Europeans such as Pavel Bure. In the almost twenty years that he represented players, Gillis swore that, if given a chance to run a team, he'd use Detroit's example of skill at the expense of brawling and physical play. "In Detroit, it began with how they treated their players. How thoughtful they were. The atmosphere they created in the organization allowed them to compete every season," Gillis noted of the Wings.

That was the recipe he would use to start his tenure as GM. Where it went after that was going to depend on a whole lot of working parts.

2

The Man with the Plan

A**S THE HOST** of Vancouver's top-rated morning radio program, Rick Cluff of the CBC is used to talking with the city's movers and shakers. But even he was a little curious when he received the call from Vancouver Canucks owner Francesco Aquilini to sit with him for a parley at the Shore Club, a noted restaurant in the city. "It was just after he'd hired Mike Gillis to be the general manager in 2008," recalls Cluff. "The team had missed the playoffs, and there was some feeling that changes were coming. No one was surprised that Dave Nonis was let go. But nobody in the city really knew much about Gillis. Who was this guy? There was a real range of opinions about whether he was a good hire or a disaster in the making."

The pair met and talked about the hiring, the position of Aquilini's Canucks in the city Cluff had moved to in 1997, and any advice Cluff might have. "I told him to trade Luongo," says Cluff with a smile. Cluff discovered a hockey owner eager to engage in debate, sure of himself and charming in the way that people of power and influence can be. "He and his family are very important people in the city. It was interesting to me that he actually wanted to know why I felt the way I did."

In fact, Cluff was one of several journalists Aquilini had invited to break bread and talk about his team as it seemingly rolled the dice with a former agent—who had no managerial experience—as his general manager. In his straightforward approach, the business magnate was working the room, sounding out how his bold move was being received. And, if possible, convincing hockey people he hadn't lost his mind in selecting Mike Gillis.

The evidence suggested Aquilini had acted quickly, calling in Dave Nonis on the Monday after the 2007–08 season ended. Three hours after the meeting started, Nonis was let go. "I think this important change in leadership is critical to the future of the team and the direction we need to take," said Aquilini. "It's not acceptable to our fans or to us as owners that our team isn't in the playoffs. As owners, we made a commitment to deliver the kind of hockey our fans deserve. At the same time, with leadership comes responsibility. So our search begins today for a new general manager, and our focus going forward is on a winning season in 2008–09."

Few journalists saw the Nonis firing as a positive. Ed Willes of the *Province* called it "the latest act in an ongoing farce... Given the Aquilini family's track record, and given what's just happened to Nonis, is there a competent hockey man out there who'll work for the Canucks?"

Influential columnist Cam Cole of the *Sun* cautioned that fans should "be afraid... be very afraid" of Aquilini's leadership. CKNW's Neil Macrae dubbed the Canucks owner "Francesco Aquiloony." And Tony Gallagher of the *Province* said it was style as much as substance that sank Nonis. "It's one thing to lose, but quite another to lose in boring fashion. And if there is one thing an owner cannot have, it's watching his customers fail to be entertained, and on many nights this season that was certainly the case, this team often excruciatingly boring even on nights when they won."

It would be safe to say that few of those dissenters changed their mind in the face of the Aquilini charm offensive. "So, Francesco, tell us how you slept last night?" radio broadcaster Tom Larscheid asked Aquilini at the press conference to announce Nonis's firing. Both sides understood that the test of his dramatic shift for a club that had never won a Stanley Cup in its thirty-eight-year history would lie in how the Canucks fared in the standings and—assuming they could get back to the post-season—in the playoffs. But challenges and bucking convention are nothing new for Aquilini or his family. It could be said that, having charted their own course as outsiders among the Vancouver social elites of yacht clubs and private establishments, the Aquilinis had long ceased to care what Vancouver public opinion felt about their decisions. They would do what they saw as proper for their business. And the Canucks have long been a family preoccupation. "My brothers Roberto and Paolo and I were fans long before we became owners," Francesco told reporters, "so I know how Canuck fans feel. They deserve a better season than the one we gave them."

TO UNDERSTAND THE Aquilinis and how they came to own the city's premier cultural engine, you must go back to when Luigi Aquilini first immigrated to Canada in 1953. Having fulfilled his military service duties in Italy, Luigi set out for Canada's West Coast to join his wife, Elisa. As the legend goes, he arrived penniless on a Friday; by Monday, he had a job in a foundry. In the intervening years, Luigi left the foundry behind to move into landscaping and then the building of homes and apartments. He began investing in real estate. Where others fell by the wayside, he prospered. He even survived being unfairly labelled a "slum landlord" in the media. By the turn of the twenty-first century, the Aquilini Investment Group had become very wealthy by being synonymous with successful real estate developments across the country. The family owns everything from high-rises

20

to hotels to golf courses to the Pizza Hut franchise for B.C. It's also responsible for a series of philanthropic ventures, creating Il Giardino Italiano in Hastings Park and preserving wetlands in Pitt Meadows that the family owned. Aquilini Renewable Energy is seeking to burn Vancouver's trash in a sustainable model that also produces energy. There's also been controversy over workplace safety and environmental issues arising from their Golden Eagle Group investments.

Along the way, Luigi and Elisa had three boys, Francesco, Roberto, and Paolo. Even as the family's fortune increased, the Aquilinis remained in their old blue-collar East Vancouver neighbourhood in the shadow of the Pacific Coliseum, home of the Canucks till 1995. Francesco, the eldest, was, by his own admission, less than a devoted student, preferring to be a football player. He was reportedly a fine player till he wrecked his knee. He also likes to tell of using the family property as a parking lot for Canucks games, and of the time that Canucks hero Lars Lindgren autographed his stick as he emerged from the Coliseum one day. (Lindgren is now a Canucks scout.)

The transition, he told journalist Gary Mason for an article in BC Business magazine, came in his last year at Templeton Secondary School. His parents were summoned by the school to be told that Francesco wasn't going to amount to much at the rate he was going. "Well, my dad went absolutely ballistic on me," Aquilini said. "He was so mad. It was so bad I think I even ran away from home for a couple of days. My dad, when he got angry, could scare the living shit out of you. But he does it in such a way that he demands respect, even to this day. But that day was a turning point in my life, no question."

In short order, Aquilini pulled up his socks, got a bachelor's degree in commerce and a master's in business administration, and started working with his father and brothers. In the process, he became a powerful but private figure in the city's economic and social life. He developed a reputation as a hard-nosed

21

negotiator and a force not to be crossed. While Vancouver morphed into the multicultural stew that it is today, with the power elite now spread across several linguistic and cultural lines, the Aquilinis—with Francesco often leading the way—came to represent the Italian face of the city. In this climate, there was no need to pay fealty to the old gods of the city. Francesco's family could be their own men.

While Francesco is the public face of the family, father Luigi and his brothers are integral to the running of the company. Any decision, from a condo purchase to buying the Canucks, is the product of a group process. Whenever a new direction is planned, the family confers, with Luigi usually being given the decisive word.

One of the new ventures was the acquisition of the city's erratic hockey team. Francesco Aquilini had never forgotten his love of sport. For a young man with ambitions in the B.C. market, that sort of connection naturally leads to the Vancouver Canucks, who were then owned by the McCaw family, Seattle-based communications billionaires who had purchased them from the Griffiths family in 1997 when a declining Canadian dollar and other business pressures forced them to sell their interest. When the Canadian dollar rebounded, the McCaws subsequently lost their enthusiasm for running the team as outsiders. They made it clear that some or all of the team could be had. Enter Aquilini, family friend Tom Gagliardi, and business partner Ryan Beedie. The trio pursued a bid to buy a portion of the team, putting it in Vancouver hands again. After tensions arose between the group and the Canucks, Aquilini pulled out of the consortium in March of 2004. Gagliardi and Beedie tried, without success, to consummate a deal on their own, and Francesco Aquilini emerged with his family's own bid to buy into the team in November. They subsequently purchased a 50 per cent share of the club from the McCaws, assuming full control in 2006.

If Aquilini had any misconceptions about the visibility of being the Canucks' owner, he was educated by the furor that erupted after McCaw accepted his initial offer to buy into the Canucks. His former partners, Gagliardi and Beedie, expressed shock and promised legal action at what they described as a double-cross. And these were not simply business partners. Luigi Aquilini had done business with three generations of the Gagliardis, and the families were collaborating on a plan for a resort on Garibaldi Mountain at the time. Beedie's father, Keith, had become B.C.'s largest industrial landlord. It was the stuff of TV melodrama as Gagliardi and Beedie sued.

The Canucks' ownership had no problems with the deal. "At all times we fully complied with all our legal and ethical obligations, and we dealt with the other party in good faith," said Stan McCammon, then Canucks president and CEO, in a statement. "We simply failed to reach an agreement with [Gagliardi and Beedie]. We had the full right to begin negotiations with Mr. Aquilini, and we did so."

The dispute generated ten published judicial decisions between 2006 and 2009 and occupied fifty-nine court days. It wasn't till January of 2008 that B.C. Supreme Court Justice Catherine Wedge finally threw out the suit, removing the last hurdles to the family buying full control. "The relationship among Gagliardi, Beedie and Aquilini was not one of partnership or joint venture," wrote Wedge. "None owed duties of loyalty or good faith to the others. Each was entitled to withdraw from the group at any time and pursue the opportunity for himself."

The decision was appealed all the way to the Canadian Supreme Court, in vain. The legal costs, borne by Gagliardi and Beedie, were in the millions. As one website noted, they might have saved themselves a lot of money: Self-Counsel Press's do-it-yourself kit on partnerships costs "$16.95 plus taxes, available at any local stationery store."

The emotional toll was even more severe. Francesco Aquilini's reaction to the judgment was muted. "We did a fair deal,"

23

he said. "We acted with integrity... I think it's time to move on. It's time to get back to business." His brother Roberto gave a different portrait of the toll the suit had taken on his brother. "I was there [in court] all the time and I can say the real cost here was seeing my brother being cross-examined by experienced, skilful questions from the other side to the point where my brother, who is inexperienced... it was painful to see him put through that line of questioning. He did nothing wrong.

"The accusations of bad faith, it really hurt," continued Roberto. "Hurt me, deep down, to see him have to go through that."

When the Aquilinis at last gained control of the Canucks, they became one of an often wealthy, diverse, fractious—and, on a few occasions, criminal—group known as the NHL Board of Governors. From just five owners in 1917, when the league opened for business, supplanting the old National Hockey Association, there were now thirty owners spread across financial, demographic, and cultural lines all over North America. The longest-serving owner, Ed Snider of Philadelphia, dates to 1967; most of the owners, like the Aquilini family, have been around less than a decade.

From being fans who once simply watched games from the luxury box, owners have lately evolved into hands-on participants in the daily operation of teams. The huge salaries made by players have changed owners and the way the league is run. Massive losses became the norm for owners who neglected to become immersed in their teams' business. In this climate, new ownership for NHL franchises in the 2000s fell several notches below the Rockefellers. While Canadian teams' equity was boosted by the rebounding dollar, Commissioner Gary Bettman's effort in the U.S. to recruit capitalized owners was fraught with problems. Despite what was supposed to be a rigorous vetting process, William "Boots" Del Biaggio was allowed to buy into a struggling Nashville franchise. Only later

24

did the league discover that Del Biaggio's riches were illusory. Del Biaggio went to jail. Del Biaggio was convicted of fraud and sentenced to more than eight years in prison and ordered to pay over $67 million in restitution. Hollywood mogul Oren Koules and ex-NHLer Len Barrie bought the Tampa Bay Lightning, a partnership that ended in chaos and controversy when Barrie's financial assets in B.C. melted like the spring snow. In the most extreme case, the NHL abandoned Atlanta as a market for a second time, sending the Thrashers into the loving arms of Winnipeg, which might have been a tiny market but at least had rich owners and real fans. The Florida Panthers, St. Louis Blues, New Jersey Devils, Colorado Avalanche, and New York Islanders have all experienced financial crises in recent years that left people wondering whether they could continue.

The most spectacular failure—and Bettman's most trying challenge—occurred in Phoenix, where the former Winnipeg Jets were sunk by a real estate deal. (The NHL loves ownership deals tied to real estate development the way Wayne Gretzky liked defencemen who couldn't skate backward.) As a result of the Coyotes debacle and the other collapses or near-collapses of franchises, Bettman became expert in crisis management for his owners—a practice that endeared him to them and gave him added clout. As one team after another ran into trouble, Bettman sprang into action, finding new capital and owners drawn by the promise of riding an equity train to the stars. When members of the hockey media predicted that no person in his right mind would take on a failing NHL franchise, Bettman would invariably produce a new eager figure with money to burn. In Ottawa, Buffalo, Tampa, New Jersey, and St. Louis, owners raved about Bettman's unceasing efforts to keep them afloat.

So while the fortunes of the tentative markets rarely improved, the league continued with thirty teams. As always, there was the promise of more expansion at the end of the rainbow, perhaps to southern Ontario or Seattle or Quebec City,

25

and new national TV contracts (which became $2 billion over ten years with NBC and $5.2 billion over twelve years with Rogers in Canada).

Little mention was made of unsustainable business models or escalating payrolls.

The financial squeeze driven by rising salaries has also brought the owners into more daily contact with their clubs' operations. "It's amazing how the dynamic has changed," says former Columbus GM Doug MacLean. "It wasn't the GM who changed the business. It was the evolution of the first president of a team. I don't know who started it, but it went from the owner and the GM to being the owner's guy running things. It changed the GM's role. In Columbus, Mike Priest was the owner's accountant. He became president of one of our owner's side corporations. And when I got fired, he became the president of the team. I watched how he got involved in the hockey operation.

"So you don't just blame a GM for a trade or a signing since then. Since salaries took off, there's a lot more people involved in making those decisions. In some cases, it's not even the GM's call. Because of the evolution, a lot of GMs have changed into assistant GMs. Other guys have the owner's ear."

Like most men unaccustomed to the full-bore media maelstrom that is the hallmark of a Canadian NHL city, Aquilini was obliged to learn some hard lessons in spin from the people who "buy printers' ink by the gallon" in Vancouver's press circle. The details of Francesco's costly 2013 divorce were splashed across the newspapers, with breathless references to expensive homes and wine cellars. No wonder Frank Giustra, a close friend, had warned Francesco about it upon purchasing the team. "I told him he was going to be in the spotlight constantly," Giustra recalled to Gary Mason. "And it won't always be pleasant or fun. I wanted to be sure he thought that through. Up until that time, Francesco was a fairly private person, perhaps even more so than me. So I wanted to prepare him for what to expect."

But Aquilini didn't get to the top by worrying what others thought. His family had never been the darlings of the Vancouver elite, and they might never be. What had always served Luigi and his boys had been the power of their own counsel. And the loyalty of those around the close group around them. Dave Nonis was, by many, accounts, a capable young NHL executive on the rise. Schooled by the previous GM, Brian Burke, and respected by many, he was the kind of talent that teams hope to find and nurture. (In 2013, he succeeded Burke as the general manager in Toronto.)

The problem for Nonis was that he was not the Aquilinis' choice, having been inherited in the 2004 purchase of the club. Furthermore, he was, in their view, a product of conventional hockey thinking. What had taken the Aquilinis to the top was an ability to reinvent and recalibrate situations. "It's about leadership," Aquilini stated in 2012. "They step up and take the risk. Someone who's willing to step up, take a chance, that's the kind of person you want. You don't want someone who takes the safe route. Work hard and get to what you think is the right decision."

The Aquilinis are helped, believes Ray Ferraro, by their self-assurance. "I get the sense the Aquilinis have a plan for growing the brand, what they want to do next. Aside from just success on the ice. Part of that comes from their upbringing, where they accumulated their money. Through construction and real estate and acquiring things, that's how I see their vision and how the business will grow. I see MLSE [Maple Leaf Sports and Entertainment] in Toronto and I say that's coming here, that's going to happen here."

David Kincaid, managing partner and CEO of Level5 Strategy Group, sees that comprehensive approach in the Canucks' operational structure. "The Canucks understand that your brand is a system—it's all integrated packaging across a system from your team to the merchandise to the TV product to the bottled water under your label. The Canucks have done that very well."

27

Brian Cooper, CEO and president of S&E Marketing Group, concurs. "The Canucks have done a tremendous job. They are one of the more sophisticated Canadian teams in the NHL, along with Maple Leaf Sports & Entertainment, in how they market to the community. They've brought in outside sponsors and done a lot of research to back their value and position in the marketplace. They concentrate on the fans' passion points. They use metrics and analytics that a lot of teams don't. In our dealings, we found they are more interested in understanding your business. They take two or three meetings to find out how the sponsor can be helped by dealing with them. The benefit of that thoroughness and being with the Aquilini brand in B.C. is substantial in their marketplace." No wonder the Canucks shot from seventh to second in NHL team revenues over the Gillis tenure. Estimates had them make as much as $70 million from the 2011 postseason.

The key to the strategy is having a winning team to sell. Especially in a Canadian town that has yet to lift the Stanley Cup. When the Canucks stumbled on the ice under GM Dave Nonis in the early years of the Aquilini ownership, that spotlight got even hotter. To create a winner was going to take a new approach, concluded Aquilini.

There were advantages to be gained from taking the club's thinking outside the conventional NHL culture. Aquilini was looking for someone to run his hockey team who would not spend his time obsessed with the media chatter (as Burke had been) and not be blown off course. "There's one thing you can't accuse me of and that's not being confident," Aquilini remarked for a *Vancouver* magazine article in 2011. "Sometimes I'm overconfident. I run a number of businesses, and I make fifty decisions a day that affect a lot people and their jobs. You get used to it, you do your work and then follow through with it. You can't agree on everything, that's not healthy. It's easy to have 20/20 hindsight." Enter Mike Gillis.

28

3

Go West, Young Man

FOR THOSE WHO make a habit of watching hockey practices, this sleepy Monday morning workout during the heart of the Vancouver Canucks' 2011–12 season was unique. In the midst of chasing a second consecutive Presidents' Trophy, the Canucks were at work on the ice, despite having come off a taxing road trip the night before, the kind the Canucks are always facing. For about ten minutes, each player in turn skated from the centre red line to a pylon deep in the defensive zone. Then they looped back and skated to the red line again. Usually, NHL players whip through these drills with blinding speed and purpose, as much to get them done as for any reason. What distinguished this skate, in the view of those watching, was that the Canucks were doing this drill at half-speed. It looked almost like a warmup.

But the team was deadly serious. Inside each player's helmet was a little foam pad that measured the player's heart rate and skin temperature. The data gathered from the Canuck players skating through the innocuous drill was being relayed to a computer. With so many quick turnarounds from travel, getting players to recover faster from jet lag is a huge asset in hockey.

"I guess they would just like to see where we're at in the season," winger Chris Higgins told reporters afterward. "They want to see how fatigued we are and how well we respond to a little bit of a workout. It wasn't anything too tough. I wish our September workouts were similar to that one. I'd be a lot happier."

"Apparently, the [data] tells them how alert we are and how ready we are when we first step on the ice," Kevin Bieksa explained. "You feel a little bit like a guinea pig, but whatever is going to help make us better, we're all for it. We're fine with it, we accept it, and there is 100 per cent buy-in around here. Ownership and management have shown they're looking into every possible way to gain an advantage."

The architect behind the slow skating and the helmet monitors was Mike Gillis, the heretic in the church of hockey. Like his boss, Francesco Aquilini, he believed in adapting what works best in his own businesses. From the day Aquilini offered Gillis the job as GM of the Canucks, the pair were determined to conduct new research to help alleviate the Canucks' traditional disadvantages of time, travel, and distance that come with playing in the Pacific Northwest.

"I've been working on a human performance plan that we've started to implement to try and address those issues," Gillis said from a seat halfway up the bowl of Rogers Arena as he watched the Canucks go through their drills. "I think dealing with fatigue from sleep deprivation and travel was the first stage. Now we're moving on to some new stages, like how you deal with the ups and downs of a season. The amount of travel we do [120,000 kilometres a year], compounded with the types of games we play, we need to find a better way to deal with that, we have to find it quickly, and that's what we're trying to do."

An adherent of Brian Tracy's seminal *How the Best Leaders Lead,* Gillis believes that safe is death in pro sports management. "Move out of your comfort zone," wrote Tracy. "You

30

can only grow if you are willing to feel awkward and uncomfortable when you try something new." It was the curse of the conventional that hampered Gillis's own progress as a player. A first-round draft pick of the Colorado Rockies in 1978, his career was ended six years later by severe leg injuries and by hockey's general reluctance at the time to address the complex concepts of maximizing the performance of elite athletes. "I understand now that I would have been far better off staying in the minors to develop," he said as the team began shooting drills. "Too many young players, especially first-round picks, are rushed, they lose their love of hockey and they're finished at the age when they should be just establishing themselves. If it was up to me they'd all start in the East Coast League and just play."

He knew enough former teammates who'd never get over what happened to them in their teens and twenties. Instead of feeling self-pity over how his own career ended through injury, Gillis turned his mind towards getting the most from the players he had on the Canucks. "We're trying to see if, maybe through a bit more scientific approach to different elements, we will be able to get our team in a better situation to have success here as we move forward," then coach Alain Vigneault told the media scrum after the practice when asked about the slow-skating drills.

In the old-boy culture of hockey, the willingness to tinker with and even break the model came in for ridicule. In many corners of the traditional hockey clan, the sleep research was met with mirth and criticism. In a business that has always shunned too much innovation, the Canucks' attempts to rethink the possibilities put them on the very fringes of respectability. That college-boy stuff was the object of great yuks from those who believed the old ways were the best ways. Years later, former Canuck Willie Mitchell talked about giving one rookie all the team's sleep monitor watches to take to the hotel so they could go out drinking beer after a game.

"There's a deep anti-intellectualism in hockey," notes author and columnist Roy MacGregor. "It's not a game that likes deep thinking. It isn't too fussy about intellectuals like Ken Dryden. They roll eyes at his thoughts and call him a bore. It's the same with Mike Gillis."

Former NHLer Ray Ferraro, now a TSN analyst, agreed. "Hockey's always been miles behind everyone else," he said, watching the Canucks go through their drills. "It's the same today. Baseball has been using sleep stuff for years. The Canucks are at the forefront of it. Teams in other cities like to mock it, but why would you not try it? Take advantage of all the research that's so readily available today. It's not like you have to invent the wheel. The stuff is there. They've been open-minded enough to say, 'How can we sleep better? How can we rest better so we don't have all these man-games lost during the year?'

"When Euros came over in great numbers, that was the impetus for us to change our training habits. I used to do bench presses, building up my upper body. That's great if you have a big guy land on you and you have to push him off. But the Europeans had these strong legs and strong core, and we went, 'We're way behind.' "

The goal for Gillis was to win the first Stanley Cup for the "mad scientists" of Rogers Arena. All NHL GMs begin with that as a goal, of course. But Gillis's intellectual pursuit was to understand why, not just how, his team might win a Cup and to maximize the conditions that would repeat success. "When it comes to innovation and creativity," agent Anton Thun told *Maclean's,* "Vancouver has taken it to a whole new level."

FOR SOMEONE WHO often holds himself back from the hockey culture—he travelled less with his team than do most GMs—the sport is in Mike Gillis's DNA. From playing the game himself to being an agent to managing the Canucks, his whole life has been touched by the business. The middle child of three growing up in Toronto (brother Paul played in the NHL from 1982 to 1993 and has been the head coach of the Odessa Jackalopes of the North American Hockey League), Gillis was a hotshot scoring prospect coming out of Toronto's minor system, the same system where his nephews Matt, Michael, and Adam Pelech have starred on their way to the pros. In 1975, Gillis landed in Kingston with the Canadians of the Ontario Hockey League, where he scored at more than a point a game on left wing, amassing 132 points in 111 games. It was in Kingston, however, that the leg injuries that curtailed his career first began. He missed all but seventeen games of the 1976-77 season because of a broken ankle. A broken collarbone hampered his final year in Kingston.

Mike Simurda, who played junior hockey with Gillis in Kingston, remembers a young guy who quickly gained acceptance from a team that featured future NHLers Tony McKegney, Mike Crombeen, Behn Wilson, Tim Kerr, and Ken Linseman. "I knew Mike would make it after how he was embraced as sixteen-year-old by the veterans," says Simurda, a portfolio manager for RBC Dominion Securities who handles the investments of some of Gillis's former clients. "I'd describe Mike as a straight-line guy. You know that expression 'bull in a china shop'? That was Mike. He wasn't an intimidating guy, but he'd go right over you to get the puck. It got people's attention, but it also ended up with him getting hurt a lot, too.

"I'm uncertain what kind of a corporate or criminal lawyer he would have made, but having met most of his clients while [he was] a player agent, it was clear they and their families were very happy with the final deals he got for them. I'm not sure the GM he was up against was equally as thrilled."

Player agent Rich Evans, who went to Queen's University law school with Gillis, says his sober exterior hides a wry sense of humour that allowed Gillis to fit into hockey's boys' club. "Mike had, and still has, a sense of humour that was appreciated by all the guys. He is a straight shooter and 'does not suffer fools gladly,' which is a trait that was shared by most of the guys that we hung around with at Queen's."

After being selected fifth overall in the 1978 draft by the Colorado Rockies, his career was blighted by his knee problems and eventually a spiral fracture of his left leg. In his rookie camp with the Rockies, he tore knee ligaments, an injury that plagued him in his early NHL career. While in Colorado, he was coached briefly by Don Cherry, who had been recently fired by Boston. "He'd always tell us, 'Don't feed [his dog] Blue, don't feed Blue,'" says Gillis with a chuckle. Being young hockey players, someone would feed him anyway. His two years with the hapless Rockies were a roller coaster of demotions, injuries, and the team's erratic development philosophy. "I wasn't playing that much, but the GM, Ray Miron, also didn't want to send me down because of how it would look to the fans and media if their first-round choice was being demoted."

Partway through his third year in Colorado, Gillis was traded to Boston for Bob Miller. The Bruins of that era were a successful veteran team, under GM Harry Sinden, that was accustomed to winning and hard living. For a time, the twenty-one-year-old roomed with salty veteran Wayne Cashman, a member of Canada's 1972 team that beat the USSR in the Summit Series. It was an eye-opening experience on and off the ice. When a young Gillis took the Bruins to arbitration, Sinden sent him to the minors. "They made an example of me as a young player, fighting for a small sum of money," he says. "It was an introduction to what happens as a player when you have no rights."

A left winger, Gillis also took some shifts on defence. After his uneven start, he finally appeared to get his career restarted when the Bruins sent him to Baltimore of the American Hockey League in 1982–83. On a team with Stan Jonathan, Rod Schutt, and Dave Barr, he blossomed with thirty-two goals and 113 points (totals that were franchise records). He appeared ready to find a place with the Bruins. Then, in training camp in the fall of 1984, a fellow Bruin fell on his leg (Gillis says he can't remember who it was), causing a fracture that doctors determined was career-ending.

It was a crushing blow. "I had high expectations for myself, and I didn't reach them," he says today. "I was my own worst enemy sometimes, coming back too early from injuries. The knee injury in Colorado, I was back in three months with an injury that today would be a whole year off. What I know now is that you need to be more patient with young players. But there was no waiting for you to develop in those days. You had no say. It was play as soon as you could. The hardest part looking back is how little control I had over what happened. Then it was over."

Gillis took stock. He had continued to pursue his education even while playing, but as a married father of a young son, he needed a plan for the future. There was some—though not all—of his NHL disability insurance from the career-ending injury to use as a stake. Gillis was accepted into law school at Queen's University in Kingston, the same city where he'd played junior hockey. "Mike was married and had a son when we all started law school," recalls Evans. "So it is not surprising that he took law school more seriously than those of us who were single, who had never had a full-time job, and who had entered law school immediately after earning our first degree. Most of us were still living the 'student life,' and Mike had responsibilities. So I think he was more studious than most of the guys who hung around together. Also, since Mike had earned money playing in the NHL, he had a house with real furniture, and Mike and Diane were often gracious hosts for the group of guys who went through law school together."

Used to competing with testosterone-choked boys from the Soo and the Pas in pro hockey, Gillis found himself surrounded by a different class of competition at Queen's. His instinct was

35

that he wouldn't survive on intellect alone in this heady company, so he would be all about the details. "It's how I coped," Gillis recalled in an interview with *The Globe and Mail.* "And those things really formed the basis of the philosophy I brought to the Canucks. I built a game plan and I decided there was no detail too small to worry about, because it might give us an edge. But it really has its origins at Queen's, where I had to come up with a survival strategy."

Post-NHL life seemed to be unfolding as planned, with Gillis living in Kingston and helping former teammates such as Geoff Courtnall with their NHL contracts as he finished his law degree. "I had no real plan to be an agent then. I was just helping out Geoff. Then it became his brother Russ, and one guy after the other said, 'Can you help?' It just happened."

In 1993, Gillis was contacted by reporter Russ Conway of the *Lawrence Eagle-Tribune* in North Andover, Massachusetts. Conway had just published the first part of what turned out to be an eight-year output of stories (in collaboration with CBC Television) about corruption at the NHL Players' Association. Conway told Gillis that his mentor, Eagleson, who had also been Gillis's union head at the NHLPA, had probably ripped him off while pursuing Gillis's disability claim. Gillis refused to believe Conway, whom he'd known briefly as a reporter on the Bruins beat. Conway persisted; Gillis resisted.

One day, inspired by reports on CBC Television about Eagleson's behaviour, Gillis's wife, Diane, re-examined the books in the basement. Sure enough, Eagleson had diverted $41,500 of the disability money to Kingsmar, a company he controlled. The deduction, Eagleson later explained, had been to pay for legal and accounting advice to pursue a claim that the insurers thought was dubious. But a little bit of investigating showed that the claim had already been approved by the insurers. There was no need for outside help; Eagleson had simply claimed a portion of his client's disability insurance.

The case ended up in court. Gillis, a young lawyer, was suing for the rest of his disability insurance plus costs. Eagleson, friend to prime ministers and sports legends in Canada, was countersuing for a quarter of a million dollars. If Gillis lost, he'd be broke. No one in hockey's cozy world would side with an outsider against Eagleson, the man who'd created the Canada Cup and international hockey for Hockey Canada. He and his wife were on an island. For six weeks, the trial continued in Toronto. Expenses mounted. It was a contentious case, replete with contradictory evidence of Gillis's word against that of Eagleson and his business associates and friends.

Besides Gillis; his wife, Diane; Eagleson; the lawyers (including Eagleson's son Trevor); and the judge, Joseph O'Brien, there were rarely more than a handful of spectators to watch as the Eagleson empire began its slow erosion under questioning from Gillis's unrelenting lawyer, Charles Scott. Susan Foster, companion of former Maple Leaf Carl Brewer, showed up, as did reporters such as Mary Ormsby of the *Toronto Star.* But rarely were more than two or three in attendance at any one time. Had they known that Eagleson would never again offer evidence under oath, even when convicted of fraud in 1998, perhaps more people would have come to watch the spectacle.

But for those weeks in June of 1995, it was a small band that had the perspective of the nape of Gillis's neck for extended hours. I confess to knowing far more about his financial life than his hockey life during that first day in court. Till then, he'd been just one of the names I'd seen of players who had been the victims of Eagleson's slick handling of their insurance matters. A cursory look at Gillis's record on HockeyDB.com, the database of stats for players both retired and active, showed a first-round draft pick who'd been selected by the hapless Colorado Rockies and then dealt to Boston, where he could never seem to stay healthy enough to get his career established. There were stints in the minors, rehabs from injury, and a final total of seventy-six points in 246 NHL games. The cold bottom line showed him retiring in 1984 after being released by the Bruins. Sadly, there were hundreds just like him.

Had someone suggested that first morning that Gillis would use the trial as a springboard to one day become a highly influential player agent and later the president and general manager of the Vancouver Canucks, I might have laughed out loud in the courtroom. That Gillis would attempt to launch a *Moneyball*-style movement in NHL management upon taking over the Canucks in 2008 seemed equally unlikely that morning. Who was this upstart? On the opening day of the trial, Gillis was stacked up against the NHL establishment. Eagleson's lawyer hinted that major NHL figures would be called to testify on behalf of the embattled union head and against this generic hockey retiree. I also knew that tangling with Eagleson could leave a mark. In 1993, I had questioned him at the press conference he held to announce his retirement from the NHLPA. When asked why he, a Canadian based in Canada, had taken his salary and pension in U.S. dollars, Eagleson asked me in front of a large media scrum, "When did you stop beating your wife?" When I protested I hadn't done so, Eagleson said, "We've heard you do. Prove that you don't."

Gillis sat stoically, day after day, quietly making notes on a legal pad next to his lawyer as those supporting Eagleson implied that Gillis was a malingerer who just wanted to cash out on a failed career. Or that he was making up a vindictive story about the mighty Eagleson because he'd taken his eye off the ball on his own finances and needed someone to bail him out.

"He became most incensed when there was a suggestion from the Eagleson side that his wife, Diane, was not testifying accurately, which was plainly not the case," recalls Scott. "He became privately exercised when we discussed the latest evidentiary denials and prevarications from the Eagleson camp. But in court, he maintained his composure entirely. Most

38

importantly, he maintained his resolve and his analytical approach through an improbably long trial and increasingly expensive legal process."

When the judge finally announced his verdict, it completely vindicated Gillis against a man he'd trusted implicitly since his own father, Patrick, had died. The key evidence, said O'Brien, was a disputed doctor's appointment. Eagleson insisted that Gillis had come to his Toronto office to hear that "the meter was running" on costs associated with the claim immediately after seeing Dr. Charles Bull. Mike's wife, Diane, insisted that their son Max had been so unruly at the doctor's office that the family had gone home instead. No meeting. O'Brien chose to believe the recollections of a young mother coping with a cranky child over some pencilled notes in the doctor's daytimer. Calling Eagleson a liar with a tendency to arrange facts, O'Brien awarded Gillis his money—damages and court costs.

Asked years later about how it felt to hear such hurtful things said about him, Gillis paused, collected his thoughts, and laconically described the dissociative state of hearing Eagleson's legal team blunder and stumble as they attempted to rewrite the past. He might have been angry, but he avoided launching into profanity, the usual default language for hockey folk pushed to the limit. "Everything in my legal training told me things would work out. I had faith that the system would operate properly."

"It was a remarkable demonstration of fortitude against a powerful adversary," says Charles Scott. "A fortitude that came from within and was ultimately and thoroughly vindicated by the trial judge's decision. If one could win a Victoria Cross for bravery and resolution in the face of legal adversity, Michael Gillis would have been awarded his medal for that fight."

39

Owners, commissioners, general managers, and coaches who encountered Gillis from then on were faced with the same cool, unimpeachable adversary who would not be swayed by loyalty to the NHL crest. "Mike is not very sentimental about that stuff," says Mike Simurda, who had a brief pro career in the AHL. "He'd rather just get on with business. Maybe because he knows these guys, he is able to separate the noise from the reality when it comes to making a deal."

"His reputation with the 'hockey establishment' was impacted by his legal pursuit of Eagleson," says Canucks assistant general manager Laurence Gilman, the capologist Gillis imported from Phoenix. "I'm certain there were some agents and club executives who hoped Mike would go away." He did not. In his most unsparing moment, he induced the New York Rangers to pay Bobby Holik $45 million over five years, a deal Evans calls his best. Some believe that, for Bettman, the Holik deal—more than any other single contract—led to the 2004-05 lockout and resulting salary cap.

Craig Button remembered dealing with Gillis when Button was the general manager in Calgary and Gillis represented Valeri Bure. "When you talked to Mike, there wasn't a lot time wasted on pleasantries," says Button. "It was 'What are we going to talk about? How are we going to do this?' Because of his experience, he could recognize your position, and he understood other people's situations. So he understood Val Bure's leverage. He understood ours. When we traded Val to Florida, it was good for him, good for the Flames, and good for Florida."

"He's a cerebral guy, and you see things that reflect his personality," says former client Mike Cammalleri. "With guys like me and Schneids [Mathieu Schneider] and Holik, he heard from us so often our opinion on how things were going. So when it comes to how he's running things, he's in touch with the current player and able to understand that. There's still an establishment, an old guard in our game—I'm not saying it's bad, but you see his team reflect a newer guard, a newer persona among players. That's probably why they're hated in some quarters.

40

"What impressed me most is that Mike is a fiery guy, an intense guy, very opinionated. As an agent, he needed that to fight for his players. But as a manager, he doesn't need to be the same person. You rarely see him making bold statements like he did as an agent, when he wasn't afraid to shake things up. But I think he's identified that as a distraction for his team. It's been interesting for me to watch how he's handled the career change."

As an agent till 2008, Gillis worked alone from a small office in his Kingston home with no full-time employees. (A brief episode when he tried to help the clients of the notorious David Frost ended with Gillis being fired for trying to get between Frost and clients like Mike Danton, who later went to prison in the U.S. for attempting to have Frost murdered.) Gillis's home was not adorned with hockey memorabilia; more often, it reflected the impeccable designer taste of his wife, Diane Coffey (they'd met as teenagers), or pictures of his three children, Max, Kate, and Spencer. While Diane, a former Olympic long jumper who was affected by the ill-fated 1980 Moscow Olympic boycott, and daughter Kate were successful athletes, the Gillis home was better known for gourmet dinners, vintage wines, and tasteful art on the walls.

By the time he moved to Vancouver in 2007 to follow daughter Kate's progress with the national field hockey team, Gillis had assembled a midsized client roster that included such stars as the Bure brothers, Markus Naslund, Tony Amonte, Mike Richter, Holik, Cammalleri, and more. He eschewed the practice of recruiting players at age fourteen; rather, he collected NHL players who'd left their existing agents. That policy of accepting players disillusioned with their current representation did not endear him to some of his peers. Even though he insists he never accepted a client till the player had left his former agent, Gillis was called a poacher—much as he would later be accused of orchestrating his takeover of the Canucks' job

41

from Nonis. He brushed aside the criticism. Despite his support of the NHL Players' Association's hardline executive director, Bob Goodenow, Gillis had also rejected flirtations with other positions in NHL management. A possible role with the NHLPA in the wake of the disastrous 2004-05 lockout was similarly rejected. It looked as if Gillis might simply ease gently into retirement, managing his clients and enjoying his three children. All seemed settled. The West Coast was a comfortable fit for Gillis, who loves the outdoors. Kate was becoming established on the field hockey team. The fishing was excellent.

Men at Work

@sportsnetmurph Vigneault with a chuckle: "Mike Gillis has
input on everything and he's not afraid to share it"

IN APRIL OF 2008, the Vancouver Canucks missed the
playoffs by three points after winning just one of their final
eight games. In a foreshadowing of events to come years
later, seeing a certain playoff spot disappear in April was a bitter disappointment to the fans and the owners of the Canucks,
particularly after a promising postseason run the year before. In
the aftermath of the meltdown, the Aquilinis fired their young
general manager, Dave Nonis. There were calls for coach Alain
Vigneault to follow Nonis to unemployment. There were no
apparent favourites for the job, only a restless undercurrent of
doubt in the city where Gillis had been living the past year.

"I knew from [client] Markus [Naslund] a little bit about the
workings of the team," Gillis says. "There were problems, but I
could see the upside, too."

In this atmosphere of flux, Gillis received an unexpected
invitation to visit the fashionable Italianate home of Francesco
Aquilini, who had taken full control of the Canucks in 2006.
While he was familiar with the previous Canucks ownership,

43

Gillis had never met Aquilini before, so the call was perplexing. Perhaps the inquisitive Aquilini was expecting a low-key discussion about the hockey-mad market of Vancouver; he was known to consult from time to time to gauge public opinion. Maybe they'd discuss Gillis's client Naslund, who appeared to be at a crossroads with the Canucks after starring for many years and setting many of the club's scoring records.

As Gillis acquainted himself with the impeccable surroundings, it soon became apparent that the talk was about much more than Markus Naslund. Gillis was about to embark on a sit-down that, in Canuck and NHL circles, is now referred to as "The Meeting."

"At the time, we were looking for someone for our general manager position, so you always have that in the back of your mind as you're talking to him," says Aquilini. "I wanted to get to know him personally. Is he a person of integrity? That's the first thing I look for when I hire someone. Mike struck me as someone who had the utmost of integrity." So did Aquilini call the meeting with hiring Gillis in mind? "Obviously, we hired him, so we must have been thinking that," says Aquilini with a smile.

"I liked what I was doing at the time," Gillis says. "I was happy being an agent, I was starting to slow down a bit, had really good clients. When the conversation began to take a turn about me and not about other things, I had to find out what the Aquilinis were all about. At the end of that meeting, I put it to them: Were they about doing what it took to win?"

The two sides—Gillis and the Aquilini family—discussed a philosophy of what it would take to return the Canucks to the playoffs and, possibly, deliver the club's first Stanley Cup. Gillis had ideas—different ideas from what many in hockey held dear. Aquilini was intrigued by the preparation and no-nonsense, straightforward approach to turning his hockey team into a winner. It was not the first time Gillis had considered opportunities on the management side. There had been a flirtation with the

44

Atlanta Thrashers. Gillis had also come very close to accepting a front-office position with the Toronto Maple Leafs when Ken Dryden was their president. So far, he had resisted the temptation. Gillis wanted control and resources. The earlier offers had supplied one, but not the other. In Vancouver, there were both.

"I can't imagine how Mike sold the Aquilinis on his plan to get that opportunity," says Ray Ferraro. "You're not hiring him and 'I'll give the details later.' You have to give Francesco a plan, and here was this guy who'd never been in management anywhere. You really have to believe in what you're selling. Mike is very sure of his vision. I played on a lot of teams that had the 'No Plan Plan.' We're going to be big this year. Next year, we're going to be skilled. If you jump around like that, you have no chance. You can't win. You can adjust, but at the core you have to believe in one way to play."

Gillis's brother Paul says it's not easy to resist the pack mentality. "If you're ever hanging out with scouts at a game," he told Vanhockey.com, "one guy has an opinion and everybody else has the same opinion. The thing in hockey is nobody wants to step out on a ledge and put a different opinion out there. Mike does have a lot of confidence in himself and puts a lot of thought into what he does. And if you feel confident about yourself, you don't care what other people think."

It would be distorting the record to say that Gillis, with no direct experience in NHL management, was the favourite in Vancouver when candidates to replace Dave Nonis were listed. (It's not clear whether any other candidate was seriously considered by the Aquilinis.) Hadn't Aquilini himself told a press conference days earlier that his new general manager would have on-the-job experience? "Absolutely. I mean, to have that experience in hockey, that's for sure. They'd have to have extensive experience and really understand the game."

Brian Burke's name was immediately bandied about as returning to Vancouver. Brian Lawton's name made the rounds.

Then the usual suspects. As a born-and-bred Ontarian, Gillis's only connection to the Vancouver market, besides daughter Kate, was representing two of the Canucks' greatest players, Pavel Bure and Naslund. In a community where suspicion, even hostility, towards easterners is widespread, being an outsider was a considerable hurdle.

But the Aquilinis' resources, their commitment to winning, and the talent base of the team proved to be the ideal spot for the Sudbury, Ontario, native. The team was a blank canvas on which to create his dream. With no Stanley Cups in team history, there was the chance to write history with a championship. After considering his options and consulting with family, Gillis told the Aquilinis he was in. Despite his unconventional path to the front office, on April 23, 2008, Mike Gillis was given a five-year contract for the plum general manager's job in a Canadian market, the tenth man to hold the position in Vancouver.

The response was instantaneous. NOW THE LOSING BEGINS, read the headline in the *Vancouver Sun*. The reaction of the hockey community to Francesco Aquilini's flyer on the untested player agent was off the hook. Who was Mike Gillis? A first-round NHL draft pick who could never get his career going over 246 games because of injuries. A successful agent, yes, but that was taking care of one player, not twenty-five. He'd never managed a hockey team, not even a junior team. Were the Canucks crazy? Three-quarters of the respondents to a poll on the host radio station, The Team 1040, opposed Gillis's hiring. Wrote Iain MacIntyre in the *Province*, "It's hard to fathom fans here tolerating two or three years of grief and losing badly." Said one online poster, "One small step backwards for hockey, one giant leap backwards for Canuck fans."

46   The vitriol gave Gillis a first taste of the rabid Vancouver hockey market, a city with an aching in its heart for a first Stanley Cup. "I think between the successful teams I had in the 1990s and the success of others after us, the expectations

began to grow in Vancouver," noted Mike Keenan, who'd been Vancouver coach and de facto GM of various teams between 1979 and 1999. "The fan base became more vibrant. The hockey base has really expanded since I was there. Not that they weren't excited by their team then, but now they're more rabid. Their expectations get skewed."

"It just seems to be that way around teams until the losing cycle is broken," says Ferraro. "And for the Canucks, that's what it's going to take. The Canuck fans have no connection to what happened in the past. But everywhere they go, people talk about how inept the franchise has been. 'When you going to win, when you going to win?' After a while, you cry 'uncle.' "

To the NHL's catty culture, Gillis had stabbed Nonis in the back after plotting secretly for months with Aquilini. How could there have been a proper job search in the week between Nonis's firing and Gillis's hiring? Hadn't he once talked to the Canucks' former CEO, Stan McCammon, about the team before Brian Burke was hired? It was widely believed that he'd spent the entire year in Vancouver, secretly meeting with Aquilini to undermine the current administration of the team. "That's simply not true," Gillis says evenly. "I met Francesco five or six days before that meeting for the first time. Never talked to him or met him before that. Then I met his father, Luigi, and his brothers, Roberto and Paolo."

The link between owner and prospective GM might best be explained by Aquilini's friendship with Geoff Courtnall, a former Canuck who was also Gillis's first client as a player agent. Courtnall had long sung Gillis's praises as an agent and a hockey mind, some of which had sunk in with Aquilini.

At Gillis's packed introductory press conference, his mission statement was simple. "I'm hoping to bring a different perspective," Gillis told the overflow crowd of reporters and team employees. "I'm hoping to bring different ideas to the draft table and to player development. I'm hoping to be able to attract players here because, in dealing with them for the last seventeen years, I understand the message they want to hear and what is important to them."

Gillis was straightforward about the club he'd taken over. "I think this team needs to get faster. It needs more grit; it needs to be more competitive. We have a solid defence and solid goaltending. But there are a number of areas that need to be addressed. If they get addressed well, this team won't be far [away]."

Gillis's matter-of-fact approach was bracing for Vancouver's longtime media members. In contrast to the effusive Burke, Gillis's approach was not cultivated for the ten-second TV clip. "The best thing I remember was his first press conference," says player agent Rich Evans, who has known Gillis since law school. "That was pure Gillis, with his short, blunt answers to some of the questions from the press. Our law school buddies loved that press conference."

"Humble is not Gillis's strong suit," wrote *Maclean's* in 2012. "In his maiden press conference in 2008, the rookie GM took a shot at the powerful Brian Burke–Dave Nonis duumvirate—the pair were fired by the Canucks ahead of his arrival, both moving on to the Maple Leafs organization—calling out their woeful recent drafting record, spotty player development and a lack of competitiveness."

Where many saw a supremely confident rookie GM ripe for a fall, Laurence Gilman knew better about an agent who'd been analyzing thirty teams, not a single organization. "He understands how players and agents think and knows what they look for in teams. He developed this insight from having watched and studied many organizations over a long period of time. His approach has been very refreshing. Mike's advantage is that he's an independent thinker and a great manager. He provides tremendous leadership and support, yet has the ability to listen to his staff and follow their counsel."

"His vision was cultivated from his experiences as both a

player and as an agent," says Evans. "There is a real advantage for a GM to have been an agent, in that a GM who has been an agent has a particular understanding of what motivates players and what is important to them."

Player agent J.P. Barry, who represented the Sedins, saw the advantages in having an agent in the GM's job. "I think a very experienced player agent ultimately knows players," Barry told the *Vancouver Sun*. "He knows how players think, he knows veteran and younger players having had very close relationships with them. That would probably be asset No. 1. And then obviously having a very strong knowledge of the business of hockey in all facets is important... and Mike is a former player, so he has that experience also."

Gillis was hardly the first player agent to be hired as an NHL general manager. Burke, Pierre Lacroix, Peter Chiarelli, and others had made the switch across the aisle. But there had never been anyone so pro-player, so hostile to management, who made the switch. "Mike's reputation as an agent was that of an extremely hard bargainer," says Gilman. "He implicitly understood his client's leverage and maximized it in each and every negotiation. He was viewed as an independent operator and a staunch supporter of players' rights." NHL commissioner Gary Bettman, who'd watched Gillis extract $45 million over five years for workmanlike centre Bobby Holik, was reportedly stunned that an owner was bringing him into the inner sanctum of management.

The teams that Gillis had taken to the cleaners in negotiations scoffed, saying the then forty-nine-year-old would now get a taste of his own medicine. "When Mike Gillis was hired, he had a lot of enemies and people who didn't like him, and they may still feel that way," TSN's Bob McKenzie reflected in 2011 for Jason Farris's book *Behind the Moves*. McKenzie knew that it would be tough to get a break from those people had the Canucks won the Cup that year. "There will be people who will say, 'You have to give him his due,' and there will be others who say, 'Well, two-thirds of his team came from Dave Nonis and Brian Burke.' So a GM can't win or lose."

Gillis and the real estate magnate's family quickly plotted a course that would defy hockey convention. The goal, says Gillis, was "to make Vancouver a destination for players around the league. A place where players tell their agent they want to go." If you could attract the best players, the thinking went, the winning would naturally follow. While other sports had been opening up to new possibilities of doing business, the concept of a hockey version of the *Moneyball* revolution—so called after Michael Lewis's book of the same name, which documented how the small-market Oakland A's had dramatically rethought player evaluation via computer models—was unthinkable that spring. But Gillis had absorbed the fundamental message of Lewis's book.

"The message I got was, in such a tight market for talent, you needed to look beyond the conventional means of thinking," he says. "In hockey, people have not wanted to go beyond their experience to find new solutions. Some hockey people dismissed *Moneyball* because Oakland never won using it. But the A's were a small market, and when they taught the big guys how it works, their advantage was gone. The Red Sox did adopt those principles and won two World Series. Being a small market who can't compete is not a problem we have here in Vancouver."

The progressive model in hockey was embodied by the Detroit Red Wings. As a cold-weather city with a fading economy and not much sex appeal, Detroit had still become the destination of choice for many top players. "Why do people want to come to Detroit?" asks GM Ken Holland. "In the nineties and early 2000s, it was to play with Stevie Yzerman and the Russian Five. In the 2000s to today, it's to play with Nick Lidstrom and Pavel Datsyuk and Henrik Zetterberg. Great players help to lure players to your team. And we're a hockey area, too, where people play the game. We were one of the first ones to have our own plane.

"Our owners are first class, and you have players recruiting players. So we had Marian Hossa come for a year, and Brian Rafalski and Dominik Hasek. We also have a great coaching staff. Mike Babcock is tough on the players, but he knows when to back off, when to give them space. When you come into downtown Detroit on a road trip, that's not all there is to the city. The suburbs are great. We have a lot of people come to Detroit and stay there after they retire. Michiganders are fabulous people. Our players pass that on to other players."

The end goal was to do the same for Vancouver, a team hobbled by its onerous travel schedule. As an agent, Gillis knew what players really wanted in a market, and so the team consulted sleep experts about travel, dietitians about better eating, sports psychologists about stress.

Continuity would also be a hallmark of the team Gillis and his management wanted to build. "If you look around at successful sports franchises, the most successful, by and large, have stability and continuity over a long period of time," Gilman told the Vancouver *Province*. "The Pittsburgh Steelers have had three coaches over the last forty years [Chuck Noll, Bill Cowher, and Mike Tomlin]. That's the way we've modelled ourselves." Gillis wanted players to talk that way about Vancouver and set about doing it from day one.

Upon taking the reins of the Canucks in 2008, Gillis wanted to emphasize skill, speed, and a progressive mentality about player development. It was not always easy to get an accurate reading in the early years. "The process becomes more important. What you're seeing against what you're hoping. Hope doesn't work in this business. You have to be very in tune of where you are in the curve of winning. It's up to us to create a culture that allows us to continue the process."

51

With thirty teams squeezed under the NHL's salary cap, the chance to gain an advantage, however slight, can be the difference between making the playoffs or not. While Gillis did not conduct business in a white coat, he and the organization used their team as a laboratory to challenge the conventional from day one of his mandate. Some of their research was made public. Other experiments were kept on the QT, away from prying eyes till the research was done. Why give away your secret weapon to opponents who could beat you with it?

For that reason, the Canucks would seek out players who were, if not educated, then open to concepts that might have them ridiculed in the nasty echo chamber of the NHL. "We want players who'll keep an open mind when we approach them about something that's out of the norm," said Gillis. "The last thing we want are players who tell guys on other teams about how crazy the organization is. We hope that they'll absorb what we're doing on travel, for instance, and realize that we're making an investment in them as well as in the team."

While Gillis was cautious about the base he inherited, the 2008-09 Canucks certainly had potential. They had a veteran core in goalie Roberto Luongo; the Sedin twins, Daniel and Henrik; emerging centre Ryan Kesler; and veteran defencemen Mattias Ohlund, Willie Mitchell, and Sami Salo. However, the farm system—which lost top defence prospect Luc Bourdon in a fatal motorcycle crash during Gillis's first summer with the Canucks—was felt to be bereft of emerging talents after Brian Burke's bumptious tenure as GM in Vancouver.

Gillis believed turnover in the roster was important, but that a total rebuild was unnecessary. He instructed Gilman, ex-Islander player Lorne Henning (director of player personnel), and former client Dave Gagner (then player development head) that they'd have "three drafts every two years," combing the ranks of unsigned college and junior players for talents passed over to supplement the drafted prospects. They and their scouts were to find gems who'd been passed over. They would play the long game, refusing to rush the future. "The best teams don't have one dramatic spike and then disappear," Gillis said. "Too many things can go wrong if you load up for a single year or two. Injuries, a bad year from your goalie. Teams like Detroit put together a foundation that allows them to be competitive every year. They don't sacrifice development to take a shot on a rental player. If it works, we'll be in the playoffs, and once in a while that will result in a championship."

As an example, the team discovered undrafted defenceman Chris Tanev playing in anonymity for Markham of the second-tier Ontario Junior Hockey League in 2008–09. Tanev, who had grown late into his six-foot, two-inch frame, had played with top prospects Steven Stamkos and P.K. Subban as a young man. But then he'd left elite hockey for a time, before ending up at the Rochester Institute of Technology and in the OJHL. He was as far off the conventional radar as any player could be. Yet by the 2011 playoffs, he was getting regular shifts on the Canucks' defence. Darren Archibald was another undrafted free agent, signing as an overage junior in 2010 and making it to the NHL in 2013.

To back up his promise of action, Gillis immediately executed an offer sheet for St. Louis restricted free agent David Backes in the summer of 2008. Signing an RFA to an offer sheet is the general manager's equivalent of peeing in the pool. In the live-and-let-live climate of NHL managers, it's simply rude to force your colleague into matching the offer, a gamble that will be reciprocated at a future date. Unsurprisingly, the Blues were not amused, matching the Canucks' three-year, $7.5 million proposal. (The Blues would later retaliate, signing Vancouver RFA Steve Bernier to an offer sheet, forcing Gillis to match.) But Gillis had sent his message to the fan base that he would not be complacent.

Yes, that would be the Canucks' notorious passive-aggressive fan base. Perhaps Gillis's biggest challenge upon taking over

53

the Vancouver job was to change the culture surrounding a team that hadn't won a Stanley Cup in its four decades of existence. "The one thing that surprised me is how focused the media is on negativity," Gillis told the *Province*'s Ben Kuzma in the fall of 2008. "Like past events that occurred long before I got here and that seem to have set a tone. I'm surprised, when you change over 30–35 per cent of your team, that it's not enough. We've made changes in literally every element of this organization. I read where we haven't done enough, and that it's been all talk and no action, and I find that pretty disappointing. We're trying to do the things that people have really wanted for some time."

But Vancouver is a different market in many ways. Some teams raise statues to great scorers. Others to great goalies. On April 7, 2011, the Vancouver Canucks raised a statue to a former coach holding a towel on a stick. The iconic gesture belonged to Roger Neilson, coach of the improbable Canucks of 1982, a ragtag team that somehow ended up in its first Stanley Cup final against the New York Islanders, the dynastic team of the era. During the third period of a Campbell Conference final game in Chicago, as Vancouver took yet another penalty, Neilson waved a white trainer's towel atop a hockey stick in mock surrender to the officials. Several Vancouver players followed suit (all were tossed from the game), but a movement was born.

"I've never seen that before," said a stunned announcer Don Wittman on *Hockey Night in Canada* as Neilson brandished his makeshift flag in protest. Neilson's white towel soon became an iconic symbol of solidarity for the Canucks' irate fans, emulated by thousands at the next game in Vancouver. The Canucks won the final three games of the series against Chicago, and Towel Power was born. Something in Neilson's defiance touched a nerve with the citizens of Vancouver and B.C. The team had been a passion for the community till then, but Neilson's underdog insubordination took the connection to a new level.

The Canucks have always seen themselves as outsiders. By the time Gillis was hired in 2008, the province of British Columbia had long epitomized outsider status within Canada. Studies show that, while all western provinces are miffed over their standing within the nation, B.C. is the most disaffected. West Coasters can point to disproportionate representation relative to Quebec and the Maritimes in both houses of Parliament or to the Torontocentric coverage of *Hockey Night in Canada* to buttress their claim that they're hard done by. The put-upon feeling about the province's place in Confederation mirrored the sentiments of the average Canucks fan faced with repeated disappointments from the home side, both before and after the 1982 miracle Cup run. It took Vancouver twelve years to return to the Cup final, and a further seventeen before their almost-victory against the Bruins.

From 1967, when they were omitted from the NHL's first round of expansion in favour of such hockey hotbeds as St. Louis, Oakland, and Philadelphia, Canucks fans have always felt somehow cheated by the process. The Canucks were like Sam in *Casablanca*: bit players in a larger drama. Always there, but never the focus. The team's pugnacious image epitomized the team's early decades, one that wholly endorsed the NHL's code of conduct on and off the ice.

"It was a crowd that appreciated the blue-collar guy, the hard worker like Gary Lupul or Cliff Ronning or Stan Smyl," says Canucks TV voice John Shorthouse. "Look at the ring of honour. Guys like Harold Snepsts, Orland Kurtenbach—real hardscrabble guys. There were a lot of years of ineptitude. I think they shared the record with the Seattle Mariners for the most sub-.500 seasons. They were lovable losers. For the first decade, it was the novelty of seeing the Beliveaus and guys like that."

"When the Canucks came into the NHL, they were so bad for so many years," recalls Ray Ferraro, a native of Trail, B.C., who played 1,258 NHL games with six teams. "That *Hockey Night*

55

in Canada ad would come up and say, 'This week, it's Toronto versus Boston, except in Vancouver, where you'll see Oakland versus the Canucks.' I'd go, 'Oh God, not again.'"

Shorthouse, who grew up in the Lower Mainland, shared Ferraro's pain. "The thing about hockey in Vancouver in the first twenty years is that the team was awful. Nineteen eighty-two was an aberration, a fluke. That's all we had to hang our hat on. There was nothing to like about the Canucks except Jim Robson, who was the best broadcaster in the country. He was the best thing about the franchise."

Outside of the *annus mirabilis* in 1982, when they snuck through the flotsam of upsets in the Campbell Conference, the Canucks were just a team that started their games awfully late by Toronto or New York standards. The Edmonton Oilers and Calgary Flames had highly skilled teams in the eighties and nineties. Vancouver pulled off upsets, but they were largely roadkill in the Smythe Division whenever they pushed past Winnipeg into the playoffs. "In those days, the Oilers and the Flames were good, they were really good," recalls Stan Smyl. "When we'd go in to play them, our dressing room was pretty quiet. The only way we could beat them was to keep it close. Any time we didn't keep it close, they turned it up." Historically, the Oilers are 2–0 against the Canucks in playoff series, while Vancouver is 2–4 against the Flames, many of those series dating to Smyl's heyday.

In fact, the iconic image of the Canucks in those early decades was the "Electric Kool-Aid Acid Test" jersey the team adopted in 1978. Having worn sober blue-and-green jerseys from the time of their origin, the Canucks suddenly incorporated all the worst aspects of disco, pop psychology, and Sherwin-Williams paint chips into their uniforms. The team look—designed by Beyl & Boyd of San Francisco—was suddenly a pizza confection of yellow, red, and black vomited over the shoulders of the players' jerseys. A stylized *V* hung around

56

the necks of the Canuck players like a millstone. Management's expressed rationale for the suits, seemingly reached after an expedition to Big Sur, was that the mellow hues of the former uniform were not exciting enough to propel the Canucks to Gretzky-like heights of accomplishment. If the unis could only make the eyes bleed, the garish garb could humble the Great One and vault Thomas Gradin to Cup immortality.

"I was a rookie the year they came out, so I didn't say much," recalls Smyl. "I'd played in New Westminster and had seen a lot of the games. I loved that logo with the stick in the C. People forget that we played the exhibition season wearing the old green-and-blue jerseys. No one saw what the new jerseys looked like till opening night. I still have the number 47 blue and green I wore that final preseason game. Then, wow. I'll never forget it. They put the same V design on the socks, and guys would tape them over so you couldn't see it. That made it even more wild." To this day, when lists of the worst jerseys of all time are compiled, the Canucks' Pizza Pop outfits are regularly included among them.

Smyl epitomized the Canucks' blue-collar identity in its first twenty years: a stocky spark plug known as the Steamer, he was gritty, underrated, and unprepossessing. At five feet, nine inches and 190 pounds, he hardly constituted a dominating presence, but his relentless style and leadership made him a ready-made captain. He retired with franchise records in every major statistical category: 262 goals, 411 assists, and 673 points in 896 games played. On November 3, 1991, he also became the first Canuck to have his jersey number, 12, raised to the rafters. "Stan Smyl was going to run over you not go round you," says Ferraro. "The people took him to their heart. But then the team would go backward again."

57

The lunch-pail Canucks of Smyl, Harold Snepsts, Tiger Williams, Darcy Rota, and "King" Richard Brodeur passed from the scene after the near-miss in 1982, the team lapsing into also-rans who made the playoffs just four times the rest of the decade without ever winning a series. A series of misbegotten trades didn't prevent the decline. After drafting B.C. product Cam Neely in the first round in 1983, the Canucks' new GM, Jack Gordon, dealt the young winger to Boston in 1987 for Barry Pederson. Neely went on to lead the Bruins to the Cup final that same season and enjoyed a Hall of Fame career. The injury-plagued Pederson was a spent force who kicked around the NHL till 1991 without ever duplicating his pre-trade skill. Adding to the insult, Gordon also gave up Vancouver's 1987 first-round draft pick in the deal, with which the Bruins chose the fine defenceman Glen Wesley.

The 1990s produced young, skilled players such as Pavel Bure, Trevor Linden, Geoff Courtnall, and Kirk McLean, coached by Pat Quinn. Part of the credit for the change in the Canucks' image belongs to the emphasis on skill brought by Bure, the Russian Rocket (later represented by Mike Gillis). While Trevor Linden was the favourite of Vancouver fans, Bure was Vancouver's first bona fide NHL superstar. "Trevor was the backbone, but Pavel was the superstar who put the Canucks on the map," says Shorthouse. "They'd never had a player like that before. They became a team you wanted to see when they were on the road. If you'd been in the building in November of 1991, when he played his first game, it was just electrifying. The number of times he picked up the puck and went end to end in a game, you needed more than the fingers of one had to count. It was edge-of-the-seat, and he was accepted immediately by the fans."

On one of the rare occasions when the Canucks were blessed by good fortune, the team stole Bure in 1989 with a sixth-round pick in the draft. (Detroit was poised to surreptitiously choose him in a later round in a draft that had already netted them Nicklas Lidstrom, Sergei Fedorov, and Vlad Konstantinov.) Most teams believed Bure wasn't eligible for the

58

1989 draft, but Canuck scout Mike Penny discovered a loop-hole that allowed Bure to become a Canuck.

A dynamic skater whose brilliant career was eventually side-lined at age thirty-four with knee problems, Bure (along with Linden and McLean) pushed the team to three straight winning seasons and back-to-back Smythe Division titles from 1991–92 to 1993–94. The rebirth resulted in a second visit to the Stan-ley Cup final, this one much closer than the rout of 1982. In one of the best finals ever, the New York Rangers, led by the old Canuck killer Mark Messier, outlasted Vancouver in seven games in 1994, ending the Rangers' own fifty-four-year Cup drought. Not for the final time, it was someone else's day.

As opposed to the one-off 1982 squad, the 1994 team seemed well positioned for a lengthy run of success with young talent on the ice and Quinn calling the shots. But after los-ing in the second round of the 1995 playoffs and first round of the 1996 playoffs, the Canucks missed the postseason alto-gether till 2001, deepening their fans' gloom. In that time, the Canucks acquired Messier and Alex Mogilny and almost obtained Gretzky. Mike Keenan, who had coached the Rang-ers against the Canucks in the 1994 final, was hired partway through the 1997–98 season when Tom Renney was fired as coach. It was hoped he would re-create his New York miracle for the team he had beaten three years earlier. He later served as the de facto GM between the Quinn and Brian Burke eras. "The team was in flux because it had gone to the Cup finals in 1994 and Pat Quinn's management style—which had paid off in the past—was that he was very loyal and patient," recalls Keenan. "Even when he had the flexibility to move players, he didn't want to do that if they'd had success with him. When Pat came [into the] league, there was a sense of loyalty to players. But I was there when the team and the league were in transition away from that. It was perfectly clear that the young stars like Pavel Bure and Trevor Linden and Todd Bertuzzi and Bryan

McCabe were at a point in their contracts where they were capable of asking for more. And yet the older players wanted more money, and it wasn't possible to pay everyone."

The biggest source of conflict for Keenan was Linden, a godlike figure to many Canucks fans, who had given up the captaincy to Messier. The bitter feud between the two resulted in Linden heading to the Islanders in what eventually became a productive 1998 trade for Vancouver that netted Jarkko Ruutu, Todd Bertuzzi, and Bryan McCabe.

Nothing seemed to work under Keenan, and the departure of Bure in 1999 symbolized the meltdown of a promising era. The Russian star grew disenchanted with the attitude of the Vancouver front office ("The management team here seemed to think it had to control and dominate its players to keep them on their toes," wrote Tony Gallagher of the *Province*) and with his contract. Bure fired his agent, Ron Salcer, and engaged Gillis to force a trade (to Florida, where he won back-to-back goal-scoring titles).

Fans and local media in Vancouver quickly turned on Bure. *Province* writer Elliot Pap declared, "Let me say, Pavel Bure's No. 10 should never be hung from the rafters unless the punk is still in it." (Bure eventually had his number honoured in 2013 and, with Pap looking on, was not required to be hung with it.)

For fans who had seen the Canucks lose with little top-flight talent in the 1970s and '80s, it was galling to see the club losing now with what seemed like real talent. The only bright spot was the move from the decrepit Pacific Coliseum to GM Place (later Rogers Arena) in 1995, a move that, ironically, forced the Vancouver-based Griffiths family out as owners when the costs of the new arena and other family holdings became too onerous.

60   The arrival of Brian Burke from the NHL head office to become general manager in 1998 and the hiring of former Canuck Marc Crawford as head coach in 1999 sparked yet another turnaround by the dawn of the new century, one that

saw the Canucks return to the postseason for the first time in five years. Through drafting and trades, Burke assembled a core of skilled young talent that included Markus Naslund, Brendan Morrison, Todd Bertuzzi, and the Sedin twins, Daniel and Henrik. Naslund, Morrison, and Bertuzzi formed the West Coast Express line, one of the top threesomes in the NHL.

All the team lacked for an extended playoff run was an elite goalie. Never was that clearer than in 2002, when Crawford's team had the Red Wings powerhouse at their mercy after winning the first two games of the opening series at the Joe Louis Arena in Detroit. But a soft goal on Dan Cloutier from centre ice by Detroit's Nicklas Lidstrom in Game 3 flipped the momentum in the series, and the Red Wings went on to win by capturing the next four games. The series also produced a vintage paranoid rant from a frustrated Burke, who, summoning the spirit of Roger Neilson, bitched that the Canucks were not getting a fair shake from the referees. "I want to point out to the officials that Todd Bertuzzi does not play for Detroit; it just looks like that because he's wearing two or three Red Wings sweaters all the time... Sedin is not Swedish for 'punch me' or 'headlock me in a scrum.'"

Despite his legal background, Burke was not the bookish type. His emotional style (he famously claimed to want "truculent" players) was reflected in a team that had edgy players such as Bertuzzi, Matt Cooke, Brad May, and Jarkko Ruutu sowing mayhem with opponents. With an attack that featured skill and intimidation, the Canucks seemed poised to win the Northwest Division for the first time in the spring of 2004. But the testosterone-heavy atmosphere Burke preferred caught up with the Canucks after Colorado Avalanche forward Steve Moore delivered a heavy check to the head of Canucks captain Naslund on February 18, an injury that caused him to miss three games. "There's definitely a bounty on his head," Vancouver's Brad May said of Moore. "Clean hit or not, Nazzy is our best player, and you respond. It's going to be fun when we get him." With the Canucks losing the March 8 game 9-2 to Colorado in the third period, there was time for more punishment. Despite warnings from the officials, Crawford put Bertuzzi on the ice late in the third period. Bertuzzi stalked Moore, tugging at the back of his sweater as they skated up and down the ice. He then swung a gloved hand into Moore's right temple. The Colorado forward fell forward, defenceless, onto his face. Bertuzzi attempted to pull Moore's head up off the ice, but he was restrained. Moore remained face down on the ice, having suffered two broken vertebrae in his neck and a deep concussion.

The roof fell in on Bertuzzi and the Canucks, with the media leading the charge, replaying the incident on a loop to appalled viewers, many of whom were not familiar with the nuances of the NHL's brand of anger management. Burke swung into action to protect Bertuzzi and his team, excoriating the media for "crucifying" the six-foot, three-inch, 240-pound forward. "You've taken this opportunity to kick the crap out of him, and I think it's been just shameful." The police charged Bertuzzi criminally, and civil suits from Moore and his family followed not long after. While far from the only team that played by the sword, Burke's Canucks came to personify intimidation and violence in the eyes of many. Before the media maelstrom died down, Bertuzzi was suspended for the rest of the regular season and playoffs.

Without their star winger's scoring and physical presence— and traumatized by the scrutiny from nearly everyone outside hockey—the Canucks stumbled to the finish line, scarcely hanging on to the Northwest Division title everyone had conceded to them weeks before. In the first round, the Canucks faced the Calgary Flames, who had barely scraped into the playoffs for the first time in eight years. Led by the brilliant goaltending of Miikka Kiprusoff, the Flames pushed Vancouver to a seventh game in Vancouver. Calgary held a tenuous one-goal lead until

62

very late in the charged contest. With star defenceman Ed Jova-novski in the penalty box watching the final seconds tick off, Calgary captain Jarome Iginla (who'd scored earlier) missed an open net and then tripped over his own dropped stick. Moments later, the Canucks' Matt Cooke tied the game with less than a minute left in regulation. GM Place threatened to come off its moorings as the Canuck fans' luck finally looked to be changing in 2004. With Jovanovski still in the penalty box, the game then went to overtime. In a cruel turnabout typical of the Canucks, a former local hero, Martin Gelinas, brought down the room as he scraped the puck behind Alex Auld from the right side of the net. The winner for Calgary eliminated Vancouver. Once more, a promising Canucks scenario was ending in disappointment.

The team that had shown so much promise was never quite the same again, as the NHL shut down business for the 2004–05 labour lockout of players. Burke never made it past the lockout, replaced as GM in 2004 by his assistant, Dave Nonis. The Bertuzzi cloud seemed to hang over the Canucks until the summer of 2006, when Nonis dealt him for Florida's star goalie, Roberto Luongo. Coach Marc Crawford was fired when Vancouver missed the 2006 playoffs. In the three seasons after the lockout, the team alternated between missing the postseason and suffering frustrating playoff losses. A fan could get a complex.

There were elements of progress. The Sedin twins morphed into durable, reliable eighty-point players on the first line. New addition Luongo gave the Canucks their best goalie since Kirk McLean—perhaps their best ever. A veteran defence augured well if the team could make the playoffs.

Still, as Gillis assumed office, there was a deep psychosis among Canuck fans. A longing unfulfilled. "There was no great era of Canuck hockey," says Ferraro. "Now is the best time ever for hockey in this city."

63

5

New Recruits

"The minute I'm making speeches in the dressing room
is the minute I don't have a coach."

MIKE GILLIS

IN MOST NHL changeovers, the new broom sweeps clean. In some areas, Gillis was active with the broom in the summer of 2008. He chose not to re-sign his former client Naslund, who went to the Rangers as a free agent. Fan favourite Brendan Morrison, too, was allowed to walk. But Gillis said he would otherwise keep an open mind. "I have not made any predisposed decisions based on anything I have heard. This is a clean slate moving forward. People will be evaluated on their performance. There may be some people who do not want to be here because I'm here. I don't know that yet. But we will find out. There are a lot of loyal people that have been here for a long time, and they need to be treated fairly." Predictably, some familiar names did leave after Nonis's departure, including Steve Tambellini, who eventually became the Edmonton Oilers' GM. Yet others, such as Canuck legend Stan Smyl, stayed in player development.

Would coach Alain Vigneault survive the Gillis takeover? "It's a safe bet that he hasn't decided to go all in or fold his cards on Vigneault," proclaimed the *Vancouver Sun*. "If, in fact, losing boring was a factor, it would not augur well for Vigneault and/or his staff," pronounced Tony Gallagher in the *Province*. It was not a decision, Gillis told reporters, that he was going to hurry along—a first taste of the deliberative Gillis style. "Of course we want to resolve it, but I don't want to rush to make a mistake. There are a lot of factors, and it's complicated. We're well along in the process, and I'm very comfortable that the process will play itself out." Vigneault himself felt he deserved a further chance with the team. "Given the circumstances, the job was well done," Gillis said. "The question is if it will continue to be done."

After a brief NHL playing career with St. Louis, Vigneault had turned to coaching in the Quebec Major Junior Hockey League with Trois-Rivieres, Hull, and Beauport. In between, he spent time as an assistant in Ottawa with the Senators. His head-coaching debut had come in the hothouse of his native province of Quebec, with the Montreal Canadiens. At first, things went well. He was nominated for the Jack Adams Award as coach of the year in 2000, but, plagued by injuries to key players, Montreal missed the postseason in two of his seasons as coach. Partway through his fourth season, he was fired, and he returned to coaching in the QMJHL with the Prince Edward Island Rocket. "I never thought of giving up," he recalled later. "I learned a lot from my time in Montreal, and I knew I could still coach at that level."

In the summer of 2005, the Quebec City native was back in pro hockey, tabbed to coach the Manitoba Moose, the chief farm team of the Canucks. When Marc Crawford was fired as the Canucks head coach the following summer, it was next man up for Vigneault. His patience and determination during the stint in junior and the minors had paid off. Significantly. General manager Dave Nonis rewarded Vigneault with a franchise goalie, acquiring Roberto Luongo from Florida. While Luongo gave the club instant credibility in the competitive Western Conference, the years under Nonis had mixed results.

Year one saw the Canucks set a new record for wins in a season under Vigneault as they captured the Northwest Division title. This time, Vigneault won the Jack Adams Award. The club made it to the second round of the postseason, beating Dallas in seven games before getting dumped by Anaheim, the eventual Stanley Cup champions. With the Sedin twins maturing and Luongo backstopping a veteran defence corps, it appeared that the team was poised to break through under Vigneault.

It would take a few more years before that breakthrough occurred. As encouraging as that year seemed, 2007–08 was bitterly disappointing as the injury-racked Canucks missed the postseason after a disastrous end to the season. It appeared that the jinx surrounding winners of the Adams Award might strike Vigneault just as he appeared to have found a nice perch in Vancouver.

For his part, Vigneault knew the fate of many holdover coaches when a new GM comes in. "Usually, the new guy wants new people," Vigneault reflected a few years later. "I didn't know Mike. Even though he was a top agent there for years, our paths had never crossed. But Mike made it clear that he was open to talking. We met every day for three weeks talking about philosophy, discussing our ideas about the game. He made it clear that he wanted to make Vancouver a destination of choice in both the conditions the players had, but also in the style we played."

In the end, Gillis decided Vigneault would continue, along with assistant Rick Bowness. (Two other assistant coaches were dismissed.) The former Montreal coach bought into Gillis's system. "Alain's a very smart guy," says Gillis. "When we explained what we wanted to do, he came on board." The coach's contract was extended for an additional year. "I can't answer on ifs and buts... I can just answer on what happened," Vigneault told reporters, "and what happened is that Mike decided I was the

66

guy. It was a good process. We covered every base, and I felt as if we were moving forward. It looked to me, without any confirmation from Mike's part, that I was becoming his guy."

With Gillis stressing skill, it was thought that Vigneault would be a poor fit for the Canucks' new era. But Vigneault said that the team's defensive emphasis before Gillis's arrival was more a function of talent than attitude. "Actually, not much really changed in the scheme after Mike came in. What changed was the skill we had. The level was not good enough to play that way before. But now, we had guys like the [Sedin] twins and Kesler there for five or six years, coming into their own who could play a more attacking style. So I didn't really change my coaching philosophy all that much." In fact, Vigneault would soon show his own progressive streak in his innovative uses of ice time and zone starts.

The coach and his new GM quickly settled into a working relationship. "We have a good rapport, and Mike empowers his staff. He listens and takes his time; he's not rushed into things. He's good at managing up. So the transition was smooth, and he's made every move to have the operation be first class. Whether it's the sleep doctors or the Nike evaluation camp in Oregon, he's always trying to make things better."

While the GM had definite ideas about what he wanted from his team, according to Vigneault he was not like Billy Beane in *Moneyball*, throwing furniture and water coolers in the dressing room when unhappy. "Mike's around the dressing room, but he's not overly present." Said Gillis, "The minute I'm making speeches in the dressing room is the minute I don't have a coach." Still, there were many in 2008 who thought the two men might not coexist for long. Given a string of losing games, went the thinking, Vigneault would revert to type as a defensive coach. Five years later, they were still waiting for the schism. "Vigneault was perfect for this market," observes John Shorthouse. "He doesn't care what anybody says, anybody writes. He laughs at it.

I've never met anyone who doesn't care what people think about him, his decisions, [whether] he should be fired. He doesn't care. That's the attitude you have to have in a place like this."

In his introductory press conference, Gillis hinted that "a couple of very good decisions, or a couple of really bold decisions, might put this team in a position to win immediately." To make that point in year one, he turned his focus on Mats Sundin, the Toronto Maple Leafs' iconic team captain. In recent years, Sundin had frequently turned down trades to contending teams, preferring to stay with the underachieving Maple Leafs. It was often thought he'd never leave the Leafs, despite the team's poor record. After thirteen seasons and 420 career goals in the blue and white, Sundin had become a free agent and retreated to Sweden. Now, the reluctant Sundin was being wooed by Gillis, who offered him two years at a whopping $20 million. Montreal, which had traded for his rights shortly before he filed for free agency, and the New York Rangers jumped into the fray, but Sundin remained, tantalizingly, in Sweden, unsure whether he had any more hockey in his system.

Gillis persisted with Sundin and his agent, J.P. Barry. On December 18, after much procrastinating and press speculation, Sundin finally signed a one-year contract worth $8.6 million, prorated over the remainder of the season—a $1.4 million pay cut from the Canucks' original offer. In negotiations, Sundin had decreased his asking price in order to give the Canucks salary-cap space to bolster their lineup before the end of the season. Gillis tried to dampen Mats Mania in Vancouver. "What we want to do is get in the playoffs and win round by round," he cautioned upon the signing. "For me, it's the process of how the team plays and the integrity it plays with. I know we will get results if we play that way. I think Mats is a great player that joins a good group of players that are committed to winning. I think we are a better team for sure. I am not going to place that label [contender] on any team."

While the Sundin move didn't ultimately pay off in a Vancouver Stanley Cup, it sent a message to the league that the Canucks could and would compete for the best players.

The successful wooing of Sundin was just one feature of a whirlwind of activity designed to defy convention and show that, as a new boy in the GM fraternity, Gillis would not be pushed around. Toronto president/GM Brian Burke was caught on Leafs TV discussing a rumoured deal on draft day in 2008 that would have seen the Canucks send Kevin Bieksa, Alex Burrows, and their top pick to the Tampa Bay Lightning in an attempt to grab Swedish defenceman Victor Hedman with the second-overall pick. This after Maple Leafs head coach Ron Wilson had told a Toronto radio station that the Leafs would be interested in going after the Sedin twins during the free-agency period.

Gillis reacted. "There are certainly some issues that the league needs to take control of when players' names are being thrown around," he told The Team 1040. "You're talking about lives and families, and those things need to be kept confidential when you may be discussing a transaction of some type. There was a mention of players' names, which was very upsetting for them, and it doesn't make me feel very good."

The Canucks filed tampering charges against their former GM and his new organization. "Listen, I don't anticipate a fight with anybody; however, we're going to protect the integrity of this organization and our players," Gillis told The Team 1040. "If anybody wants to take a shot at them inappropriately, we're going to protect our interests." The NHL fined Wilson $10,000 for his part in tampering with the Sedins, while Burke and the Leafs management were given a warning for the draft incident.

Some whispered about the impertinence of calling Burke on charges of tampering, but those who'd known Gillis a long time were not surprised. *Maclean's* pointed out in 2012 that he "has never been one of hockey's favourite sons. As an agent, the too-clever-by-half lawyer took on the league's general managers,

69

talking them into the kind of bloated contracts that led directly to 2005's lockout. As a GM, he's done it all over again, creating a destination franchise in what once was the league's Left Coast laughingstock, where the game's stars are practically begging to be underpaid."

The dyspeptic Gillis didn't describe them as miracles, but as results of a "process." One of those in the hockey biz who'd known Gillis for a while and shared his ideas about the "process" was Laurence Gilman. Out of work at the time of Gillis's hiring after being fired by Phoenix, Gilman was the quintessential new-era hockey executive. He'd never played competitive hockey in his hometown of Winnipeg. He'd been hired by the Jets as a cheap source of contract work. But in organizations full of hockey evaluators, having some sophistication in contract work became increasingly important. When the league adopted its hard salary cap (forcing all teams to stay under a total payroll) in 2005, teams needed Gilman and his brethren even more to keep order on the books. Gilman and Gillis had sat on opposite sides of the table on several occasions, such as when the Coyotes signed Gillis client Tony Amonte, but they had developed a healthy respect for each other. He'd followed the Jets to Phoenix when the team moved to the desert in 1996. Now he was on the Left Coast.

"I first met Mike at a Sports Lawyers Association conference in Boston in 1995," Gilman recalled. "I was working for the Winnipeg Jets at the time. We sat together while watching a Stanley Cup playoff game. He came across as reserved and guarded. However, he also seemed very intelligent and possessed definite views on how poorly run most NHL teams were at that time. I liked him. Several months later, I was working on a contract negotiation and had reached a stalemate with the agent for the player in question. I wanted insight from someone who worked on the other side. I called Mike and reintroduced myself. He was very guarded at first and didn't want to answer my questions. Eventually, he warmed up, and we had a very intellectual and philosophical discussion. Our relationship took off from that point."

With Gillis's hiring, Gilman fulfilled a promise. "Mike often told me that one day he would finally accept a GM position and that, when he did, I would be the first person he'd hire. Given that I was employed for most of that period, I never really gave it serious thought. Then I was let go in Phoenix. He accepted the Canucks GM job on Tuesday, April 22, 2008, called me on Friday, April 25, and I was in Vancouver by Sunday, April 27. Needless to say, I am extremely grateful that he kept his word."

FOR GILLIS, THE lone wolf, managing a large staff and roster of players would prove to be a seismic shift, both personally and professionally. His time was no longer his own. Having never suffered the criticism of media or fans in his days as an agent, it was a stressful transition for him, being seen by TV cameras in tense times in his booth at the arena. "It can be uncomfortable sometimes, because I've never sought that out," he said one day while lunching at the Italian Kitchen in downtown Vancouver. "I never aspired to that type of attention. It's something I didn't necessarily understand when I took this job—the amount of public awareness, the visibility. At the end of the day, people are supporting what we're doing. People have been very kind to Diane and me. I can't complain one bit." Sure enough, the maître d' and several fans stopped by Gillis's table at the restaurant to pass on best wishes to the club, which he accepted pleasantly.

In addition to transitioning his team for the future, Gillis had to be the public face of the franchise. That became a heavy burden after the unexpected deaths of the Canucks' former No. 1 pick Luc Bourdon (killed in a motorcycle crash) and Pavol Demitra (killed in the September 2011 Russian plane crash that wiped out the KHL team Lokomotiv Yaroslavl), plus the suicide of Rick Rypien, who died in the summer of 2011 after leaving for the Winnipeg Jets. Another Canuck draft pick, Yann Sauve, was hit by a car in the fall of 2010. It was Gillis's job to offer the right words in trying times—hardly what he had in mind when he took the position.

6

Accidentally on Purpose

"You see your best guy pulled and your captain sitting.
You think that isn't [depressing]?"

DON CHERRY

MIKE GILLIS PROBABLY understood "uneasy lies the head that wears the crown" as he sat on the sofa in his Vancouver home in the winter of 2009. In his first season as president and general manager of the Canucks, things had hit rock bottom. The club was in the midst of a lengthy winless streak, and the residents of Vancouver were not happy. The esoteric concepts of the previous summer were being tested on the rack of an NHL regular season. An exhausted Gillis sat back and sighed as the TV in his living room pitilessly showed the highlights from the Canucks' previous game, a 5–3 loss to the offensively challenged Nashville Predators. The TSN announcers talked darkly of a coaching change or major trade to shake up the reeling Canucks.

Gillis turned down the volume. His team was playing Minnesota that night, and another loss would make it eight games without a win—including an ugly six losses at home. He finally had his starting goalie, Roberto Luongo, back from a leg injury, but the team captain had lost four straight since his return. Even the arrival of Maple Leafs legend Mats Sundin had failed to ignite the club. Management was conducting individual interviews with players to divine the cause. One defenceman, Gillis later admitted, started crying when confronted about his recent play. "He felt he was playing tough enough, but when we showed him what we wanted, he got upset.

"I wish there was something magic I could do. We just have to stay with it. I've had people call me [from] around the league, telling me about how they went through the same thing. We're a good team, we'll get out of this. But it feels terrible."

Things did not improve that night against the Wild. The Canucks overcame 2-0 and 3-1 leads to tie the Wild with just fifteen seconds left. A palpable sense of gears shifting and luck changing was felt in the stands. And then Daniel Sedin took a penalty in overtime. Canucks forward Ryan Johnson's shot block went right to Marc-Andre Bergeron, who one-timed it past Luongo for a stunning 4-3 loss at home. The Canucks had thrown thirty-seven shots at Minnesota goalie Nicklas Backstrom and still lost. The Vancouver fans, inured to failure, silently trooped out of the arena, no doubt thinking, "Here we go again." In his office beneath the stands, Gillis leaned forward on his desk to change channels on the TV. A bottle of California red wine, untouched, sat beside him. The rookie GM was stoic, but even his ironclad self-confidence was being sorely tested. "That's what happens when you're going bad," he allowed as the highlights showed Bergeron's shot bulging the back of the Vancouver net. "We're a good team just getting in our own way."

Game 9 of the streak, against the Carolina Hurricanes two days later, found the Canucks tied again, this time with 1:22 left in the game. They were also killing a penalty. But Alex Burrows popped free on a breakaway, beating 'Canes goalie Cam Ward cleanly to end the streak. "Tied at three after fifty-seven minutes and we have to kill a penalty, and they already had two goals on their power play. A lot of people probably thought it was going to be another one of those games we wouldn't be able to close," Burrows told reporters afterward. "But we found a way to get it done, that's the bottom line, and now it's a lot of pressure off everybody's shoulders."

None more so than the rookie GM. "I'm going to try to get some sleep," he allowed as he departed GM Place, confident that for one night, at least, the world was not about to roll over on him. The time of innovation and promise from the previous September seemed a long way away.

IN HIS CAMPAIGN to show the media and the fan base that it was not business as usual, Gillis had been full of surprises in his first months as GM. He and Vigneault had appointed Roberto Luongo as the team captain, the first goalie in the NHL to hold that distinction since Bill Durnan, shortly after the Second World War. This was done in spite of league rules forbidding goalies to act as captains during the game. "I discussed with the team the number of games that we thought he could play," Vigneault told reporters afterward. "I talked to him about the leadership within our team, I asked him who he thought would be a good captain, good assistants, and he came up with the people you see around us here—then I went through with Roberto the characteristics I mentioned, and I said all those guys have those qualities, but there's one individual that has them on just a little higher level than anybody else. It took him a little while to figure out where I was going with this, and he said, 'You mean me?' And I said, 'Yes, and if you want the job, you want the responsibilities that go with it, I am offering it to you.' It took him about .01 seconds to say yes, he wanted the opportunity."

75

Because he couldn't operate as a captain on the ice, Luongo painted the *C* on his mask and let veterans Ryan Kesler, Willie Mitchell, and Mattias Ohlund perform the duties during

Canucks contests. "Opening faceoffs will be done by Mattias," said Vigneault, "because he's the longest-running Canuck, and since Willie likes to talk the most, we'll have him talk to the referee." Needless to say, the decision nettled the traditionalists, like *Hockey Night in Canada*'s Don Cherry. "You see your best guy pulled and your captain sitting," Cherry said. "You think that isn't [depressing]?"

But Gillis was unfazed. In addition, the team would carry no "designated heavyweight" fighter. Everyone on the roster would sink or swim on his skill. Yet, as he discovered during the long losing streak in January, simply having novel ideas and shaking up the status quo guarantee nothing in the NHL. Sometimes you have to hunch your shoulders into the wind and move forward, no matter how much it hurts to hear and see media reviews of your work.

Gillis's relationship with the media was perhaps the biggest challenge to his nature. Cordial and bemused in his first years as GM, Gillis did not court the Vancouver press who preyed upon his team and, by extension, him. His weekly radio spots on The Team 1040 were typically taciturn and replete with pauses and sighs. Press conferences were often like briefings from the politburo, with reporters left to fill in the blanks. He professed bafflement sometimes at things that fascinated the press corps, but, if given a well-timed question, he could be expansive and insightful. Early in his Vancouver tenure, Gillis declared a boycott on his players talking to *Hockey Night in Canada* because the Canucks protested that the telecast had smeared Alex Burrows in what he felt was a one-sided intermission feature.

Through all the prying cameras and reporters' questions, Gillis said he never regretted the trade-off he made. "I decided this is the job I wanted, I don't want to go anywhere else. Not being able to go fishing or hunting when I want to is challenging. But I can do those later. The chance to win a Stanley Cup and be influential in the hockey business by doing things right and creating a different environment is more important at this point in my life."

As tempting as it might have been to do so during the losing streak, Gillis and his management crew tried not to look back to the Burke and Nonis regimes to assign blame. The infamous "blame the predecessors" note remained unopened for now. "Even though there was massive external pressure about the coach and the players, we had a good team, not a great team, and we had a plan we wanted to stick to," Gillis recalls. In fact, the losing streak proved to be the last sustained stretch of mediocrity in 2008–09 (and for several years after). The Canucks went from a franchise record for consecutive home losses (seven) in January to a franchise record for consecutive home wins (eleven) in March. From the Carolina game on, the Canucks were the best team in the NHL, winning the Northwest Division over Calgary to return to the playoffs. The strong finish vaulted them into a first-round playoff blitz of St. Louis, beating the Blues in four straight while allowing just five goals. The new-look Canucks then faced Chicago in a bitter six-game series that saw the Blackhawks come back from a 2–0 deficit to win the series 4–2.

"I felt we were probably two years ahead of where we thought we'd be," Gillis reflected after the Chicago loss. "We had a chance to win that series, but weren't mature enough, experienced enough. We didn't have the right mix to overcome the adversity we encountered in that series. Based on our core, we were ahead of where we thought we'd be, but we still had a lot of work to do to compete for a Cup."

Year two saw more progress. In spite of a fourteen-game road trip necessitated by the 2010 Winter Olympics in Vancouver, the Canucks again finished first in the Northwest. They beat Los Angeles in six games in the first round, but were again upended by eventual Cup champion Chicago in six games—the final game a dispiriting 5–1 loss at home.

Through the first two seasons of the new regime, the "sins of the past" gave Gillis a firewall behind which to experiment and operate as he thought best. The importation of Sundin and former Gillis clients Mathieu Schneider and Pavol Demitra, the losing streak in year one, the hiring of Ryan Walter as assistant coach—none had worked completely as planned. But the team was winning series in the playoffs. In the glass-half-full mindset of the early years, they were seen as trying to break the loser mould. To most fans and media, there was something refreshing about the trial-and-error process that translated as a break with the past. It wouldn't always be that way.

ONE OF THE challenges for the Canucks in those playoffs had been the extensive travel involved. As a first priority, Gillis embarked upon solving the club's travel problems. As a player agent, Gillis had heard from his clients about the brutal travel West Coast teams such as the Canucks were subject to; he also knew that regular five-, seven-, or even ten-game road trips were a handicap to signing the best free agents. "The one thing that really hurts us in attracting players, especially ones that have played in the East their whole careers, is the issue of our travel. And our schedule," said Gillis in 2009. "We are at a severe disadvantage, because people just presume we are on the road all the time." Said former Columbus general manager Doug MacLean, "With Mike and the Canucks' travel situation, it's definitely something they have to focus on if they're not going to lose an edge on the ice and in competition for talent."

Gillis also was coming to appreciate the value of proper rest for a team, as opposed to working them harder. For instance, a two-hour nap can reverse the negative effects of a missed night of sleep. Proper hydration and rest at key moments are far more beneficial than extra training. In its understanding of sleep and rest, soccer has often been in the forefront of pro sports. Manchester United star Wayne Rooney describes the importance of getting eight hours at night: "To do your best in training, eight hours is fine... I can't lie in bed and force myself to sleep. I'll wait until I'm tired, normally about eleven or twelve, then get up around eight. You do notice the difference if you can't sleep for that long, which is normally after a night game. You don't get home until twelve and can't sleep until about four. Then you're tired."

The Canucks—whose nearest opponents are on the other side of the Rockies, in Alberta—log about 120,000 air kilometres a season and regularly experience lengthy road trips, such as the 2010 Olympic trip bookending the Games in their hometown. Vancouver players sleep in their own beds only about 50 per cent of the time during a season. There are no bus rides, no train trips, no getting back from a road game that same night. By comparison, a team located in the northeast of the continent has only a few dozen days during a regular season in which its players can't expect to sleep at home. They also take buses and ride trains to games, while the Canucks fly almost everywhere during a typical season.

During the 2011 Stanley Cup final, the Canucks and Bruins were four thousand kilometres and three time zones apart. (Only the 1905 Dawson City Nuggets travelled farther in a Cup-deciding series.) But while Boston's longest playoff trip before the final was to Tampa Bay, in its same (Eastern) time zone, Vancouver had already played two series in the Central time zone (versus Chicago and Nashville) and just once in their own Pacific time zone (San Jose). The shortest flight was to play the Sharks—about two and a half hours.

In the 2012 playoffs, while the Western Conference champion Los Angeles Kings had flown to series in Vancouver, St. Louis, and Phoenix, their Eastern counterparts in New Jersey had only taken buses in the final two rounds as they remained in the Eastern time zone exclusively through three series. "The toughest part is not going, but coming back," said Kings coach

Darryl Sutter. "Everybody's different, but when you look at the schedule, the Saturday–Monday is a tough turnaround, for both teams. If you go eight o'clock, then five o'clock, that's a tough turnaround. Even if it's just a normal game and you only play three periods, you're not getting out of there until midnight. So you're getting in here at three in the morning, with the time change, and then you turn it around and play the next day at five. That's the toughest part of the series, right there."

In the years before the Canucks adopted their travel regimens, NHL players largely self-medicated when it came to getting enough sleep and then getting ready for games. The combination of games and travel produced tales of Guy Lafleur drinking ten cups of coffee before a game and players using antihistamine-containing products such as NyQuil to get a pre-game boost. One former NHL trainer talked of going to the home of a player in the early hours of the morning to tend to a defenceman whose heart rate did not return to normal after he had consumed too many stimulants before a game. Likewise, players needing to get sleep after a game used other narcotics to counter the effects of adrenaline and caffeine consumed to get up for the game. The process repeated itself for morning practices, where groggy players trying to catch the coach's eye would use artificial stimulants to boost their energy levels. It becomes a vicious cycle of dependence fuelled by alcohol, drugs, and energy drinks.

In response, the Canucks sought healthy ways to reduce this dependence. They also appreciated that every player had different tolerances for travel; a one-size-fits-all approach could not work effectively for the whole team. So Gillis looked around at other industries—such as the military, trucking, airline, and railways—that deal with travel dislocation all the time. How did they minimize disruption and maximize productivity when crossing time zones? Enter Fatigue Science, a Hawaii-based firm that had also worked with the Australian Olympic

Committee and several professional rugby teams. The firm advertises a system it developed to monitor athletes' sleeping habits, one that is "dedicated to providing world class technology and consulting services for the analysis and prevention of mental fatigue related incidents... Simply put, lack of sleep impacts the performance of professional athletes by slowing player reaction times during games, often making the difference between winning and losing."

Sleep deprivation affects the general population, reports the *Wall Street Journal:* "Nearly a third of working adults in America—roughly 41 million people—get [fewer] than six hours of sleep a night, according to a recent CDC [Centers for Disease Control and Prevention] report. That number of sleep-deprived people is up about 25% from 1990. About 27% of workers in the financial and insurance industries are sleep-deprived, according to the CDC, while nearly 42% of workers in the mining industry share the same complaint. A 2011 study published in the journal *Sleep* found that insomnia costs $2,280 per worker in lost productivity, adding up to $63.2 billion nationwide."

Fatigue Science helped the Canucks' physical therapists, Roger Takahashi and Glenn Carnegie, to monitor conditioning by collecting data on road trips. As they slept, Vancouver players wore wristbands designed to monitor how they were sleeping—whether they were in a deep sleep or a light sleep. Fatigue Science then analyzed the data to produce a plan on how to travel and what times to practise. The system was also instrumental in dietary matters and determining which players should room together on the road.

"They look at all the guys, how they're sleeping, and it shows if you should stay over in a city or fly right after the game," Daniel Sedin told NHL.com. "It works especially if you've been on a four- or five-game road trip. It really decides if we're going to stay over and fly the next day, or fly right after the game." Said Alex Burrows to *The Globe and Mail:* "They've given us tricks

81

to control our breathing, methods to help us sleep, whether it's iPhone apps or other things to lower your heart rate and allow you to get better sleep. It works."

The only ones objecting to the policy were the weary wives of players who wanted their husbands home the same night, not later the next day, after a long road trip. (There was no research on how to successfully deal with domestic bliss, however.) The overall success of the program led Fatigue Science to brag, "The Vancouver Canucks have turned a 40-year history of the worst travel schedule in the National Hockey League into a competitive advantage."

Once the Canucks formalized their travel regimen, other teams—such as the Calgary Flames, who had previously rejected travel stress management—followed their lead in trying to smooth the bumps of a daunting travel schedule with another firm. (Fatigue Science has an exclusive contract with the Canucks.) Travel had also become an issue in collective bargaining. "The more guys are tired, the more likely they are to get hurt. This is going to be an issue [in the negotiations], maybe not the biggest issue, but it's something a lot of guys are talking about," a player representative from an Eastern Conference team told *The Globe and Mail*.

In fact, the Canucks soon found their methods (or those from other sports) being adopted by the competition. While hockey is notoriously hard to quantify and reluctant to change its habits, there has been movement from some teams to look into different techniques. From travel advice to metrics to nutrition, the race is on to stay ahead of the Canucks and progressive teams such as Pittsburgh and Detroit. (In 2013, the Penguins disclosed that they had used a hockey metrics company to help them assess the trade for Brenden Morrow from Dallas.) And to keep your secrets away from the opposition. "You used to know how other teams operated," Dallas Mavericks owner Mark Cuban told the opening panel at the 2013 MIT Sloan Sports

Analytics Conference. "Now you have to reverse-engineer what they did to see how they do it."

American pollster Nate Silver, who, in part, used sports-research theories to guide the Democrats to the White House in 2008 and 2012, told the same panel, "There's not the low-hanging fruit anymore of having some teams that are totally stupid." In other team sports, the introduction of owners who used metrics in their businesses on Wall Street (Joe Lacob of the NBA's Golden State Warriors and Stuart Sternberg of baseball's Tampa Bay Rays) saw those owners adapt their experience to the sporting realm. Jonah Keri's book *The Extra 2%* documented how Sternberg turned the hapless, small-market Rays into a contender by using the lessons that had made him rich at Goldman Sachs.

The Canucks may have been there first in several cases, because of the eclectic approach of Aquilini and Gillis. But it was only a matter of time till others tried to overtake them using new skills.

7

Transition Game

"In Philly, when I started in 1984, one agent might have three
clients and the total salary was about a million dollars. Now you might
be negotiating $100 million with that agent for one or two players."

MIKE KEENAN, FORMER NHL COACH AND GM

THE BUSINESS-CLASS section of the Lufthansa flight to Frankfurt on June 30, 2009, was a busy place. Walking to his
seat for the seven-and-a-half-hour flight was noted hockey
player agent J.P. Barry of Creative Artists Agency. CAA controls
one of the most powerful player portfolios in the sport. The
boisterous, squarely built Barry (a lookalike for comedian Will
Sasso) played hockey himself and still looks like he could crush
an incoming forward with a check. Once a lawyer for the NHL
Players' Association under Bob Goodenow, the New Brunswick
product had taken over the player portfolio of Mike Barnett's
company, IMG Hockey, when Barnett moved into NHL management in Phoenix with his client and pal Wayne Gretzky.
While Barnett's Coyotes cratered in the desert, Barry built himself a strong business. When IMG decided to get out of hockey,
Barry and his partner, Pat Brisson, took their portfolio to CAA,
best known for representing such actors as Tom Cruise, George

Clooney, Jennifer Aniston, and Penelope Cruz. Prospective hockey clients from Saskatchewan to Slovakia can now find their photos listed among Hollywood's greatest film stars in company literature.

At the time of the Lufthansa flight, Barry and Brisson could boast a client list that included Sidney Crosby, Evgeni Malkin, Mats Sundin, Dany Heatley, Patrick Kane, Claude Giroux, Jonathan Toews, and dozens more NHL stars. (In a few years, they'd also lure a very prominent Canuck.) As he made his way down the aisle of the plane this night, still tired from the recently concluded NHL Entry Draft, in which CAA client John Tavares had gone first overall to the New York Islanders, Barry was headed to Stockholm via Frankfurt on a mission for his two (literally) inseparable clients, the Sedin twins, Henrik and Daniel.

To say that the Swedish brothers are indistinguishable understates the case. Teammates, broadcasters, and coaches can be flummoxed by exactly which of the twins they're talking to. Had they been more anarchistic, the two might have played some of the greatest practical jokes ever on the hockey world. But they are the quintessential Swedish stereotype: balanced, unassuming, and with a wry sense of humour. The Sedins have played together since being paired on the same line as fourteen-year-olds in the small northern Swedish city of Ornskoldsvik. Through the diligent efforts of then Vancouver GM Brian Burke, who traded up to obtain both brothers with the second and third picks in the 1999 draft, the Sedins were kept as a matched set, like designer luggage. They were still playing together on the same line with the Vancouver Canucks ten years after that memorable draft.

From shy, unprepossessing twenty-year-old rookies, they had grown into shy, unprepossessing dynamic scorers in the world's greatest league. Their innate chemistry on the ice, finding each other in the chaos of the opponent's zone, is unparalleled in sports. Like bridge partners who have played together

85

forever, they are always seemingly one move ahead of the opposition. All in spite of being disparaged as soft and easy to intimidate by the troglodyte element in the sport.

Barry's mission to Sweden was to find out whether the pair would continue their unique magic in the uniforms of the Canucks, the only NHL team they'd known. Henrik and Daniel were set to become unrestricted free agents in forty-eight hours, unless negotiations started to pick up. "By the time we got to the 2009 draft, the Canucks hadn't moved off what we thought was an unacceptable number for us," Barry recalls. "The length of negotiations without progress was weighing on the twins, and for the first time they started to think they might not stay in Vancouver, even though that's their wish."

As Barry entered the cabin, he was met by two familiar faces already seated in the plane's plush seats: Canucks GM Mike Gillis and his assistant general manager, Laurence Gilman. Without asking, Barry knew that the club executives were also ticketed for Stockholm to see the Sedins. Barry and Gillis knew each other well from years as friendly rivals in the agency business— Gillis the cool, deliberate outlier with the uncompromising veneer; Barry the buoyant, irrepressible deal maker who moved easily among management figures to negotiate contracts. Both men had played hockey (Gillis in the NHL, Barry in university), and there was no question of their competitive nature.

Stories had Barry asking for twelve years and $63 million each for the twins; the Canucks were looking for a shorter term. While outsiders dismiss agents as leeches or worse, their importance can't be overstated in complex negotiations for franchise players. "As the salary scale increased, the agents became very big," says Mike Keenan, who was GM in Chicago, Vancouver, and Florida. "In Philly, when I started in 1984, one agent might have three clients and the total salary was about a million dollars. Now you might be negotiating $100 million with that agent for one or two players. So his power base in the structure of an individual team is quite significant. If an agent has enough clients on one team, he might be as powerful as the manager."

Needless to say, Barry was going to have a very large say in the business of the Canucks. So were the Sedins. "When owners hand out guaranteed contracts for $100 million, then that individual is now a major partner in the ownership of the team," says Keenan. "That's why the evaluation process on the player is so important. If your hands are tied by a long-term deal or no-move clause, it's hard to convince fans that you're improving. If the agent says, 'My client isn't going to move,' you're locked in. That's why you need to make hard, in-depth decisions early on in the drafting of the contract. You better get it right on the player when you give him $100 million, because you're almost making that player a partner in your group."

A new wrinkle in the Sedin drama had emerged to put added pressure on the two negotiators. Newspapers in Toronto were full of stories describing how Brian Burke—now the general manager of the Maple Leafs—was also on his way to Sweden to pounce upon his former employees should they become available on July 1.

With just forty-eight hours till the twins became unrestricted free agents, Gillis had been convinced by Gilman and player-personnel director Stan Smyl that a personal trip to the twins' home might get things moving in the right direction. "I'd been on the other side, so I knew it could go down that way," Gillis recalled afterward. "It didn't upset me. They were the most important players on the team to establish a culture. I had to be sure they wanted to be the go-to guys who'd lead the team. I had to be sure they wanted to be in that role, be in the limelight. I don't think in the history of sports that there have been two twin brothers, that close, who were going to absorb a significant portion of our [$48 million] salary cap space. How were you going to make it work?"

"I rolled into business class for the flight, and they were sitting there beside me on the plane," Barry recalls with a chuckle.

"We talked as the flight went along, and I told them they'd have to wait till I had a chance to talk to the guys and their wives. We ended up going to dinner at a very nice place in Stockholm the first night and had the meeting with the twins the next day. I think Mike and Laurence getting on a plane to go to Sweden turned the negotiations."

The importance of the newly minted general manager, just a year into his term, signing up his franchise players can't be overstated. For Gillis, who had sat on Barry's side of the table for two decades, the urgency was complicated by the economic realities of the modern NHL, with its salary caps and floors, unrestricted free agency, and salary arbitration. It might have been easy to bestow a huge payday on the Sedins, in much the same manner that other teams had rewarded their franchise players. Calgary, for instance, was paying Jarome Iginla $7 million a year. Detroit had given Pavel Datsyuk and Nicklas Lidstrom $6.7 million and $7.45 million respectively. Pittsburgh was saddled with similar $8.7 million-a-year salary cap hits for Sidney Crosby and Evgeni Malkin (thanks to Barry and CAA).

The Sedins were on the verge of joining that category of player. Gillis's task was to pay the Sedins enough to want to stay in Vancouver, but also to leave salary cap space for the other elements Gillis wanted to add for a contending team. Barry was aware of Gillis's desire for a competitive team, but he was also under an obligation to cash in for his clients at the peak of their earning power. When the Sedins renegotiated in 2014, as thirty-four-year-olds heading into the back portion of their careers, their leverage might not be as great.

The discussions the sides had held had also been complicated by the financial health of the Canucks, the NHL, and the North American economy itself as it lurched out of the great economic collapse of 2008. Says Barry, a schoolmate and still a friend of Bank of Canada governor Mark Carney (who became governor of the Bank of England in the summer of 2013), "My argument was the strength of Canada's economy was an important factor. Those were scary numbers about the economy at the time. But in some way, hockey in Canada is immune to the economy. If people are talking about a few dollars to spend, they're going to put it to hockey. The revenues in Canada overshot the losses in the U.S. by a long shot."

For his part, Gillis was more bearish about the economic prospects facing the NHL clubs as he and Gilman settled in for the flight. "It was hard," says Gillis. "J.P. and I did a lot of fighting. We'd known each other a long time. I have a lot of respect for him and the way he does the job. At the end of the day, we had to understand the external stuff. How everyone was going to operate in this context, what everyone was committed to, was far more important than the actual dollar figure. We asked them to take less money here in order to make it work, and they were prepared to do that. They were also prepared to be the cornerstones of the team."

SINCE THE NHL had locked out its players twice before to impose greater constraints on salaries after their precipitous spike in the mid-nineties, the competitive difference between the top and bottom teams in the league has narrowed. Competition for the sixteen NHL playoff spots is governed to a larger extent by injuries, referee calls, and what the players call "puck luck." This has made a science of squeezing the most value out of the fewest dollars under the NHL's salary cap. The rise of the Los Angeles Kings, the eighth seed in the 2012 Western Conference playoffs, to Stanley Cup champions is proof of how little there is to choose between teams in the salary cap era. Where the champion Montreal Canadiens of the seventies or the Edmonton Oilers of the eighties would make mincemeat of playoff Cinderellas, winning by large margins, now teams seemed to feel that if they could just get into the playoffs, they could do as the Kings did. All it might take to push them over

89

the top was to shoehorn one more high-priced player under the salary cap.

The squeeze has seemingly produced a competitive frenzy in the final six weeks of the season, as only a handful of teams are truly eliminated before the stretch run begins. While this parity has been promoted to fans as a panacea by the NHL when it locked out players—an equalizer between large and small markets—the effects of salary caps on competitive balance aren't necessarily reflected in which markets make the playoffs. Major League Baseball, for instance, has no salary cap, just a luxury tax on free-spending teams. In theory, MLB teams can spend whatever they want—and the New York Yankees annually do just that, often paying a tax on the extra spending on players that virtually give them an all-star lineup.

So there should be a discrepancy between leagues like the NHL, which have salary caps, and MLB, which has none. In 2012, twenty-seven of thirty NHL teams had captured one of its sixteen playoff spots since the 2004–05 lockout; twenty-seven of the NBA's thirty teams had qualified at least once for the sixteen available playoff spots in the previous four years. Meanwhile, twenty-two of thirty MLB teams had made the playoffs in the previous six years—in a playoff format where only eight teams make the postseason. To reinforce the point, small-market Cincinnati, Oakland, St. Louis, and Tampa Bay all made it to the 2013 MLB playoffs. But its big dogs get to eat as well, driving the MLB revenue model. The last small-market NHL team to win the Stanley Cup was Carolina in 2006.

In the NHL, you are what your salary structure says you are. Forwards with first-line salaries playing on the third line make for a recipe for disaster. Ditto defencemen paid like a No. 1 or 2 who are performing on the third pairing. The Canucks under Gillis planned to operate under a meritocracy that rewarded core players, but they weren't going to hobble the team with a couple of weighty contracts. Thus it became incumbent upon

Vancouver to be as thrifty as possible with the Sedins while trying to keep the core players at home. Pay them too much, and you couldn't afford the extra parts needed to compete. Neglect drafting and player development, and you'd be forced to go into the expensive free-agent market to get the pieces you need. Rely too heavily on trades—always a 50/50 proposition—and lack the stability in the clubhouse that develops a winning chemistry. It is a balancing act that only the best franchises manage. Gillis had watched them all from his perch as a player agent in the 1990s and 2000s. He'd seen teams like Detroit, which had sustained a championship-calibre team into a third generation. He had also seen franchises like Colorado, Dallas, and Calgary lose their status as elite squads because they stopped developing talent or hobbled themselves with onerous contracts. Then there were the likes of Columbus, Edmonton, and Florida, who, despite getting top draft picks, could never seem to get the equation right.

As he spied Barry across the cabin of the Lufthansa flight, Gillis was cautiously optimistic about the base he'd inherited when he accepted Francesco Aquilini's offer. The key from day one had been to sign his offensive catalysts, the Sedin twins, to a deal that would establish the team's salary grid. It was a negotiation that would define his success in managing the payroll in Vancouver.

J.P. Barry might have been a longtime friend of Gillis's, but he had made it clear there would be no friendly deals. The Vancouver media—custodians of the team's long and persistent culture of failure—would be ready to speculate and savage any false steps in the process. Canuck fans, accustomed to failure, could be counted on to think the worst as the deadline got closer.

It was a rapid introduction to the spotlight for the agent who had always worked behind the scenes. "He was a new GM trying to figure out his team and his team's salary cap," recalls Barry. "Mike was thinking the cap was moving down because of the 2009 financial collapse. We tried to start off keeping it friendly. We're both pretty intense, and we had some difficult meetings. We both didn't budge for a long time."

That's because the Sedins may be the most unique talent combination in hockey history, perhaps sports history. Once they began playing on the same line in Ornskoldsvik, it was clear they were going to present a challenge to the NHL, one summed up by Canucks scout Thomas Gradin. "They're good enough to play with anyone, but separately their capacity might decrease by 10 or 15 per cent." Henrik was seen as the play-maker while younger brother Daniel served as the scorer. There was also a generally held perception in the cozy NHL culture that the two ginger-haired brothers might be too soft for the rigours of the NHL. Even though they'd been playing in a men's league since 1996, the Sedins' artistic, offensive style was considered a product of the big European ice. Confined to the smaller rinks in the NHL, many thought they'd have no room to operate. Moreover, they'd be easy candidates for intimidation. If so, drafting both would represent a waste of not just one, but two picks—an insurmountable setback for a club. And finding a way to obtain two of the top three picks in any NHL draft is nearly impossible.

Their agent at the time, Mike Barnett, conspired to keep the Sedins together by suggesting a series of poison pills to discourage clubs from splitting them up. They had the option of not signing with the teams that drafted them, or of playing junior hockey for two years and then signing as free agents with the same club. But the Sedins had no interest in the Canadian junior system. Barnett also proposed that just one twin enter the draft while the other waited a year, forcing the hand of his drafting team. In the end, Burke was able to assemble consecutive picks at numbers two and three, but it wasn't simple. He sent defenceman Bryan McCabe and a first-round pick in 2000 to the Chicago Blackhawks for the fourth-overall pick in the current year. Burke then sent that draft choice and a pair of third-round picks to the Tampa Bay Lightning for the first-overall pick. Finally, he sent the top pick to the expansion Atlanta Thrashers for the second-overall selection and a conditional third-rounder the following year. The understanding was that the Thrashers would take Patrik Stefan first overall, leaving the Canucks to take the two Sedins. The key for Burke had been convincing Tampa Bay GM Rick Dudley. "I told him, 'Nobody is leaving with these kids except me.' And finally I told him we had two of the top four picks [third and fourth overall] and he said that [trade] hadn't come across yet. I said it was registered a couple of hours ago."

Finally, Burke was able to choose the pair, who looked like characters from the Quebec humour website *Têtes à claques* as they pulled on their Canucks jerseys. (They were also the only picks in the top ten of the 1999 draft who didn't flop. Stefan, for instance, is considered one of the biggest busts in draft history.) Burke compared the PR notoriety of the twins to Mario Lemieux or Eric Lindros. "There's a mountain of pressure on the twins already," Burke said.

After staying for another year in Sweden, the pair debuted in Vancouver in 2000–01. Their early years in the NHL were marked by increasing point totals and a vicious campaign by the sweats of hockey to impugn their toughness by labelling them "The Sisters." The frustration of teams mugging the young Swedes was famously captured by their GM, the voluble Burke, during the 2002 playoffs when he chided the referees and the league for their double standard. "Sedin is not Swedish for 'punch me' or 'headlock me in a scrum,' " Burke complained. But it soon became apparent that the two people least affected by the intimidation were the Sedins themselves, especially when they made the offenders pay with a power-play goal.

As time passed, their lethal effect on the power play forced a change in opponents' behaviour. Playing behind Vancouver's top offensive players, including Markus Naslund, Brendan Morrison, and Todd Bertuzzi, in their early years, the Sedins first became reliable second-line scorers, and then graduated to first-line threats who gave Vancouver the league's elite power play. When the Bertuzzi incident destroyed the heart of the 2004 Canucks, the twins seamlessly assumed the mantle as the next generation of core players. In the 2006–07 season, Daniel established himself as the Canucks' top scorer with thirty-six goals and eighty-four points, leading Henrik in Canucks scoring. In 2007–08 Henrik was the leading Canucks scorer, and second in the league in assists. Even better, the "soft" Sedins were rarely out of the lineup as their superior conditioning and Vigneault's management of ice time kept them healthy. The biggest obstacle to their gaining greater prominence was the Canucks' failure in the playoffs, which led their critics to charge the twins were just regular-season players, not stars who would shine in the rough and tumble of the postseason.

Behind all this, the feints and dodges of the Sedin negotiations had continued throughout 2008–09, the final year of their contracts. Considering the team's playoff shortcomings, Vancouver's media speculated endlessly on whether the twins were worth the commitment, and which free agents might replace them if they rejoined Burke, now in Toronto. Both Gillis and Barry felt the twins had the ability to up their scoring, but as they headed to Sweden for the showdown, Barry was basing his pitch upon the promise that Henrik and Daniel could take a step up to the very top tier of NHL superstars, with point totals in triple digits. "The charts that we had showed the twins were going to another level," recalled Barry. "It wasn't about what they'd done the year of negotiations, but that they were tracking to a new level. They had a chart that was going straight upwards in terms of production."

Barry's faith would eventually be borne out by the explosion in the Sedins' output in the consecutive years of 2009–10 and

2010–11, when they took turns winning the Art Ross Trophy as the NHL scoring champion. But in 2009, not knowing the future, the Canucks assumed a more measured approach. "We understood that the twins were essentially loyal, conservative people whose families liked the Vancouver community and the schools in which their children were registered," Gillis would later say. While they were prepared to consider another team, the Sedins were reluctant to leave the only city they'd known as NHLers. It was especially important that their families be happy with the deal.

As the parties sat together on the plane, waiting for the engines to roar and take them to Sweden, the deal could not have been shaved finer. "It came really close," Barry says. "We had our final meetings at the weekend of the draft in June, and it didn't go well. We were feeling a lot of tension. I told Mike that weekend that we were done, and I was headed to Sweden to prepare for free agency. Negotiations had completely broken down that weekend."

The two sides passed the time on the flight discussing issues and trading hockey gossip. But Barry could give no assurances that night. It remained for the untested GM to lay out his plan for the Sedins, the club, new approaches on travel, and the signing of the rest of the Canucks' core.

The meeting with the Sedins and their wives, Johanna and Marinette, turned the tables. "Mike spent a lot of time explaining why the Canucks wanted to keep them, that they were the most important part of the core," recalls Barry. "After that, they moved on their offer for the first time ever." Gillis says now that he didn't feel any undue pressure closing the deal with the popular players with Burke poised nearby to snap up his prize assets. "I didn't have any knowledge till after the fact what other people were doing," remembers Gillis. "I'd been there before, I knew they were going to have options. Stan Smyl and Laurence Gilman felt it was the final thing to allow them to make the right decision. It was a whirlwind trip. We sat down and asked them their objectives and do they fit with ours. When we left, we didn't have a contract, but [we were] very confident we'd have one the next morning."

Gillis was correct. The next day, as the clock ticked down towards the Sedins becoming unrestricted free agents, they said yes. "The Sedin contract allowed us to create a culture about the team, not individuals. We live in a salary cap world. My position with every player is we're going to pay you the most we can within this context. If it gets beyond a context that doesn't let us win, we may have to take a step sideways, but we're determined to have this plan."

In the end, the pair left money on the table to stay with a promising franchise and a city in which their families were comfortable. Their five-year deals averaged $6.1 million per year. Sometimes, players hitting the mother lode will plateau or even regress as they try to cope with the pressures of their new status—and of being so highly paid. To reward the Canucks, however, Henrik and Daniel went on to consecutive scoring titles. Henrik also won the 2010 Hart Trophy as league MVP. "It would have been nice had they done that the year leading into negotiations," laughs Barry.

The Sedins were the foundation of Gillis's financial plan, but by no means was that the entire story. They also served as examples in the community. In March 2010, Daniel and Marinette, along with Henrik and Johanna, made a joint $1.5 million donation to the B.C. Children's Hospital's $200 million project for a new building. They requested that it be put towards a pediatric intensive-care unit and a diagnostic imaging area. Both sides agreed it could not have worked out better.

HAVING ESTABLISHED A benchmark for his core players, the Canucks GM set about getting his other elite players under contract. Next on the list came goalie Roberto Luongo, who'd been obtained by Dave Nonis in 2006 after spending six years in the relative anonymity of the Florida Panthers (he'd been drafted by the New York Islanders in 1997). Luongo was no secret to hockey people, however. He and agent Gilles Lupien had rejected a $30 million deal in Florida because he felt the team was not sufficiently committed to winning and getting into the playoffs. Luongo was also demanding that his backup goalie, Jamie McLennan, be re-signed and that his goalie coach, Francois Allaire, be hired. Unable to get Luongo to sign, former Canucks coach Mike Keenan traded Luongo to the West Coast for Todd Bertuzzi, Bryan Allen, and goalie Alex Auld.

A perennial choice behind Martin Brodeur for Team Canada's goalie, Luongo was rated among the top five netminders in the world and one of the most durable, too, playing over seventy games in each year from 2003–04 to 2007–08. His coach, Alain Vigneault, speculated that Luongo's workload might be hurting him late in seasons or in playoffs. But Luongo himself was not backing off on his desire to play as often as he could. He was also the type of personality that the Canucks' new management was seeking to build upon. Like the Sedins, Luongo was family-oriented, according to Lupien. "For some players, it's only money," Lupien told reporters. "They play hockey and they want the value, the money. For some players, it's family. Roberto's Italian. His wife's Italian. They want their parents around, grandfather and grandmother, kids all around the house."

As the 2010 expiry date for Luongo's four-year, $27 million deal drew near, goalie contracts were all over the map. Brodeur—Luongo's former neighbour in the Montreal suburb of St. Leonard and the top goalie in the game—was being paid $31.2 million over six years. Calgary's Miikka Kiprusoff's deal resulted in an annual cap hit of $5.833 million till 2014. Pittsburgh's Marc-Andre Fleury was in for an annual cap hit of $5 million. Meanwhile, the Islanders' oft-injured goalie Rick DiPietro was on a fifteen-year, $67.5 million deal signed in 2006.

DiPietro's lengthy deal was widely mocked in hockey circles when it was signed, but it had in fact served as a template for long-term contracts, such as the one the Canucks were contemplating for Luongo. To give their goalie his due and keep the salary cap intact, a team could simply amortize the proper compensation over a longer term. The NHL hated these deals and attempted unsuccessfully to label them as non-compliant with the CBA. But as long as the team could make the case that the player might viably play till age forty-one or forty-two, the contracts were grudgingly approved by the league for the moment (while planning their revenge for another day on teams like the Canucks).

What to do for Luongo? Under his previous deal, Luongo had averaged $6.75 million a year. But with the twins taking a hometown "haircut" to stay in the $6.1 million range, that was out of the question. Something was needed to give the goalie a raise while keeping everyone in the dressing room happy. Satisfying the media and fans about Luongo's worth was probably not in the cards: despite being nominated for the Vezina Trophy during his Vancouver stay, Luongo had critics in both the press box and the stands after he performed erratically in the 2009 playoffs, especially when Chicago blew out the Canucks 7–5 in Game 6 of the Western Conference semifinals. With prospect Cory Schneider expected to arrive in the next couple of years, the critics wondered, why tie yourself to Luongo in a lengthy deal?

Gillis disagreed, pointing out that dumping Luongo would send a bad message to his other core players—and, moreover, to players around the league who might be contemplating Vancouver as a future destination. A hair-trigger executive style does not reassure top players of the stability of a franchise. So Gillis came up with a two-pronged approach to establish that Vancouver wanted Luongo and that the Canucks didn't abandon their players on a whim. The first move had come the year before, when he and Vigneault named Luongo the team's captain. The move was designed to recognize Luongo's role as a team leader and to emphasize that the Canucks were not going to be hidebound by tradition.

In this climate, the Canucks and Luongo's agent, Lupien, started hammering out an early extension to his deal, to take effect beginning in 2010. "If we put one player ahead of rest of the team, it begins to fall apart really quickly," said Gillis. "With Roberto, we set out the same set of facts as we did with the twins. And he was prepared to accept that." In the end, the Canucks and Luongo settled on a twelve-year, $64 million extension that was heavily front-loaded, with Luongo getting $10 million in the first year of the contract and decreasing amounts thereafter. It also included a no-trade clause, a detail that would eventually haunt the team. The Canucks, meanwhile, got Luongo for a manageable salary cap hit of $5.333 million over the life of the deal, allowing them flexibility to ink other players to their winning core. The NHL deplored the contract with its extended term and front-loaded payments, but lacking—for now—any specific weapon in the collective bargaining agreement to fight it, the league reluctantly approved the deal. In a few years, the Luongo deal would prove a poisoned chalice for the Canucks. But for the time being, the comfortable cap hit was nice for the Canucks' short-term plans. Even better was the example of players taking hometown discounts to stay with a winning program. There were some complaints about the length of the term (Luongo would be in his forties when the deal concluded), but many applauded it as another Gillis masterstroke.

In the next few years, Canuck regulars fell into line with the pay grid. In March of 2009, Alex Burrows had already signed a four-year, $8 million deal that featured the added perk of staying on the first line with the twins (a previous beneficiary, Anson Carter, had chased free-agent dollars after scoring thirty-three goals with the Sedins, and he promptly dropped out of the league). Burrows then produced offensively at a rate that would have brought him as much as twice that amount in free agency. Ryan Kesler, the strapping second-line centre who was, as much as the Sedins, the key to the Canucks' offence, signed a six-year contract with an annual cap hit of $5 million in March of 2010. Kesler, who had been a workmanlike player till then, exploded with forty-one goals in 2010–11. Defenceman Kevin Bieksa, one of the core players in the dressing room, was re-upped for five years at a cap hit of $4.6 million.

Not every move worked. Gillis brought in two former clients, Mathieu Schneider and Pavol Demitra. Schneider clashed with coach Vigneault and, in a bitter moment, asked his former agent for a trade. Demitra played brilliantly—for the Czech team at the 2010 Olympics. For the Canucks, however, Demitra was an injured, indifferent disappointment as a secondary scorer.

If the object for Vancouver was to give itself as many top players as possible under the restrictive cap, then the Sedin and Luongo deals seemingly positioned them well for the future. The dollars the Canucks' contract strategy saved enabled them to afford three defencemen capable of playing on top pairings—Dan Hamhuis ($4.5 million per year), Keith Ballard ($4.2 million), and Jason Garrison (five years at $4.25 million per)—as well as top-six forward David Booth ($4.25 million). With the available cap space, they also came close to signing a number of other high-profile players.

"I'm not going to make any short-term deals that endanger the structure we have in place for the future," Gillis said as often as people would listen. "Succeeding in this business isn't simply about today. It's making sure you adopt a plan that gives you a chance to be successful for a long time to come." NBC analyst and former Hartford Whalers coach Pierre McGuire says this planning kept the Canucks rolling in the first years of his administration. "Mike thinks outside the box; he's one of the most creative GMs. He understands the long-term value of team building. When he identifies a problem, he won't sit on the sidelines. He's always trying to get better. When he sees a hole in the roster, he fills it. He was a real breath of fresh air in the league. He proved that an outsider can do a good job if he's really organized and creative. That's why Mike was successful."

In his first years at the helm, Gillis's biggest challenge would come not from contract demands within his own team but from the deals signed by rival GMs around the league as they learned to manipulate Gary Bettman's magic-bullet CBA (won by shutting down the league for the 2004-05 season). The precedent of one bad contract in another city could cost his owners, the Aquilinis, millions to match.

As year three of the Gillis regime dawned, the Canucks were now a coat he was wearing in the public mind. Reciprocity was a thing of the past. Not that Gillis complained. He understood the rules of the game from his years as an agent, watching countless new GMs come in with high hopes and then flounder on the reality. "Those of us who've talked to Mike, he believes what he believes," says Ray Ferraro. "But his eyes can be opened to other things. I think that's the thing that people don't see in the radio or TV interviews—he's gruff with media, he doesn't like doing the regular segments. But he has a side to him that is curious—'Hey, can we do this better?' When it doesn't work, other people like to take potshots at him. They'll lose a game on the road, and you'll read in a paper from another city, 'I guess their sleep doctor miscalculated.' You're not going to win eighty-two games. It's like blackjack: you're trying to give yourself the best odds as much of the time as possible."

8

That Close

"I'm not sure what it means. I think it means we lost."

MIKE GILLIS

MIKE GILLIS ENTERED Cioffi's Deli on Hastings Street and headed immediately to the meat counter. Gillis is a fine cook, has an enviable wine cellar, and insists on the best produce he can find for himself and his players. The staff at Cioffi's recognized him right away and greeted him as a familiar face. The Canucks faithful in the store, delighted by the rise of the team since his arrival, clucked happily as he moved among them. The pressure to win in a Canadian NHL city is great and very public for someone devoted to his family rather than the fame of managing the Canucks.

"It was a shift. It's been a real challenge, a very different challenge," he said as he waited for the clerk to wrap up a few steaks. "Either you embrace it or let it overwhelm you."

Laurence Gilman accompanied Gillis in Cioffi's as he settled on grain-fed beef ("Much better than AAA Alberta," Gillis deadpanned to an Albertan standing nearby). The two were the hockey version of Don Quixote and Sancho Panza, constantly bouncing ideas off each other as they wandered the hockey landscape. Gillis with his laconic, impassive exterior and Gilman ever alert, his dark eyes taking in the offerings behind the counters while discussing hockey, made for a distinctive sight. Unlike other GM–assistant GM relationships in hockey, this one wasn't threatening for Gillis.

"I've never had a difficult time making decisions," he said. "That's not a problem. Time-wise, your willingness to delegate is very important. You can't see every junior game, every AHL game, every world championship game, so I've been lucky to have excellent people working here. I allow people to do their job and have an opinion. In the end, I have to arbitrate, make final decisions, but it's never been 'I know more than you.' It's been 'We know a lot together.' "

Symbolic of the group approach was the drama surrounding his first-ever first-round pick, Cody Hodgson, taken tenth overall in 2008. In keeping with Gillis's avowed philosophy of drafting skill, Gillis had gone for the young Brampton Battalion centre, who would star for Canada at the World Junior Championships in 2009 and be named captain of his junior team. Hodgson was indeed a skilled player who seemed to exhibit strong leadership traits; that convinced Gillis to select Hodgson ahead of such future stars Jordan Eberle, Tyler Myers, and Erik Karlsson. While his skating was considered a liability (Hodgson's stride is short and choppy), the pick seemed prescient after Hodgson was selected player of the year in the Canadian Hockey League in 2008–09.

Then, in the summer of 2009, Hodgson hurt his back while training. Initially diagnosed as a bulging disc, the injury caused Hodgson to miss two months of training. When Canucks doctors and another in Toronto cleared him to participate in the team's 2009 training camp, Hodgson still seemed hampered as he faced NHL competition for the first time. He was cut, and Canucks coach Alain Vigneault casually observed that perhaps the young man was using his back pain as an excuse for his

103

tepid performance. None of which went over well with Hodgson's father, a former Ontario cabinet minister and successful businessman.

The Hodgsons then fired agent Don Meehan and went with iconoclastic Edmonton agent Ritch Winter. In addition, Cody was sent to the Cleveland Clinic, which said the young player should rest for a month. (Some undetected nerve damage in one leg was also revealed.) Hodgson in fact missed the first fifty games of the OHL season while undergoing treatment and rehabilitation for a bulging disc. It wasn't till a year later that the injury was correctly diagnosed as a muscle strain, and it was discovered that the treatment for the disc problem had aggravated his real injury.

Through it all, there was tension between the player's camp and Canucks management. The Vancouver media speculated on a rift between Gillis and his first top prospect when Hodgson declared he would no longer be training in the off-season with the team's then director of player development, Dave Gagner, under whose supervision he suffered his back injury. Canucks fans, impatient as always for success, shook their heads in resignation that the Canucks were seemingly going to miss on another draft pick.

Hodgson finally got his pro career underway with the Canucks' farm team in Manitoba, and all animus appeared healed when he even saw some playoff action with Vancouver in 2011.

While Cody Hodgson's path proved erratic (and would soon take a dramatic turn), on the eve of the 2010–11 season, the arrow for the team was clearly pointed upward. Gillis and his staff had clearly made progress with the signing of undrafted defenceman Chris Tanev and the accelerated development of young players such as Alex Edler, Cory Schneider, Mason Raymond, and Jannik Hansen. Both Ryan Kesler and Alex Burrows had become stars, and holdover Kevin Bieksa found consistency among the top four defencemen after battling injuries in previous seasons. Defenceman Christian Ehrhoff, obtained in a larcenous trade with a cash-strapped San Jose team, and Dan Hamhuis, signed as a free agent, gave Vancouver depth on defence—a weakness that had been exploited by Chicago in the two previous playoff series. The Sedin brothers were now superstars, with Henrik winning the Hart Trophy as the league's MVP and Daniel, who was injured in 2010, not far behind. Luongo was Luongo, capable of brilliance or carelessness on any given night.

The organization's swagger made many in the league openly hostile to the club, but that reaction ignored a growing sense of unity and purpose within the club. With the team in Ottawa on Remembrance Day 2010 for a game against the Senators, practice was cancelled and the team and coaches instead went en masse to see the solemn ceremony at the Cenotaph in downtown Ottawa. That included Canadians, Americans, Swedes, and yes, even the German Ehrhoff. Centre Manny Malhotra appeared on the CBC with Peter Mansbridge. "To see generations of soldiers—I can't imagine what they've gone through—but to honour those who made the ultimate sacrifice for Canada is a small gesture for us... The final parade, seeing generations going by and the pride they have in being a member of the armed services, that's the point that really hit home for me." Mansbridge was impressed. "As I said on air during the service, on that day, in that moment, there was no doubt in anyone's mind who was Canada's team. I thought it was an incredible moment—a visiting team of highly paid pro sports athletes making it very clear in a quiet but very public way that they knew what real sacrifice was."

Still, the reputation for arrogance stung. And it was no secret around the league that competitive core players such as Alex Burrows and Ryan Kesler had short fuses when hassled by opponents. While Gillis and coach Alain Vigneault admired their feistiness, it was also becoming apparent that the after-whistle jostling was distracting Burrows, Kesler, and others, taking them out of their focus. In the preseason, selected Canucks were shown video of players such as Steve Yzerman, a consummate competitor, but one who knew when to skate away from trouble.

"We wanted them to see that they could take another step in their development if they reined in some of the after-whistle stuff," Gillis explained as he sat in his office. On the TV screen across the room, there was video illustrating what he wanted from the players. "This game in 2011 is all power plays, and we want to win that battle. You can't do it if your players are in the penalty box for penalties after the whistle. We have other guys to take care of that stuff if it happens. We need them to stay focused." The self-discipline of staying out of the penalty box would manifest itself that season, with Kesler scoring forty-one goals while Burrows notched twenty-six. Better yet, the differential between PP and PK opportunities played right into the Canucks' strength on the power play.

The fortieth-anniversary campaign proved the greatest season in Vancouver Canuck history to that date. After an erratic start to the season in which starting goalie Roberto Luongo struggled to find his form after giving the captaincy to Henrik Sedin, the Canucks took off in midseason. With no fourteen-game road trips such as they'd experienced during the 2010 Olympics in Vancouver, the club became as efficient on the road as at Rogers Arena. The Canucks clinched first overall in the Western Conference on March 29 and won the team's first Presidents' Trophy (for finishing first overall in the NHL) two days later. Their 117 points were the greatest total in club history. Daniel Sedin would match his brother from the year before, winning the Art Ross Trophy as the NHL's top scorer (although he didn't capture the Hart Trophy as his brother had).

The Canucks' reward for the bullish season was a first-round matchup with the defending Stanley Cup champion Chicago Blackhawks, their greatest rivals after two straight years of acrimonious playoffs in which Chicago manhandled the Canucks. But this was a diminished Chicago team after the front office mismanaged their payroll. Missing from the team that had beaten Vancouver in six games en route to their win over Philadelphia in the 2010 Cup final were Dustin Byfuglien, Kris Versteeg, Antti Niemi, Ben Eager, and Andrew Ladd.

The series would hinge, as always, on the volatile Luongo, who'd had streaks of greatness and slumps where he had surrendered questionable goals during the season. Could he lead a team, or would he be more of a passenger on a winning team? Luongo had no playoff history in his previous stops in Florida and Long Island. He did have the Olympic gold medal as Canada's starting goalie in 2010 and one remarkable seventy-two-save performance in quadruple overtime against Dallas during his first playoff series as a Canuck in 2007. But even in that game, his teammates had carried Luongo after he allowed four goals before settling in for a truly remarkable playoff performance that saw Daniel Sedin win it for the Canucks.

The surging Canucks took immediate advantage of the eighth-place Hawks, jumping out to a 3-0 lead in the series. Just as Vancouver was gleefully writing the Blackhawks' epitaph, Chicago returned the favour, winning three straight games themselves. Gilman had a front-row seat as the series progressed. "Watching each game from our management suite feels like sitting in the crowd," recalls Gilman. "Each night, the tension was so thick that you could feel it. There were times when I looked over at Mike and saw that his skin colour was almost crimson red. However, he always maintained his composure and maintained a sense of calm."

In what would be a foreshadowing of the remainder of the postseason, Luongo faltered in those three Chicago wins. He was pulled in Game 4, a 7-2 Chicago drubbing of the Canucks, and Game 5, a 5-0 shocker before the Vancouver fans. Looking for a spark, coach Alain Vigneault also benched him for

Game 6 in favour of Cory Schneider. Schneider played brilliantly, except when handling the puck, in a game in which the Canucks had the lead three times only to surrender it. Two gaffes by the young goalie—and a penalty-shot goal—left it in a 3–3 tie as the clubs headed into a tension-filled overtime. With comedian (and Hawks fan) Vince Vaughn looking on, Chicago fought for their lives. To ramp up the tension, Schneider left the game after developing cramps in the Vancouver net. That gave Luongo a chance to play the hero in overtime and revive his reputation. It wasn't to be. With Luongo out of position on his belly after making a save, Ben Smith tied the series with a rebound goal in the first OT period. Remarkably, the Blackhawks looked as though they were ready to crush Vancouver's heart again.

In between Games 6 and 7, Gillis showed that, while he might not be mistaken for Brian Burke, he was not beyond employing an old-fashioned technique for GMs whose teams are facing enormous pressure: he made himself the story. On the off-day, Gillis stood with his back to the Canucks logo on the wall of Rogers Arena. Reporters huddled around, microphones and note pads at the ready. Brandishing a sheet of paper with research he'd developed, Gillis indicted the referees. Chicago had had 69 per cent more power plays in the last four games, he said in a steady monotone. Through six games, Chicago had received twenty-seven power plays to Vancouver's sixteen. "I'm not sure how you explain that discrepancy, but we're going to be very hard pressed to win hockey games if, throughout an entire series when the score is tight, they get 75 per cent more power plays than we do," said Gillis. "And that's just the reality. That's the facts that we're facing.

"You look at the game last night, you guys all watched it, you don't need me to comment about what occurred in that hockey game. But when you break down the video, there are some extraordinary plays to explain, given what's gone on... We were lucky to get into overtime the way things occurred during

[Game 6]," Gillis said. "We directed eighty-five pucks at their net. If we would have had any power plays whatsoever, it probably could have been a hundred.

"We've had the best team during the regular season, and that was the best game they've played last night during the whole year," he said, salting his address with a little hyperbole. "And so, for us to come away with a loss is shocking to me."

Naturally, the hockey media jumped all over Gillis. "So at the intersection of 'Homer' and 'We were robbed, son' stood Vancouver Canucks general manager Mike Gillis on Monday," wrote Mark Spector of Sportsnet, "talking to a media throng peppered with a few who must have wanted to throw their pom-poms in the air and yell, 'See! Didn't I tell you?' The local GM calling a press conference to throw chum into the shark-infested waters of the NHL's most paranoid market? Hallelujah, conspiracy theorists, maybe we've been right all along."

The league, too, took a dim view of the comments, fining Gillis for his intemperate blast. But the performance had its intended effect. While the GM took his lumps, his team flew (relatively) under the radar in the press. Luongo was back as the starter in Game 7. So were all the goblins in the Canucks past, especially regarding Chicago and its brilliant captain, Jonathan Toews. In the tension-soaked game at Rogers Arena, the Canucks scored very early in the first on a goal by Alexandre Burrows. All seemed well. Luongo was stellar. The Canucks peppered Corey Crawford in the Chicago net, but couldn't stretch the lead. Vancouver vigilantly nursed a 1–0 advantage into the final two minutes of the game. Then, as if on cue, Blackhawks captain Jonathan Toews brought the assembled multitude to its knees. The brilliant centre somehow evened the score shorthanded to send the contest to OT. It reverberated like the Martin Gelinas heartbreaker in 2004, when Calgary stole a series from a favoured Vancouver team. This time, at least, there was a chance for redemption.

109

Through the intermission, the inevitability of a Chicago comeback shattering the Canucks gripped the Vancouver crowd. Fatalistic Canucks fans couldn't understand what they'd done in previous lives to be tortured this way for a third straight year, losing to the hated Hawks. It was not much better in the Canucks' executive booth. "One memory that will always remain with me will be the intermission prior to overtime in Game 7 of our first-round series against Chicago," remembers Gilman. "Jonathan Toews had scored with a minute or so remaining to tie the game. All the life had been sucked out of our building. I sat speechless in our suite during the intermission. I was very uncertain that we would come through. Mike was standing beside me, looked over, and said with more conviction than I'd ever heard from anyone, 'Laurence, we will not lose this game!' "

In overtime, Burrows immediately took a penalty, sending yet another shiver of dread through Rogers Arena. Chicago buzzed the Canuck net in search of the winner, but Luongo stoned Blackhawk sniper Patrick Sharp, going post to post for a larcenous pad save. Back on the ice, Burrows knocked down a lob pass from Chris Campoli at Chicago's blue line, sped to the middle of the ice, and drilled a laser past Crawford high on the blocker side. On *Hockey Night in Canada,* B.C. boy and Vancouver resident Jim Hughson let the mask slip a tad, saying, "After three seasons and nineteen playoff games against Chicago, for Vancouver it's a wonderful day for an exorcism."

"Mike had momentarily left our suite when Alex Burrows scored the series winner," Gilman recalls. "The puck went in, the horn went off, and the building erupted. Mike walked in almost immediately thereafter and deadpanned, 'I guess we won.' I responded by saying, 'Yeah, we did.' We both laughed. It was an amazing moment."

In fact, Gillis had decided to use the washroom as overtime started. *Hockey Night in Canada*'s snooping TV cameras, which had sought him out in the lowest moments of the series, could not find a trace of Gillis in victory. "It was the only time I could get in there with no one bugging me," he revealed later. "I was in there, and I heard the noise. I knew we'd won. I came into the suite and Laurence and Lorne [Henning, director of player personnel] were just grinning like crazy." The Burrows goal sent Vancouver into ecstasy. For a team that had won just three play-off series since 1994, and for a fan base and media that always expected the worst, the win was a revelation. As the Canucks jumped around the ice surface, it seemed as though a large burden had been lifted. When the hockey gods favour you with such a turnaround from despair to delight, it must be a sign of something good.

Next up were the stubborn Nashville Predators, on a high after winning the franchise's first playoff series. Coached by the impeccable Barry Trotz to play stifling defence in front of the fine goalie Pekka Rinne, the Predators turned the series into trench warfare. With the games lacking the drama of the Chicago series, the Canucks were forced to rely on their system and great will to subdue Nashville and its talented defensive pair of Shea Weber and Ryan Suter. The biggest showdown in the series was forced by the ubiquitous Green Men, two spandex-clad fans who harassed Nashville players in the penalty box with gymnastic moves that mocked the Preds players. Nashville GM David Poile became so vexed about these clowns that he protested to the league, which eventually set up guidelines telling the pair what they could touch and how close they could get to opposing players.

The Canucks advanced to face San Jose in the Western final by subduing Nashville 2–1 in Game 6. Had it not been for an empty-net goal by Vancouver in Game 4, all six games would have been one-goal decisions. After his wobbly performance against Chicago, it seemed Luongo had regained his equilibrium in the net. Led by a brilliant performance from Kesler, the Canucks showed they could win with tank warfare and not just

111

their stylish passing game. (Ominously, Kesler appeared to hurt himself in Game 6, a foreshadowing of the Canucks injury jinx in the playoffs.)

Next up were the San Jose Sharks, led by their prolific offensive stars Joe Thornton and Patrick Marleau. The Sharks, like the Canucks, were burdened with a reputation as a talented team that could never win the big game, let alone win a Cup. One of the two teams would shed its "loser" image, and many predicted in the media it would be Thornton and the Sharks. They would be wrong. If playoff series are a contrast in styles, then San Jose proved a good match for the Canucks' strengths. Vancouver exploited a lack of depth on San Jose's defence, winning in five games. The series was won in overtime on a point shot from Bieksa that resulted from a fluky bounce from the stanchion supporting the Plexiglas at Rogers Arena. Few if any saw the puck go in on TV, but there was nothing accidental about the Canucks' conquering of the Sharks. In the end, San Jose proved the easiest opponent for the Canucks in the 2011 postseason.

Wrapping up the Sharks quickly was important because the grind of the postseason was starting to take its toll on Vancouver. The club had lost defensive specialist Manny Malhotra to a serious eye injury in March. With the experienced Mikael Samuelsson (who'd won a Cup in Detroit) already out for the entire playoffs, there wasn't much room for depletion. More setbacks soon emerged. Captain Henrik Sedin appeared to be favouring an injured leg, too. For its part, Boston—Vancouver's opponent in the final—had seen two of its first three series last the full seven games and had dodged elimination several times. Against Montreal in the first round, they'd fallen behind two games to none before roaring back to finally conquer the Habs. Tampa Bay then took Boston to Game 7 of the Eastern final—a game featuring no penalties, thereby negating the Lightning's productive power play. Despite the heavy load of games, Boston was a largely healthy team entering Game 1—outside of centre Marc Savard, who'd been lost to a concussion much earlier in the season.

Neither team had had a Stanley Cup final experience in a long while—Vancouver since 1994, Boston since 1990. With no track record for either side, the Canucks were given the slight advantage due to starting at home and their Presidents' Trophy performance in the regular season. Truthfully, there was no easy way to gauge a favourite given the distinct clash of styles. Former player agent Peter Chiarelli had assembled a team that was a throwback to the big, bad Bruins of the Bobby Orr era, a punishing side with both size (six-foot, eight-inch captain Zdeno Chara, bruising B.C. native Milan Lucic) and great skill (David Krejci, Patrice Bergeron). They also had agitators such as Brad Marchand to keep the pot boiling, and a stingy goalie duo of Tim Thomas and Tuukka Rask.

The Canucks, meanwhile, were the kids with the new toy, a team that could score in bunches and was happy to let the world know just how clever they were. Under Gillis, they seemingly had all the requisite parts—plus attitude from forwards Alex Burrows and Maxim Lapierre. Their goaltending, problematic earlier in the playoffs, seemed to have settled down. The Canucks were eight deep on defence, as youngsters such as Chris Tanev and role players Aaron Rome and Andrew Alberts got considerable ice time when injuries hit the Canucks during the regular season.

To the delight of their nervous fans, the Canucks won the first two games on home ice in a fashion that often indicates that the gods are picking favourites. In Game 1, Raffi Torres's goal with just 18.5 seconds left in the third period was the only score needed for a 1-0 win. Luongo stopped thirty-six shots and the Canucks killed off a five-on-three power play. In Game 2, Alex Burrows's wraparound goal early in overtime won it 3-2. The slick shift gave the Canucks a 2-0 lead in games. Only twice since World War II had a Stanley Cup finalist blown such a lead after winning its first two games on home ice.

As fans spilled out onto the streets surrounding Rogers Arena after Game 2, there was a festive air of anticipation amongst the fans. The warm summer kept many fans in the downtown to walk, talk, and bond in what looked like the vindication of their fandom as Canuck supporters. Walking past the Hudson's Bay department store, the Hotel Vancouver, and Robson Street, there was a sense in the happy faces that Vancouver would shed its loser label and forever discard the stain of the 1994 riot. Giddy fans embraced on the mall behind the art gallery, passing a joint between them and smiling into the June night. "We're going to do it, man," repeated one bearded fan in a vintage Stan Smyl jersey as he leaned against a stoplight at Howe and Robson.

But for those with a nervous disposition, signs of trouble for the Canucks started to emerge in Game 1. The Canucks lost stalwart defenceman Dan Hamhuis for the rest of the series as he suffered a sports hernia applying a hip check to Milan Lucic on the boards. The loss of his minutes and steadiness would cost the Canucks dearly. Then, in a scrum behind the Bruins net, Burrows bit the finger of Bergeron after the Bruins forward thrust it into his mouth. "Fingergate" precipitated a war of words between the coaches and an epidemic of players sticking fingers in each other's faces. While Burrows escaped suspension, the bite raised the Bruins' temperature, galvanizing a team that had its back to the wall. Former Bruin Mike Milbury, working as an NBC analyst, complained bitterly, calling it "a disgraceful call by the league ... They're impacting this series by a non-call." Vancouver forward Mikael Samuelsson, injured and out of the series, watched the Burrows bite with foreboding. "[I] was in the press box during those games, but it probably wasn't very good that Burrows bit Patrice Bergeron in the finger in the first game," he later told Hockeysverige.com, a Swedish website. "After that,

Boston was angry. You might say that was the wrong team to fire up. They play a very physical game, and I thought it would've been better to let the bear sleep, if you know what I mean."

Just how much the Bruins were inspired was apparent in Game 3. Cheered on by its enthusiastic crowd, Boston pasted the Canucks in every phase of the game. After a scoreless first, Luongo surrendered all the goals in the 8–1 laugher, being shelled by Bruins forwards. Ominously, Thomas shut down the Canucks' top scorers, stifling the team's potent power play, by stopping forty of forty-one shots. To make matters worse, in the first period, defenceman Aaron Rome felled Boston forward Nathan Horton with a devastating late check in open ice at the Canucks' blue line. A concussed Horton was lost for the playoffs. The NHL's Hockey Operations department, looking to defuse media anger over the nasty tone of the series, responded by suspending Rome for four games—in effect, the rest of the playoffs. It was another critical hit to a thinning blue line.

"Oh well, one game" was the sentiment of Vancouver fans who saw it as a temporary blip for their team's Cup hopes. Then came a second, more discouraging win for Boston as the Bruins shut out Vancouver 4–0 in Game 4. Luongo was pulled early in the third period after a shaky performance, while Thomas had another strong performance, stopping thirty-eight shots. Boston had clearly seized the momentum in the series while doubts about Luongo from the Chicago series re-emerged.

Back in Vancouver for Game 5, the nervous anticipation of Canucks fans pervaded. For a team and a region that always saw the prize slip tantalizingly slip from its fingers, the electricity was everywhere. "The 2011 Stanley Cup playoffs were an extremely electrifying experience for everyone in Vancouver and the province of B.C.," noted Gilman.

The Canucks' emotional 1–0 win in Game 5 at first seemed to lift the gloom. Lapierre's game-winner came 4:35 into the third period, and from then on, Luongo and the depleted

Canucks hung on for a win that left them just one game away from the team's first Stanley Cup. Despite his other failings, Luongo's thirty-one-shot shutout made him just the second goalie ever to record two 1–0 wins in the final.

To top it off, Luongo lost temporary control of his games-manship in a postgame press appearance after Game 5's winning goal. Thomas had ventured too far from his crease, Luongo claimed, allowing Lapierre room to circle the net. When asked if it was smart to supply oxygen to a team needing a little boost, Luongo capped the verbal gaffes by whining, "I'm just saying on that particular play I would have played it different. That's the difference between me and him. I have been pumping his tires ever since the series started so I haven't heard one nice thing he had to say about me so, that's just the way it is." If Luongo's goal had been to provide the Bruins with bulletin board material, then he succeeded.

A mix of elation, exhaustion, and foreboding blanketed the Lower Mainland of B.C. as the Canucks made another cross-country haul for Game 6 in Boston. Seeing the enervated state of the team, some in the Canucks family quietly believed that this game might be the best, last shot for the exhausted Canucks and their erratic starting goalie. Had Luongo straightened out? Should Schneider get a start? Could the power play get going? Would the team survive much more mauling from the Bruins? Would Bruins goalie Tim Thomas have a bad game and give the Canucks a few easy ones? Would the referees call the game a little tighter?

The answers for Game 6 were all no. Luongo whiffed early and often, leaving at 8:35 of the first period, already down 3–0. Powered by their raucous fans, who sensed that Vancouver might finally be broken mentally, Boston had its way in every phase of the game. Forward Mason Raymond was knocked out of the playoffs when his back was broken by a pile-driver check from Adam McQuaid that shoved him backwards into the boards. The domination was epitomized by Marchand's brazen cuffing of Daniel Sedin late in the 5–2 win. The unopposed mugging seemingly symbolized a Canucks team out of gas—and answers—for the resurgent Bruins.

Worst of all, the engine of the Canucks, its vaunted power play, was ineffective when it got its chances against Boston. At the most inopportune time, Vancouver's offence was unable to score as it headed to Game 7 before its home crowd. The combination of Thomas and the towering Chara was smothering the Vancouver forwards around the net.

Gillis and the Canucks brass hoped the energy of Rogers Arena might be enough to revive the offence in the final game, as it had in Game 5. But there was also a dread that frustration would build if the club flailed ineffectively against Thomas again. An emotionally drained Gillis was stoic. "We played all year to get the chance to win one game for the Cup. There are twenty-eight other teams that wish they were here. We had the best record in the league, the best offence. If we play the way we can we should be okay." But the Canucks were a far cry from the team that entered the playoffs on a triumphant note. Samuelsson, Hamhuis, Rome, and Raymond were out with injuries. Kesler, his hip labrum torn, was a shadow of the player who'd seemed a slam dunk for the Conn Smythe Trophy after the Nashville series. Alex Edler was playing the final game despite a broken hand. Alex Burrows's shoulder would need surgery in the summer. Other Canucks were similarly hobbled.

Monday, June 15 was a warm, promising summer evening in Vancouver. The sun glinting off English Bay provided a brilliant backdrop for a city seemingly converging on its downtown area for parties and rallies. For Mike Gillis, there was still the gnawing question of whether there was something more he could do for his team. His daughter Kate, now a veteran of the women's field hockey team, tried to reassure him. "I think, at that point, I'd finally convinced my dad that he couldn't do anything else,"

117

she told the *National Post.* "He'd put the team together, put them on the ice and, at some point, you have to remove yourself and let the boys do the work."

Estimates had the crowds downtown at 150,000 by the time the game started. The patio in the front of the CBC building had been a magnet for fans throughout the playoffs as crowds watched the Canucks' steady progress to this moment on huge TV screens. The tailgating had begun early, and by late afternoon many of the fans were intoxicated. Vancouver police, confident after its experience with the Olympics the year before, had a scant 150 officers in the area to control the estimated hundreds of thousands on the street. A fan-friendly approach was being widely hailed as making the difference between 2011 and the riot that accompanied the club's loss in Game 7 in New York City in 1994. Just in case, the team took to the local newspapers with a call for civility, win or lose.

At Rogers Arena, the exhausted teams readied themselves in an atmosphere of suffocating pressure. The depleted Canucks knew they had to grab a lead, dictate the emotion of the game, and depend on a defence that had held leads throughout the playoffs. Playing at home, there were hundreds of well-meaning friends and neighbours to deal with. The Bruins, meanwhile, were a continent away from such distractions, coming off a crushing defeat of the Canucks two days before. The recipe was to keep doing what they'd done, punishing the Canucks' offensive players while exploiting their defence with the speed and skill that had made Game 6 so one-sided. They would also get as many testing shots on the jittery Luongo as early as possible.

It was a smart strategy. Luongo had clearly not recovered from the Game 6 debacle. He lost track of the puck on the Bruins' first goal by Patrice Bergeron at 14:37 of the first period. It went downhill from there as Boston kept pressuring the Canucks and Luongo. With Vancouver unable to score multiple goals in four of the six games thus far, a deficit of two or more goals would be a death sentence for the Canucks. So when Marchand's wraparound goal made it 2-0 in the second period, Rogers Arena became quiet as a crypt. It was now going to be a matter of Boston running out the time left and claiming the Cup for the franchise for the first time since 1972. The final score, a 4-0 shutout by the Conn Smythe Trophy winner Thomas, spoke to the almost total domination Boston had enjoyed since Vancouver's wins in the first two games. Bruins captain Zdeno Chara, who'd punished the Sedins the entire series, held the Cup aloft in the eerie silence of Rogers Arena, its burgundy seats drained of most of its fans. Hollow-eyed Canucks silently watched as the Bruins skated the Cup around the ice.

For crestfallen Canucks fans, it was déjà vu. "As a Red Sox fan, there was always something going wrong," says Ray Ferraro, who covered the series for TSN. "I can see how Vancouver fans felt. Something is going to go wrong. It's always something. They weren't sure what it was. Even in the third round against San Jose, there was a segment of fans that felt it was going off the tracks. Even for Game 7 of the final, there was a feeling that they weren't going to win. And sure enough, they didn't. When the first goal went in for Boston, the air went out of the Canucks fans."

The Canucks' biggest fan may have taken it hardest. An exhausted Francesco Aquilini let a few of the reporters in the Canucks dressing room know how he felt about their coverage before he was quietly convinced to go back to his office under the stands. (Aquilini later apologized.)

As if losing the Stanley Cup on home ice in Game 7 weren't enough, the defeated Canucks then had to watch as looters and drunks, many dressed in the team's familiar blue jersey, rampaged through downtown Vancouver, setting police cars, buses, and other vehicles on fire. The mob broke into the same stores and shops it had walked past after Game 2, intimidating anyone who got in the way. By the time the overwhelmed police force called in reinforcements, it was too late to stop the disgrace of yet another hockey riot in Vancouver—although many were skeptical as to just how many in the mob were hockey fans.

"The thing that made a real impression on me was a guy who had goggles to protect himself from pepper spray or tear gas," said Gillis afterward. "I asked myself, 'Who would go to a hockey game in June with those goggles, unless you were fully complicit and wanted to be part of that?' That made a lasting impression on me that that isn't a fan of ours. That was somebody who went into that situation hoping that these circumstances would occur and participated willingly. Losing the seventh game and then having to watch that on the television might have been as disappointed as I've ever been here."

"The 2011 riot had a lot of things that had nothing to do with the hockey," says Canucks broadcaster John Shorthouse. "There were a lot of mistakes made and a lot of people looking to make trouble. It was a perfect storm. Having said that, it happened twice and there was an element of hockey fans involved. I've often wondered what would have happened had Zach Parise scored for the USA instead of Sidney Crosby scoring for Canada at the Olympics here in Vancouver. There would have been some drunken anger."

Many in the media revelled in the misery of the clever Canucks losing and then having another hockey-related riot. For much of the year, the Canucks were isolated from the eastern media by the fact that most of their games were played when it was late at night in the Eastern time zone. But as the club finally slew its Chicago jinx and rolled on through Nashville and San Jose to the final, the spotlight became red hot on a team that rarely worked in conventional ways. "The shocking part was how much Canucks hate was in the air," wrote Sportsnet's Stephen Brunt in 2012. "Even in the East, where there is no long-standing rivalry, no real shared history, no excuse for holding a grudge, something about Vancouver seemed to rub a whole lot of people the wrong way."

To the red-meat section of the hockey culture, the Canucks became "divers" who were perverting the great sport. Some criticism was sharp-edged. CANADA'S TEAM? NO THANKS, barked the front page of the *National Post*. The *Toronto Star* said the Canucks would be "the least deserving champions in NHL history." "They whine. They turtle. They want referees to fight their battles," *Edmonton Sun* columnist Robert Tychkowski wrote. "They are arrogant, they bite people, and their fans set fire to police cars." Chicago *Daily Herald* columnist Barry Rozner called them a "disgrace to the game."

Players were not shy about piling on, either. Ryan Whitney of Edmonton growled, "Ninety per cent of the guys in the league want nothing to do with seeing them win." Detroit goalie Jimmy Howard later would say: "They've got a bunch of idiots over there. There are only several good guys on that team, and they know who they are." Maxim Lapierre was chosen as the most hated player in the NHL in an informal poll. Said Florida's Krys Barch of Lapierre, "I'd be embarrassed to be his father."

The narrative quickly became the team that got what it had coming on the ice. A 2012 Angus Reid poll said that only 35 per cent of Canadians rooted for Vancouver as the country's hope in the playoffs, compared with 70 per cent for the Montreal Canadiens.

"There is always a Vancouver–Toronto rivalry," sighs Ferraro. "When Leafs don't make playoffs, radio show hosts in Vancouver can't get enough of it. And vice versa when the Canucks were in the playoffs—they couldn't write or talk enough about how the Canucks were hated around the country. It feeds on itself. There's a real rivalry. Toronto views itself as a small New York, and Vancouver views itself as not Toronto. It was awash with anti-Canuck stuff when they made their run."

"It was amazing to all of us the amount of anti-Canuck sentiment across the country," says Shorthouse, who called the Canucks' games. "It was media-driven, with certain writers fanning the flames. That made it grow bigger and bigger. When you're on the cover of *Maclean's* as Canada's most hated team, where did this come from? What drives me crazy is when the Sedins are cited in these articles. [The *National Post* deemed them "too bland" to cheer for.] Are you kidding me? Are there two better people in hockey? And for them to get thrown under the bus it really drives you crazy."

For Gillis and the Canucks, the ensuing riot seemed almost too much to handle after the nightly grind of pressure and travel since mid-April. He bridled at the national media scrutiny. "The whole notion that we weren't Canada's team, we never aspired to that," he responded that summer in a *Vancouver* magazine article. "We're a hockey team located in Vancouver. Nobody asked to be Canada's team. That was concocted by writers not in this community. If they knew what these players and organization do in this community, the amount of time and their own money they gave back this community, I think it'd be embarrassing for them. We didn't aspire to that."

The riot, too, left its mark on Gillis and the organization. "We don't believe the people who behaved that way reflect us or our community," he said. "I said I hope that they get prosecuted to the fullest extent of the law, they get found out, and get embarrassed, as we were about their behaviour. With media the way it is today, it was portrayed as it should have been. But then it gets repeated and repeated in every different media.

"I know there are things we'll do in the future if we're in [a] position to avoid that. And I think the city will be in a position to avoid that. Very disappointing, but also very enlightening that we can't take anything for granted and we'll have to adjust for that in the future."

One thing was certain in the NHL's big picture, where success is slavishly imitated. Despite the fact that the Canucks were just sixty minutes from the Cup, savants were declaring their skill and offensive thrust a failure. The Bruins, went the thinking, had exposed the flaws in the system favoured by Gillis and Vigneault. Brawn was in and brainpower was out. The Canucks' fancy-pants schemes were for losers. If you wanted to win the Cup in 2012, teams would need to emulate the Bruins' combination of tenacity and truculence. Which would be fine if every team could find a goalie as hot as Thomas had been. No matter: Boston had been the admittedly better team in the final and all else that came before—including Boston's harrowing seven-game escapes in three playoff series—was relegated to irrelevance.

Asked what the draining 2011 final represented, Gillis allowed himself a small smile as he looked out into a blue Pacific sky high above Kitsilano. "I'm not sure what it means," he said. "I think it means we lost. At times, it's incredibly frustrating. At times, it's incredibly gratifying. You ride the roller coaster of emotion, of doubt and success that don't give you much time to reflect. I learned an awful lot about what it takes to win. We'll be a lot better for it. I just don't know if it'll happen right away in the next season." Even the ever-confident Gillis might have been surprised at how long he'd have to wait.

9

Once More Unto the Breach

"The Detroit Red Wings probably spend about seven dollars on the offices. They put all the money into scouting and development. I played in Atlanta, and man, we had great offices. Our team stunk."

RAY FERRARO, TSN ANALYST

B Y SEPTEMBER, the legacy of the June 15 loss and ensuing riot still hung over Vancouver like the clouds over Grouse Mountain. The riot had left 140 people injured, one critically; four people were reported stabbed in the melee. Nine Vancouver police officers had been injured in the burning and violence that snaked through the downtown. Critics were howling for Vancouver police chief Jim Chu to finally do something about arresting the rioters who'd torn the city apart on the night of Game 7. Four and a half months later, police had begun circulating photos of the rioters, asking for citizens to identify them. Photographs of sixty-four suspects were posted on the Vancouver Police Department website, resulting in twenty-eight suspects turning themselves in, being arrested, or being placed under investigation. Still, more was expected by the citizenry.

While the VPD was taking a deliberate, time-consuming approach, there was little time for complacency on the part of

Vancouver's hockey team before the next season rolled around for the exhausted Canucks: just 119 days separated Game 7 of the final and the first game of the 2011–12 season in October. The most severely injured Canucks—Ryan Kesler, Alex Burrows, and Dan Hamhuis—were going to miss some games at the start of the season after summer surgery. Others would have their traditional training regimens curtailed by the short rest between seasons. Almost every Canuck would also have to deal (quickly) with the emotional fallout in the brief June-to-September layoff.

It was a wall many teams had found hard to hurdle. "I just remember when we lost in the seventh game of the 2004 finals with Calgary," recalls former NHL defenceman Rhett Warrener. "There was no way I would have been emotionally or physically ready after what we'd gone through, losing to Tampa. Fortunately, or unfortunately, the owners locked us out that fall, and I never had to find out."

But these were the lab-coat Canucks, and the bounce-back from a near-miss of the Stanley Cup was simply another challenge to be studied and, eventually, conquered through better science. In their efforts to monitor players, the Canucks wanted to push past where most sports teams had ever been. Could the data help them assemble a better team? Were the current methods of evaluation just scratching the surface of predictive behaviour? Specifically, they asked themselves, "Can we determine which of our players best copes with the stress and pressure of close playoff games?" or "Can we make success repeatable?" And, because obsolescence is always stalking sports teams, "How do we rebuild, even as we compete at the top end of the NHL?" Maybe, the Canucks hypothesized, current hockey scouting techniques could be augmented in the same way that Billy Beane's Oakland A's expanded on the understanding of baseball scouting. Namely, by crunching the NHL equivalent of on-base percentage, walks, and strikeout/fly-ball tendencies.

125

Advanced training with team and personal trainers has been around the NHL for about a generation. The burst in curiosity about improved conditioning corresponded to the enormous jump in salaries at the same time. Players suddenly looking at as much as $10 million a year sought out methods of prolonging their careers—and their earning potential. It was no longer enough to use training camp to get in shape; players needed to be ready to compete on the first day of camp. With the money they made, they employed trainers such as T.R. Goodman in Los Angeles, who designed rigorous programs that allowed players such as Chris Chelios to play till the age of forty-eight. Goodman moved players away from the ripped-body model of NFLers into a more subtle understanding of the proper hockey body (something Europeans had known about for years). That meant core strength, flexibility, and explosiveness. It took three years, for instance, to finally get Chelios conforming to the model Goodman wanted. Other NHLers, hearing of Chelios's legendary durability, flocked to Goodman or similar trainers to get with the program. Soon, the off-season regimen included ferocious daily routines ranging from muscular endurance to muscular strength and high performance. Dietary habits also evolved to support such training.

The time lost to injury and the extended playoff runs were going to challenge the summer routines of the Canucks, most of whom adhered to the new training standards. Recovery and rebuilding of a Canucks team physically and emotionally depleted by the loss to Boston was the foremost challenge as camp opened in Whistler in September of 2011. Gillis and his team set out to find a better mousetrap to return them to the Cup final. They discovered that too much training can sometimes be as harmful as not preparing enough. As early as the 1930s, Canadian Hans Selye, a noted endocrinologist, was instrumental in identifying the ways in which stress affects the body and its performance. Through the work of Selye at McGill and the Université de Montréal, coaches and managers came to understand how too much training—with its resultant stress—can be harmful to an athlete.

According to the U.K. website Peak Performance, stress alters the body's hormone balance. "Not only adrenaline, but substances like testosterone, human growth hormone, the glucocorticoids and mineralocorticoids show an increased output, while the production of others falls. It doesn't matter what the stress is—it may be problems of moving house, working for exams, playing too many games of football, or simply worrying about something." Stress can be a double-edged sword, delivering greater energy and increased awareness but overloading the system. "This has an effect on the entire metabolism, including the rate at which our cells grow and are repaired as well as the production of the cells in the immune system." Prolonged cortisol secretion due to chronic stress can result in significant physiological changes.

Imagine how that stress is compounded when it's a hockey player facing the seventh game of the Stanley Cup final. There is fatigue from the long playoff schedule, nagging or even debilitating injuries that must be accepted, and then there is the psychological stress of the media spotlight, the expectations of families and friends, plus the self-critical stress the athlete imposes upon himself. Exterior pressures exist, too, when a coach or GM pushes past the limit of endurance in an attempt to keep his job. Or when a franchise in financial distress needs an extended playoff run to stay financially solvent. It has been documented that extreme levels of stress can contribute to higher rates of injury.

Seeing athletes fail in the stress of the Cup final or Olympics has led to the development of a number of techniques such as imagery, reframing, thought stoppage, and creating a positive environment. For instance, cognitive restructuring enables you to think through a situation, turning negativity into a balanced response while helping you plan for future situations.

127

"Research has discovered that there's a point at which stress simply takes over and blocks any coaching or instruction," Gillis said, sitting back in the chair behind his desk at Rogers Arena. Behind him and on his desk were clinical studies and research manuals from exotic-sounding institutes and impressive schools. "If the part of the brain responsible for dealing with stress takes over, the player will revert to instinctive behaviour—and that's not always positive. If you look at champions in any sport they're often people who've learned to conquer that moment of flight, stop the brain from taking over. That allows them to stay on program for what has worked. By the same token, there are players who never overcome that and can't win."

Thus the time-honoured notion that teams can't win the first time in the playoffs because their players haven't yet reached that critical moment of stress in a championship game. The secret to overcoming this might be preparation. A 1988 study of Canadian Olympians found that those planning for their competition, as well as how to deal with disruptions, were significantly more successful than those who hadn't planned ahead. Manchester United's Wayne Rooney illustrated the value of planning, right down to what jersey he'll wear in competition. "I always like to picture the game the night before. I'll ask the kitman [equipment manager] what kit we're wearing, so I can visualize it. It's something I've always done, from when I was a young boy. It helps to train your mind to situations that might happen the following day. I think about it as I'm lying in bed. What will I do if the ball gets crossed in the box this way? What movement will I have to make to get on the end of it? Just different things that might make you one per cent sharper."

Gillis also found research from Britain, as yet unpublished, that showed the effects of stress can also be traced to the positive and negative coaching of athletes. "The research shows that coaching can affect the adrenaline and cortisol in the system," explained Gillis. "For instance, the worst thing you can do on a game day is show an athlete images of his opponent succeeding. That increases the [level of the] hormone cortisol, which is released in response to stress into the immune system. They produce uncertainty and doubt. On the other hand, positive coaching results in adrenaline being produced. So on a game day or at intermission, we'll try to stress the positive aspects of a situation we faced in the game. If we're behind, we'll show how our team has come from behind in the past. If an opposing goalie is playing well, we'll find video showing us scoring on him in the past."

The Canucks weren't the only ones moving in this direction. St. Louis coach Ken Hitchcock, always looking for an edge, used this type of research to change his coaching persona. Once a fire-breathing taskmaster, Hitchcock evolved into a more soothing presence. "You don't get them out of the ditch with a bunch of criticism and a bunch of conflict," Hitchcock noted in 2013. "My job is to get them back up and running and feeling good about themselves. As much as you want them to learn from the mistakes, they've got to see the good stuff, too."

Another study showed that recordings of soothing music and calming voices help to gently contract and release muscles and promote focusing on one's breathing. Could the Canucks simulate those conditions in practice or training camp without being swept into the vortex of an elimination game? Could they help players get past their fears? "That's what we're trying to find out," said Gillis. "If we can create a program of understanding like that it could do for hockey what *Moneyball* did for baseball. Advance the understanding in a leap."

In the early days of Gillis's employment in Vancouver, the team began building a database of this research, previously not applied to hockey, that could give it a significant and dramatic advantage over its opponents. If all went well, the Canucks could then assemble the research and market their techniques while remaining ahead of the opposition.

Part of this project required players who were open to experimentation, and the club rewarded players who bought in and shipped out those who did not. If anyone wanted off the ride, said Gillis, he'd accommodate them. And so the club showed what seemed like extraordinary loyalty to struggling players while cutting bait with others, such as Cody Hodgson, who didn't buy into the organization's plans.

Thus, players skating slowly in practice, seemingly half-interested, and the reconfigured dressing-room facilities at Rogers Arena. Traditional dressing rooms, such as the one built for GM Place in 1995, were rectangular. At any time, most players could not see teammates whose stalls were along the same wall or look into their eyes at key moments. Voilà: in 2009, an oval dressing room resembling the bridge on *Star Trek,* with designer light box overhead, to produce better sight lines. Plus a new kitchen, players' lounge (to escape media), Wi-Fi workstation, and whirlpool setup. The Canucks' home dressing room quickly became the envy of players around the NHL.

There was also a mysterious back room at Rogers Arena, out of bounds to the prying eyes of media, who dubbed it the "mind room." It was part of a psychological counselling initiative in conjunction with a firm called MindRoom Sports Science. The Canucks hoped to identify which players needed help in dealing with the stress of their natural "fight or flight" moment. Using the results, a coach might decide who needs to be played more or less in the final moments of a Stanley Cup game.

"What we're concentrating on is methods to bring a more scientific and objective approach to how players are treated, how they compete, how they prepare, to give us any advantage we can possibly get with respect to performance," Gillis said. "Every element that would go into human performance, we try to analyze, get a grip on, and create a more objective standard."

That process included the owner. A rabid soccer fan, Aquilini had learned of the ground being broken by teams such as

Manchester United of the ESL and AC Milan of Italy's Serie A. Under Sir Alex Ferguson, Man U was famous for its innovative approaches to training the whole athlete. "Everything the player does on the pitch has different impacts in the performance of the team," Carlos Queiroz, Man U's assistant coach, said. "If you run and shoot, then there's the technical impact, the fitness impact, an emotional and mental impact. Human beings aren't split into different areas; we work through a complex system. My job is just to create the right harmony and make the right decisions in terms of preparation—which drills to do when, how many hours of training to do on each day of the week, etc."

In the wake of the 2011 loss in the final, Aquilini wanted to emulate this regimen with his team. After several years of wooing, Aquilini hired Bruno Demichelis away from Chelsea FC in 2012. Demichelis had created a sports-science centre known as MilanLab while with AC Milan. The purpose of the lab, says the website, is to "optimise the psycho-physical management of the athletes by entrusting this task to MilanLab, which represents the ideal combination of science, technology, IT, cybernetics and psychology." MilanLab's software program "performs neural analysis and uses artificial intelligence to transform vast amounts of numeric medical statistics into meaningful predictions through the PAS technology (Predictive Analysis Server), a system that works to predict the possible risks to the players."

Demichelis would be charged with re-creating the system in Vancouver. Specifically, it was hoped he would prolong the careers of franchise players such as the Sedins and Ryan Kesler. AC Milan defenders Paolo Maldini and Alessandro Costacurta had extended their careers until they were forty-one after working with MilanLab. Unfortunately, the Canucks were unable to obtain work permits from the government to keep Demichelis in Vancouver. Citing the availability of qualified Canadian candidates for the job, the Canucks' request was denied in late 2012. That left Demichelis, who'd moved to Vancouver, without a job.

While the Demichelis experiment did not work out, it demonstrated the resources the Canucks were willing to put towards staying ahead of the competition by optimizing sports science. There was also the latest state-of-the-art machinery, such as compression machines to eliminate the lactic acid that builds up in muscles during play, allowing for speedier recovery. Gillis pointed to data from soccer indicating how a body fatigues during the course of a game.

"We have looked at [passing efficiency] in soccer," Gillis noted in a 2012 interview on The Team 1040, the Canucks' host broadcaster, "and we put that in a very different context. We've looked at it relative to fatigue and conditioning, and how your percentage of passing success is relative to your conditioning, and the time in the game when you do it, and how many minutes you've played. There are studies that we've looked at that indicate that passing percentage in soccer goes dramatically down depending on the time in the game or depending on the conditioning of the player.

"The problem in our sport is that when you combine hitting and you combine puck battles, that takes it away from every other sport. We're trying to define fatigue levels in those circumstances, and as you know, a player usually gets hit twice when he gets hit once; he gets hit by the player and then hits the boards. How you can attribute that to success and how you attribute that to fatigue levels is instrumental in finding out when a player in the third period makes a mistake. And something happens, and I think that as we've found, in a dynamic, competitive contact sport, that fatigue levels are really a lot of the determining factor in success or failure.

"You need defencemen who can handle big minutes, because they're constantly—in today's NHL—being challenged, hit, challenged speedwise in their own zone, and then they have to make really good passes, outlet passes, and that's what differentiates those great defencemen from the ones that are really good."

ANOTHER KEY PART of Canucktivity was dietary—ground being plowed by others in the hockey business as well. The preparation most hockey players receive in junior hockey is structured to emulate the NHL rigours and prepare them for the grind of the world's top hockey league. On one hand, the Canadian Hockey League does that with its punishing regular-season schedule and additional rounds of playoffs. Particularly in the West, this forces players to travel by bus for as long as twelve or fourteen hours to get to games.

Junior hockey has advanced financially from a generation ago, to the point where teams are worth millions and make money for their owners. But the business of prepping players can still remain far behind the NHL level. Even in the second decade of the century, many junior players were still subsisting on a diet heavy on McDonald's, roadside pizza, chicken wings, and, if old enough, beer. Playing three games in thirty-six hours doesn't leave time for much else as a bus rolls through the long winter night. It's hardly the ideal way to put on the necessary bulk for the NHL, and in some cases, prospects look for shortcuts they're not getting in their diet.

Better diet is a particular obsession of former NHL star Gary Roberts, who has become a shaman in the hockey community with his concepts about nutrition, rest, and exercise and his Gary Roberts High Performance Centre in Toronto. He's been described as the Chuck Norris of nutritionists. How serious is he? "He had the team water replaced with Fiji water because it was the most pH-balanced," former teammate Tim Brent told Yahoo.com. "I thought, 'Wow, he's hardcore.' " Roberts's conversion occurred after a neck injury that many told him would cost him his career. Roberts was able to find doctors to help him rehabilitate his neck. Along the way, he also discovered the importance of nutrition to the elite athlete. Over time, Roberts remade his body. The player who first retired at thirty with neck issues finally left the NHL for good as a player at age forty-two.

133

Now, Roberts stresses to young players the need for eating the best produce while steering clear of poor food choices and alcohol. He also cites the need for proper rest and recovery time. And Roberts has also designed his own exercise program that maximizes explosiveness and agility, not bulk and brawn.

All of which has made him a daunting character to some (including Gillis, who clashed with Roberts over Cody Hodgson). "It's hardcore, absolutely," Roberts told sportswriter Sunaya Sapurji. "But these are top junior hockey players that want a life in the National Hockey League. So there are different levels of 'Scary Gary' for different ages. Like I say, 'Part-time athlete, part-time results,' so if you want to be an NHL player these days and be the best you can be, yes, you don't have to be 100 per cent of a psychopath. But you better be 75 per cent, or you won't make it, No. 1, and you won't stay there, No. 2."

While he didn't exactly see eye to eye with Roberts since the Hodgson episode, Gillis had no problems with his 2012 No. 1 draft choice, Brendan Gaunce, using Roberts's services and losing fifteen pounds in his first five weeks of training. After all, Gillis preached similar lessons on nutrition to his team and in his own diet, seeking out the best produce, fish, and meat for his own table. "The abundance of great fresh food is one of the best things about living in Vancouver," he said. "Every day, you can have freshly caught fish and organically produced meat for your diet. We try to get our players to take advantage of it, too."

So Canuck players—in particular, the unmarried ones—had their food prepared for them daily by a dietitian and the team's own chef, David Speight, when they were in Vancouver. Speight also led cooking classes, helping players make their own nutritious food—the better to have them getting proper nourishment on the way home from practice or games rather than fast food or pub grub. On the road, team meals at hotels were planned with the same nutritional standards. "Why not try?" asked John Shorthouse. "Maybe it makes the difference in a [league] where there's so little difference between clubs. Out here, you have to try these things. Travel is a significant factor. This was the first team that was daily preparing meals for players. It makes sense."

Prospects attending Vancouver's development camp in September got a full helping of the Canucks' acquired knowledge on nutrition. Frankie Corrado, the highly rated defenceman taken in the fifth round of the 2011 draft, saw the value right away. "I didn't realize how important proper nutrition is until I started playing in the [Ontario Hockey League]," Corrado, who eventually made it onto the Canucks in the 2013 postseason, told Canucks.com. "Then it took me about a year to realize the toll it takes on your body when you're not eating well. That first year wasn't pretty, but I got through it. The meals were always really basic. There was never an extra with it. No spices, none of that stuff. It's just like hockey, actually; you learn as you go. As time goes on, you have more confidence with that you're doing, so you do a little more and a little more."

Another dietary nuance was the development, à la Gary Roberts, of a unique sports drink in collaboration with scientists at UCLA. Using feedback from the players and Vancouver's training staff, a specific game beverage was created to respond to the specifics of playing in a sea-level environment and the demands of heavy travel. Players had their own unique formula for water.

Some of these techniques had been tried before. Some sprang from the minds of the Canucks and were later imitated around the NHL. But there could be no doubt that no team thought harder or longer about things that the hockey culture considered crazy. The best teams discovered innovation and spent accordingly. "The Detroit Red Wings probably spend about seven dollars on the offices," says TSN analyst Ray Ferraro. "They put all the money into scouting and development. I played in Atlanta, and man, we had great offices. Our team stunk. Where [are] you going to place your resources? You've got a relatively deep-pocketed owner who's giving you the resources to do things.

"And everything the Canucks have done has been tailored to performance. When they redid the dressing room, one of the key components was the kitchen. The players were fed after practice so they wouldn't stop on the way home for McDonald's. Everything is about, 'How can this team be a winner? How can you get to the point where you're one of the seven or eight teams that competes every year?' "

Not everyone saw the Canucks' initiatives as foolproof. Former Edmonton head coach Craig MacTavish spent a season as head coach of the Canucks' top farm team, the Chicago Wolves, in 2011-12. MacTavish told Bob Stauffer of Edmonton's CHED radio, "It's good to try and incorporate some of these new-wave ideas—because there are lots of them out there—but at times when you try and incorporate so many, and you bring in so many experts, it can be counterproductive.

"There were a lot of people around looking for players' time, trying to get in front of the players, and as you know, living the schedule and the timetable day in and day out, time is maybe the most valuable resource that we have—especially for the players. It's a lot different now, than certainly when I played . . .

"But at the same time, there's definitely a balance there. Sometimes, you can go too far and demand too much of your players [to the point] that they're burned out. And I think that's something we really have to be careful about in the NHL in general, and [referring to the lockout-shortened 2012-13 schedule] especially during a season that there's only going to be forty-eight games in such a short period of time."

136 THE FALL OF 2011 certainly represented the most daunting challenge to the Canucks' vaunted scientific approach to success. In addition to overcoming the Stanley Cup final hangover, Ryan Kesler, Mason Raymond, Alex Burrows, and Dan Hamhuis

began the year on the injured list as they rehabbed after surgery to treat playoff injuries. There was also the major problem of how to replace defenceman Christian Ehrhoff, who, along with Raffi Torres, had decided to chase the money.

In the case of Ehrhoff, whom Gillis had stolen in a deal with San Jose, it was a whopping ten years and $40 million from Buffalo. (Kevin Bieksa, who decided to re-sign with the Canucks, received four years at a cap hit of $4.6 million.) While he had disappeared during the playoffs with a plus/minus rating of minus-13, Ehrhoff had been an integral piece of the Canucks' offence and power play during the year, winning back-to-back Babe Pratt Awards as the team's top defenceman. There was hope that another defenceman, such as Alex Edler, might step up into his role when play resumed, but no one was underestimating the loss to the team and its power play. By a significant margin, Ehrhoff had led all Vancouver skaters in total ice time and even-strength ice time in 2010–11.

"We have players with injuries and some challenges," Gillis said as he looked forward to the season. "But we'll approach it a little differently next time. We'll be a lot better next time for it. You can look at [the Stanley Cup final] as the ultimate defeat or you can look at it as [being as] successful as you can get without winning. If we don't get complacent, we'll be in good shape."

When the team reconvened in September 2011, only one addition had been made to the lineup that had come so close the spring before. Another German, veteran forward Marco Sturm, was signed as a free agent after missing the previous year due to injury. With three regular forwards entering the season on the injured list, perhaps Sturm could tide the team over. Conceding that his team's lack of size hurt when the Bruins had laid on the muscle, Gillis also signed a handful of unheralded power forwards who'd spent the last couple of years either in the minors (Dale Weise, Mark Mancari, and Steve Pinizzotto) or, in the case of Byron Bitz, had been injured. Looking at the

137

opening lineup, the Canucks were going to count on the return-ing team—when it was fully healthy by November—and rookie centre Cody Hodgson to get them back to the playoffs and, with some luck, the Stanley Cup they'd missed the previous June.

There was also the question of how Roberto Luongo would recover from the trauma of being yanked during the final and how many games his backup, the highly touted Schneider, would get. Luongo professed to be unconcerned with the jeer-ing and teasing over his playoff performance, but there was no doubt it was a situation that needed to be managed properly. Vigneault said he was hoping to rest his No. 1 goalie for thirty to thirty-five games over the season, and he turned out to be true to his word about getting the Massachusetts goalie time in the net—especially after Luongo suffered his traditional slow start. What would surprise many during the year, however, was how often Schneider was started in high-profile games. And just how the emergence of the younger man would roil the Canucks' carefully constructed plans for years to come.

10

Wait Until Last Year

IF THE CANUCKS' 2011–12 regular season had a signature moment, it probably came in the only rematch with the hated Bruins. Taking place on Sunday afternoon, January 7, 2012, at the TD Garden in Boston, it was a game in which several story lines intersected for the Canucks. The first of them involved Roberto Luongo—or, rather, the absence of Roberto Luongo. Many believed that, after his playoff humiliation, the goaltender needed to win a revenge game against the Bruins to get his confidence back should the teams meet again in the playoffs. The Bruins, who had started slowly as defending champions, were back on point by the New Year, thereby offering a great test for Luongo. But the Canucks brass saw it differently, wanting to know whether their twenty-five-year-old backup, Cory Schneider, could stand the heat of a playoff-type game.

"It wasn't by accident he was played in big games [like the Boston contest]," Gillis said later. "We wanted to see if he was as good as we thought. He is. The emergence of Cory as such an outstanding young goalie has changed the landscape."

Schneider was more than ready for his closeup. The Canucks' power play, the one that had sputtered in the 2011 final, was dynamic again. It scored four goals in the charged atmosphere of the matinee at the Garden, with Hodgson notching a beauty on a great roof shot. From there, Schneider denied the Bruins in a 4–3 win that seemingly left both sides drained. After Vancouver's stuttering start to the season, the gritty road win had everyone in hockey believing that the Canucks were back—and then some—for another run at the Cup. They had two bona fide goalies now, and—for the time being—a secondary scoring threat in Hodgson. Little did anyone suspect that the win in January would be the high-water mark for the club that season.

GILLIS KNEW HE needed to add parts to his battered team in the fall of 2011. So as the cleaning staff made its way through the stands of Rogers Arena after a victory over the Nashville Predators on a Thursday night in October of 2011, he and Laurence Gilman were not celebrating. Instead, they were huddled around the speakerphone in the general manager's office below the seats. On the shelves behind them were the eclectic works of Gillis's management gurus: *How the Best Leaders Lead,* by Brian Tracy; Jim Collins's *Good to Be Great; Adapt: Why Success Always Starts with Failure,* by Tim Harford; *The Speed of Trust* by Stephen M.R. Covey; Sebastian Junger's *War.* (There was also a wine catalogue from California and a garish animal hide slung over a chair.)

The pair looked like old-time radio fans listening to one of Foster Hewitt's transmissions from Maple Leaf Gardens. While the TV on the wall showed highlights of the Canucks' 5–0 victory over the Preds, Gillis leaned forward over his phone on the desk, eyes focused on events half a continent away. On the other end of the line was Lorne Henning, the Canucks' vice-president of player personnel. Henning was not at the Predators game; he'd been watching David Booth, a twenty-eight-year-old Michigan-born winger with the Florida Panthers who had risen with Ryan Kesler through the ranks of USA Hockey. Booth had speed and had scored thirty goals for Florida a few seasons before. He might be even better known as the recipient of a vicious 2009 head shot from Mike Richards of Philadelphia that sidelined him with a serious concussion. Since the injury, Florida had tired of waiting for Booth to find his touch again.

While Henning's voice came through the speaker, coach Alain Vigneault stuck his head in the door, eager to hear Henning's appraisal of Booth. Henning described Booth as a good fit for the Canucks' up-tempo, puck-possession style. Kesler might help his old friend regain his scoring touch, and Booth could help Kesler reintegrate after his injury while adding speed to a line slowed by the absence of Mason Raymond, out with a back injury. The question was: Had Booth emotionally rebounded from Richards's dirty hit?

In return for Booth, centre Steve Reinprecht (who went to the Canucks' farm team in Chicago), and a third-round draft pick, the Canucks would eventually give up expensive veterans Mikael Samuelsson and Marco Sturm, whom they had signed as a free agent in the summer. Satisfied with what he heard, Vigneault left and headed for his car.

When the trade was announced on October 22, people in the Vancouver sports media applauded; it seemed like a huge upside for the Canucks should Booth stay healthy, and Gillis's record on acquisitions thus far was impressive. After the team's sluggish start, restless fans, too, were pleased to see management actively working to strengthen the lineup. The downside was Booth's rich contract, running through 2014–15, one the Panthers had given Booth after his big-scoring season. To justify the $4.25 million annual salary cap hit, Booth would have to make the second line a viable offensive threat, taking pressure off the Sedins. With expensive Gillis acquisitions Keith Ballard ($4.2 million) and Manny Malhotra ($2.5 million) eating up cap space without providing offensive stats, Booth needed to be a home run.

"I remember the first time I saw him was at a golf tournament," Gillis laughed. "This ball got hit into our group from behind, and I looked around to see who'd hit it. And way down the fairway, I can see this blond guy who must've hit the ball a mile. He came up afterward to apologize, and I couldn't get over how strong he was built from the waist down. He's got the legs of a much bigger person. That's what you want in a hockey player is that development in the lower body." The perpetually phlegmatic Gillis seemed pleased with his acquisition, but he also knew how many things needed to go right for Booth to help the Canucks. Indeed, as he seemed to be rounding into scoring shape in December, Booth sustained a serious knee injury when checked low by Kevin Porter of Colorado, sidelining him for a month (Porter received a four-game suspension). Coming back eighteen games later, in January, he was ineffective playing on the wing with fellow American Kesler. Booth ended up with sixteen goals and thirty points in sixty-two regular-season games. Crucially, he was a non-factor in the playoffs when Vancouver's offence shrivelled. Booth complained about reduced ice time as well. And a PR problem was touched off among Vancouver's New Age community when the enthusiastic hunter posted photos of himself with a bear he'd shot with a bow during the off-season. (It would not be the final time the eclectic Booth defied convention in his controversial stay in Vancouver.)

The real bombshell trade, however, came at the February trading deadline, shortly after the Boston game. Cody Hodgson had been supplying the team with secondary scoring from the third and fourth lines—a necessity, since a rehabbing Kesler hadn't been producing at his usual pace since his return. There had been encouraging outward signs that the past ill will between the team and Hodgson was over. But behind the scenes, Hodgson was unhappy with his ice time. He or his agent, Ritch Winter, repeatedly complained about how Vigneault was handling his ice time—even though Hodgson was still a defensive liability and received power-play time. "I dealt more with Cody Hodgson during his time with the team than with any other player," Gillis explained. "I had only two players ever ask to get out of here, [former client] Mathieu Schneider and Cody."

The general manager had some new concepts about hockey and how to treat players, but he had one old-fashioned notion: anyone who didn't want to be in Vancouver would be accommodated with a trip out of town. And so, the decision was made to boost Hodgson's trade value.

To those willing to observe, the team's actions also revealed an inside glimpse at how it evaluates and promotes the strengths of its players. From the time the team resolved that Hodgson was going to be moved, it made a concerted effort to put the young centre in a position to succeed, starting him almost exclusively on offensive-zone faceoffs.

Hockey researcher Vic Ferrari wrote about the scheme. He pointed out that, in the thirty seconds following a faceoff at either end, teams that take the offensive faceoff outshoot their opponents by a 2-to-1 ratio and outscore them by a ratio of 1.7 to 1. Under Alain Vigneault, Vancouver had developed some of the most extreme discrepancies in zone starts. "Vancouver does this more evidently than any other team in the National Hockey League," noted the *Province*'s blog. "The fact that it's been unnoticed by so many media members and fans in Vancouver is getting to be not even funny anymore." Hodgson thrived in his new role, scoring key goals in several big games. As the clock on trade deadline day ticked down to 3 p.m., Hodgson had a gaudy sixteen goals and thirty-three total points. Most observers of the team missed the significance of Hodgson's strategic ice time, but it was in keeping with how the Canucks structure their ice time.

143

"We do use advanced analytics to some measure," Gillis explained to Matt Sekeres on The Team 1040. "It's more difficult in hockey than in baseball, because baseball is a defined event. You've got a hundred different things that go into player success. Who they play for, matchups they constantly play against. Their age. Injury history. So you've got lots of things that are determinant factors in hockey that can't be properly analyzed just through analytics. In baseball, you can.

"What we've done is look at things and try to design success, particularly for younger players, based on where they're starting. And who they're playing with and what situations they're playing with and the number of minutes they play. And I've become convinced that you can really begin to enhance a young player's ability by putting them in situations where they're going to be able to succeed almost all the time, and the only way you can do that is if you have the luxury of having a good team. If you don't have... if you're in a rebuilding stage or something that might not have the luxury to design those ice times the way you'd want... but here, we're fortunate, we have a good team, we can do what we want."

The analytics are not one-size-fits-all; their applications vary across a roster. "It's different for different positions," Gillis told Sekeres. "For forwards it's a combination of shots on net, quality of shots on net, location of shots on net versus time on ice. You know, there's a number of stats that go into it, but one of the reasons that *Moneyball* was intriguing to me was that—I taught it at law school and talked about it a lot—was what happens when a team is forced to look at something differently. And forced to go against the grain and forced to change the rules to their benefit so they can be competitive.

144   "And the biggest thing that I got from *Moneyball* was not statistical analysis, but it was that ability to think differently when you're not forced to, when you want to. And when you want to create a different culture and a different environment. And the

fact that they were successful, that leads me to believe that you can be successful doing it without being forced to do it."

So in the dying moments before the trade deadline on February 27, Gillis took the less-travelled road, swapping Hodgson and defenceman Alex Sulzer to Buffalo for the Sabres' top prospect, Zack Kassian, a bruising, big-bodied forward who'd been chosen thirteenth overall in 2009, and defenceman Marc-Andre Gragnani, who had played in junior for Vigneault in Gatineau, Quebec. When he appeared for his media availability to explain what seemed to be an astonishing trade, Gillis explained that big forwards with skill were amongst the hardest commodity to find in hockey. "There were six young players that I would have traded [Hodgson] for if any of them were ever made available. One was made available at the trade deadline, and it was Zack . . . When we got a chance to grab an elite young prospect like him who could help in the physical grind of the 2012 playoffs and in the future, we jumped at the chance."

Canuck fans who had come to see Hodgson as the team's future scoring star were shocked. Even after Kassian, who is a year younger than Hodgson, scored in his Canucks debut and Hodgson went pointless in his first seven games with the Sabres, the furor refused to die down. Had their seemingly implacable GM acted in haste? "I don't regret that trade," Gillis told the media months later. "I'd do it today." The GM's confidence did little to calm jittery fans, however, especially when Kassian's ice time was eventually reduced. The player touted as providing a physical presence to counter the Los Angeles Kings' size became a healthy scratch by playoff time. Hodgson, playing on Buffalo's top line, started to find his scoring touch—an element the Canucks sorely needed as their offence went cold in the final weeks of the season.

The most pointed criticism of Gillis's big trade came after the season from ex-NHLer Gary Roberts, now Hodgson's trainer and mentor. Angered when Gillis talked about

145

Hodgson's reluctance to stay in Vancouver, Roberts snarled, "For me, I'd like to be the guy that looks at Mike Gillis and says, 'You're a moron.' It doesn't really do anybody any good other than the fact that Mike Gillis looks like, as they say on TSN, a dud." Roberts later retracted the insults, but the battle lines were drawn on Hodgson. For his part, Gillis still felt his first No. 1 pick would someday be a fine player, but with Hodgson vacillating on Vancouver, he took the chance to get something scarce (a power forward) for something he could more easily replace. "We wish Cody the best," was Gillis's terse summation after the season.

FOR THE REMAINING months of the 2011–12 regular season, the team toyed with its potential. Winning streaks were matched by ragged play that saw mediocre non-playoff teams such as Montreal, Buffalo, and Dallas leave Rogers Arena with upset wins. For every 6–2 domination of Toronto, there was a brace of close 1–0 and 2–1 wins. It appeared as if the team, conscious of the long, rugged path ahead in any playoff run, was determined to not to waste an ounce more energy than necessary in winning games.

"Obviously, we haven't been pacing ourselves, but we've been cautious," was Bieksa's description of the approach. "We're taking good care of ourselves. We're doing the right workouts going down [the stretch], so everything's geared towards Game 1 and Round 1."

Gillis would later describe his team as "indifferent" coming down the stretch, but it seemed to go deeper. The Sedins, coming off their back-to-back Art Ross Trophies, were a pale version of their dominant selves as they fell back to levels of offensive production not seen in several years (even accounting for the general drop-off in scoring across the NHL in the second half of the season). The power play, missing Ehrhoff's presence, struggled mightily. Kesler, the forty-one-goal scorer the year before

146

who hadn't returned till November (and then probably too early), lost his scoring touch, settling for twenty-two goals on the year and none in his final seventeen games. (It was later discovered he'd wrecked his left shoulder in February.) Schneider might have been the most consistent Canuck, although Luongo had long stretches of fine play, too.

The team's lethargy wasn't helped by the serious concussion suffered March 21 by Daniel Sedin on a vicious elbow from Chicago's Duncan Keith that resulted in the team's best scorer missing the final nine games of the year, plus all but two playoff games.

If there was another malaise Gillis identified as the most important in his team's failure, it was the one that set in in the days after the Boston game, when the league seemingly departed from its fastidious standard of penalizing obstruction and interference. While the NHL never acknowledged any change in the way referees called games, it was soon accepted around the league that players could get away with more against skill players. That was bad news for teams such as the Canucks, who depended on special teams for their success. "Guys have learned from the rules, and they've adapted," said Gillis. "So they use body positioning and different angles now, and we have to identify it. I'm a fan of offensive hockey, and I think the league is, too. If not, we should change the name of the game to 'goalie.' We have to keep scoring in the game. But right now, it's not happening."

(The ire of the New York Rangers' president, the legendary Glen Sather, was also directed not at referees but at rule makers who'd taken out the red line for the purpose of offside calls on two-line passes. "I don't like the dump-in style that the league has gone to," Sather would say at season's end, after his Rangers lost in the Eastern Conference final. "Dump it in and turn it over. I'd rather see puck control. The coaches have developed a style to try to win. Dump it in and try to create turnovers, block shots, six guys go the front of the net, somebody shoots it, hope for a lucky bounce—that's not a skill play in my mind.")

Ominously, scoring in general also melted away as offensive catalysts such as Sidney Crosby, Daniel Sedin, Nicklas Backstrom, Chris Pronger, and David Perron missed significant time with concussions. Even as the league convulsed over Crosby's concussion problems, it became open season on skill players—culminating in Keith's crushing elbow on Daniel Sedin in March, which garnered only a five-game suspension served towards the end of the season. While this went on, research showed that the brains of former tough guys such as Reggie Fleming, who died in 2011, showed signs of chronic traumatic encephalopathy (CTE), the brain damage formerly known as punch-drunk syndrome.

With Daniel Sedin still sidelined with a concussion, the Canucks nonetheless won eight of their final nine games, an unlikely winning streak that took them into the playoffs as the top seed in the Western Conference and earned them a second consecutive Presidents' Trophy as the team with the best record in the regular season. The spurt made them a hot commodity again. While the wins were almost all close, the refrain from the team was that it had learned how to win close games and that the low-scoring efforts were the perfect preparation for a team like the Los Angeles Kings, their likely first-round opponents. The Kings, who had blown two key games with the San Jose Sharks late in the final week of the season, had been chronically challenged on offence all season. Their goalie, Jonathan Quick, was seen as the only reason that the team fell across the finish line in eighth place, a seemingly spent force.

There were a few voices who warned that Kings coach Darryl Sutter, the former Calgary GM/head coach who had taken the coaching job from Andy Murray in December, had a master plan for the overconfident Canucks. The Kings had been building a big, fast team, and, under Sutter, they were ready to go right over the defending Western Conference champs to prove that skill was overrated in a battle with brawn. "It will be a closely contested series, but look for the Kings to prevail in six games," predicted a blogger on the *Bleacher Report* website. But most of the mainstream media and playoff poolies saw the Kings as no impediment to Vancouver rolling into the second round of the playoffs. One poll on *Hockey World Blog* had 93 per cent predicting a Vancouver win. Too much experience, too much firepower, two star goalies.

In spite of Daniel Sedin's absence, Vigneault and Gillis both felt they were better positioned in 2012 than they'd been in the magical March of 2011. "We've changed a few elements," said Vigneault, "but our core has stayed the same. The core in our team is focused, is motivated, and they're ready for this opportunity." Said Gillis, "I feel this team is better situated than our team last year going into the playoffs." Starting at home, Vigneault would control the line matchups while the Canucks' besotted faithful would provide their heroes with all the emotion they needed. Already, fans looked forward to meeting Detroit or Chicago or San Jose in the second round.

If they were to meet those teams, it would be on a golf course. In a brutal five-game beatdown of the Canucks, the Kings smashed the aura that had been painstakingly built up since Gillis took over in 2008. When the Kings' Jarret Stoll beat Cory Schneider high on the short side in overtime of Game 5 at Rogers Arena, there was no part of the Canucks' game that hadn't been exposed in some fashion. For any Cody Hodgson fans still saying "I told you so" in Vancouver, the Canucks' secondary scoring had never shown up in the series: they scored a paltry eight goals in the five games. Daniel Sedin rushed back for the final two games of the destruction, and while his brother Henrik played heroically, the team's top line was largely negated. The Canucks' defence, which had come together so well in 2011, came apart like a bad Slinky under the Kings' withering

149

forecheck. Alex Edler, whose progress had led Gillis to feel he could replace Ehrhoff, reverted to rookie mistakes, coughing up the puck as the pressure for a comeback mounted. An injured Kevin Bieksa was immobile. Canucks forwards who'd taken pride in their discipline took inane penalties as they tried to meet L.A.'s physical push. The coaching staff seemed paralyzed in the face of the Kings' meticulous game plan.

But nowhere would the loss change the face of the Canucks more than in goal. Most observers felt that Roberto Luongo, the starter in Games 1 and 2, had kept the games from getting even more out of hand than the pair of 4-2 defeats. Still, he surrendered seven goals in two games (plus an empty-net goal in Game 1), including two shorthanded scores in Game 2. The fans of Vancouver roiled over what to do as the season seemed to be suddenly escaping them.

Looking for something to spark his team after losing the first pair at home, Vigneault played his trump card by using Cory Schneider in net for Game 3. The young man from Massachusetts didn't disappoint, surrendering just four goals in three games as Luongo looked on balefully from the bench, his longtime No. 1 role usurped at the most public of times. While Schneider ably carried his share of the burden, the problem for the Canucks was that Quick was even better, stopping ninety-eight shots in the final three games. Despite losing two of the three games he started, Schneider—the man everyone assumed would be traded—had clearly made a claim on the No. 1 position. In the moments following the ritual handshakes between the teams, the discussion in Vancouver pivoted from "What will we get for Schneider?" to "Will Luongo waive his no-trade clause to get out of town pronto?" After all, Schneider's contract was dwarfed by Luongo's lengthy deal and he was seven years younger than Luongo. In a salary cap–driven league, everyone concurred, the younger man was a more efficient use of money at the same production level. When Luongo later confirmed that it was time to move on, it became clear that Gillis's agenda would be dominated by the disposition of the goalie who had been at the heart of the team since 2006. No one could have anticipated just how long and bloody the Luongo saga would be to both him and the team.

JUST AS THE Bruins had been in the 2011 final, the Kings were clearly the better team on the playoff ice when it mattered. For Vancouver players, management, and fans, there was stunned disbelief at the rapid collapse by the team that had just won the Presidents' Trophy. While a number-eight seed beating a first-place seed is not unheard of, to do so in five convincing games gave everyone in hockey pause about the true nature of the Canucks (and of the Kings, as it turned out). Were they potential champions, or simply a team that looked fine in the regular season but couldn't cope with a physical playoff style employed by Boston and now Los Angeles? So swift and complete was the defeat of the heavily favoured Canucks that no one could summon the energy to riot in 2012.

Certainly, the owner and his president/GM had no prepared speech to greet the cold, grey dawn on Monday, April 16, 2012. It was rumoured that Aquilini had few, if any, publishable thoughts after seeing the epic collapse—except perhaps to fire the coach. Despite rumours flying around the hockey world of Vigneault's imminent dismissal and Luongo's trade, Gillis waited a full week to meet the media for a post mortem. A cooling-off period, he described it, so that no decisions were made in haste.

When he finally sat before the media in an open-necked shirt, Canucks water bottle propped on the table beside him, Gillis was not accompanied by Vigneault. For a few moments, a buzz went through the Norm Jewison Media Room in the bowels of Rogers Arena. Did this mean Vigneault was toast? He had just one year left on his contract, and despite the expectations

151

of another triumphant playoff run, there'd been no talk of an extension. "Where is your coach?" Gillis was asked. "He's sitting about twenty feet away from here," the GM explained. Without saying so precisely, Gillis then made it clear that, if he had his way, Vigneault would be back as coach. Again, a frisson of nervous energy surged in the room packed with local media eager for a juicy GM–owner squabble over Vigneault.

Gillis, who was also headed into the final year of his own original contract, did little to defuse that talk. "My future will be discussed first, before we get to anybody else; we'll discuss my role and how I've done, then we'll move on to every other role in the organization. Everyone will be evaluated for how they've done and how they've performed." The scribes wondered whether the passionate Aquilini might force Gillis to resign if he backed Vigneault too strongly, but no one dared ask the question.

Switching gears quickly, Gillis was asked the inevitable question: What happened? "I really felt the game in Boston, for some reason, was such an emotional and challenging game, it was almost like playing a Stanley Cup final game in the middle of the season, and from that point on, I don't think our team ever really collectively got their emotions together," Gillis said.

Goalie Schneider agreed with his GM about the Bruins game. "I know guys were just exhausted after that game," he later admitted. "I don't think people realize the emotional intensity... guys were sore for a week after, just the physicality." Added Henrik Sedin, "He's right. For a stretch after the Boston game, our focus wasn't there. Maybe we looked forward to that game too much, and after we had trouble coming back to the team we are."

152   "We had some injuries that [affected] us," Gillis continued, "and we just didn't seem to play consistently as well from that point. There were certain points where our goaltending was so

good it got us through. As a group, I didn't think we executed as well or played as well from that point for the remainder of the season."

Gillis indicated he had concerns about the team even as it was closing out the regular season by winning eight of its last nine games. "Heading into the playoffs, we won a lot of games at the end that I thought our team was somewhat indifferent in and met a team in the playoffs that was very well coached," he said. "They played hard, they won some games that could have gone either way, and suddenly you are down 3–0 in a series and it's very difficult to climb your way out of it."

When pressed on whether his master plan emphasizing skill and speed would be junked in favour of the defensive, size-based style now proving successful in the playoffs, Gillis offered no retreat. "Success goes in cycles, and perhaps we were on the wrong side of the cycle this year. But it wasn't just us," he said, referring to the first-round shocks also suffered by highly rated Pittsburgh, Detroit, Chicago, and San Jose.

But why fly in the face of convention if you're not going to be supported by the NHL? "Well, the general managers' meeting I was at supported that view [about more offence]. I think the whole rules package that came out of the last lockout supports that view," he said. "I think that the entertainment value is born out of having momentum changes and offensive opportunities and penalties being called. That's great hockey, and I think everyone here would share the opinion that the hockey in the last three or four years has been the best it's ever been—so a retreat from that doesn't seem to make any sense to me."

Whether it made sense or not, Gillis's refusal to accept the status quo carried him straight into the crosshairs. Still, there was no flinching. "I am not doing this job to get another job in hockey," he explained privately a few days later. "I'm going to do it the way I think is right, or I'm not going to do it all. We

153

have accomplished 98 per cent of what we set out to do. I think in those circumstances most people continue on, continue with the plan, and continue to finish off the last 2 per cent. I feel very proud about what has been accomplished by the organization, on and off the ice, and I feel it's the right thing to carry on and continue to try and accomplish our goals."

11

Regrouping

*"You're going to make mistakes. In my time, you could recover.
Now you just scramble, and it's tough."*

FORMER NHL GENERAL MANAGER CLIFF FLETCHER

THE DAYS AND weeks following the Canucks' dispiriting demise in the 2012 playoffs were the most taxing of Mike Gillis's career as a general manager thus far and a progress report on Canucktivity. The enormous vacuum caused by the team's rapid exit was filled with issues both internal and external—many of them beyond Gillis's control. That these issues cropped up in the emotional bear pit of Vancouver only magnified each of them. As his team surrendered two shorthanded goals to the Kings in Game 2 on Vancouver's home ice, Gillis was watching on the other side of the country in Kingston, Ontario. One of his closest friends had died, and Gillis was at the funeral, not at the game. The personal strain of his friend's death and the extinction of a season that had seen the Canucks as the No. 1 team in the NHL regular season was considerable. 155

Friends saw how the enormity of the GM's job in a major Canadian city was taking its toll on Gillis. He reluctantly suffered his media critics, of which Vancouver had many. He was learning firsthand what the men on the other side of the desk from him had known for a while about holding one of the thirty GM posts in the NHL: you can't live with it, and you can't live without it.

"There've been moments where I reflected and wondered if the amount of energy and the amount of opportunity to be evaluated by everybody was the right thing for me," he confided later, "but I felt that it was. I felt that we had unfinished business for sure here, and this team was on the right track."

The price of involving himself in every detail was teaching Gillis to delegate as he went along. "It's too complex now. There are too many areas that require modern-day thinking to limit yourself. I think hockey was behind other sports in terms of young executives who think that way. It's like they've finally come to the realization that you need other skills than having played hockey."

"The job is so much more difficult today than even in my era back in the late 1990s when I ran Toronto," says Cliff Fletcher. "With the cap system, it's devastating, the effect of a bad signing on your ability to improve. If the player you committed the big money to can't get the job done, not only is it a bad decision on the player, but also on the cap money you carry forward. You don't have the ability to recover by doing something the way we did in my era. You're going to make mistakes. In my time, you could recover. Now you just scramble, and it's tough." Fletcher's words would prove prescient in the upcoming years in Vancouver.

For now, Gillis was still in charge. To some, the evolution of the firebrand GM of Canucktivity into an establishment figure was starting to show. "In the years since Gillis has taken over," said TSN's Bob McKenzie, who has followed Gillis for three decades, "I think two things have happened. That is, first and foremost, he's mellowed a little bit, that maybe his experiences have taught him what a difficult job being a general manager is, and he maybe comes on less strong in that area than he did before he got the job or right after it.

"The second is that, over time, I think he has become more accepted within the fraternity. Obviously, there are some individual GMs who aren't fans of Mike's, and I'm not saying they're going to vote him Mr. Congeniality, but I've been to enough annual GMs' meetings, and that's where you can really see them all in a social milieu—and I've noticed he is a much more accepted member of the group now than he was at first.

"That may be true of all GMs who are new to the club, but obviously Mike came in as a former agent and a guy who, by his own admission, was never in the business of being warm or fuzzy or trying to win popularity contests. But he's not nearly as much an 'outsider' now as he was at first." As proof of that acceptance, his peers voted him GM of the Year in 2010-11.

The "mellowed" Gillis's first priority in the wake of the 2012 loss was to meet with his owner, Francesco Aquilini. The Canucks' boss was also their No. 1 fan, and as those who encountered him in the team's dressing room after the loss to Boston in Game 7 of the 2011 final will attest, he wears his heart on his sleeve. Though Aquilini himself made no public pronouncements, the Vancouver gossip mill was alive with stories that he wasn't happy.

Since the 1994 playoffs, only ten times had the eighth seed defeated the first seed—in thirty-six series. Top seeds had a 72 per cent overall success rate in the first round. The disappearance of the team's scoring—just nine goals in five games—put the Canucks coaches in the crosshairs. In the moments after Game 5, there was a feeling that Vancouver, despite the absence of star scorer Daniel Sedin, had not been properly prepared for the challenge of the physical Kings, that the team had read the near-unanimous predictions of an easy victory for the Canucks and fallen asleep. (In the weeks following the loss, Vigneault and Gillis would admit that the uncertainty caused by Daniel

157

Sedin's extended recovery from his concussion had disrupted preparations.) It was only two days before the postseason that the coach discovered that Daniel wouldn't be starting the playoffs. "It's something that, moving forward, I am going to deal better with," Vigneault reflected during the summer. "I learned a valuable lesson on that, and I think it will make me a better coach."

Newspapers and sports-talk radio speculated that Aquilini might want heads on plates and all manner of swift retribution against those responsible for the disappointment. In the history of the NHL, incendiary moments have triggered many snap judgments to fire coaches and general managers. In 1969, an angry, well-lubricated Toronto owner, Stafford Smythe, famously fired his longtime coach and GM, Punch Imlach (who'd won four Stanley Cups in the previous eight years), in the dressing room just moments after the Maple Leafs had been crushed by the Boston Bruins in the playoffs. The next year, it was the Bruins coach, Harry Sinden, who exited the team in the days following the club's Cup win after a row with management. Ottawa Senators owner Eugene Melnyk dismissed John Muckler—whose tenure corresponded to Ottawa's best years in the NHL—shortly after his club had been eliminated by Anaheim in the 2007 Stanley Cup final.

As summer finally swept away the rainy Vancouver spring of 2012, critics whipped up support for a snap decision to make someone, anyone, wear the loss at Rogers Arena. Vancouver wasn't a town to sit still when panic was called for. In the minds of some critics the team's highly publicized improvements and upgrades went from being cutting-edge to irrelevant. "In terms of proactive management of his team, in terms of player development, trading record and free-agent acquisitions, Gillis has had little notable success," sniffed the Vancouver *Province*. "And it was also clear that no matter what you thought of Gillis, he thought plenty of himself... Maybe the Aquilinis are happy with regular-season success, capacity crowds and a handful of playoff dates every season, but they promised more than that."

In Ottawa, *Sun* columnist Bruce Garrioch was dismissive. "He always considers himself the smartest guy in the room, but giving Luongo a deal with a cap hit of $5.3 million through 2021–22 was ridiculous. Moving the contract is going to be even more difficult. Bolts GM Steve Yzerman has declared he wants nothing to do with that kind of trade. Toronto GM Brian Burke would have to swallow his pride to acquire Luongo." Makes you wonder what people would have said had the team not finished first overall for a second straight year.

Former Canuck Mikael Samuelsson, who'd been dealt early in the year for David Booth, joined the chorus, telling a Swedish website, "I didn't think very highly of [Vancouver] management, so in that way I didn't mind [being traded] . . . Disappointed is not the right word. But I liked it a lot in Vancouver. I had a pretty significant injury my second season in Vancouver, when I tore my [abductor tendon] in my groin. The rehab was going well and I felt good in camp, but when the season was about to start, the leg didn't work. Looking back at it now, it might have been good to be traded. I got extra time to rehab and come back fully fit. I liked it a lot in Florida, but it was tough leaving the Sedins, Edler, and the other guys up in Vancouver."

There were more sympathetic assessments of Canucktivity, however. "Gillis may have had an unsuccessful year, but judging by what he could have done, he really didn't go out of his way to prevent it," said the *Vancouver Sun*'s blog, *Pass It to Bulis*. "That's because he doesn't operate in one-year increments. He just builds. If, in the course of this building, the team has a down year, and the worst that happens in these down years is the Canucks win the regular season, the up years should make fans pretty happy."

Wrote blogger Thomas Drance about the financial covenant between players and the team, "That Gillis, Gilman and Co.

159

have managed to get the majority of their roster to 'buy in' on that [financial] plan and accept the Canucks' particular 'covenant' is quite the accomplishment. It's not a Stanley Cup, but it's still nothing to sniff at. And certainly it didn't just take care of itself."

Canucks TV voice John Shorthouse shakes his head. He knows there are few pressure cookers like the one in Vancouver. "There seems to be a real intense focus on even mundane moments in the franchise history," says Shorthouse. "The coverage of day-to-day—all-sports radio and TV, I think we set the record. There was a game on October 30 [of 2011], and I think that's the earliest I've ever heard [anyone talk about] a must-win game. They were off to their usual slow start, in L.A., and the words 'must win' were used." Shorthouse laughs in spite of himself.

After the raw emotion of the 2011 Cup run and subsequent riot, the mood in Canuck Nation in the spring of 2012 was more restrained but no less displeased with the team's quick exit—even if it was to the eventual Cup champion Kings, who steamrolled everyone on their way to the Cup. Amidst this vortex of second-guessing and speculation, Gillis did something characteristic, a move meant not to quench public comment so much as outrun it: he called a timeout. Gillis and Aquilini put off their meeting for almost two weeks, letting emotions cool before evaluating what had gone wrong and what had gone right.

"My preference [is] to wait a little bit longer in order to make sure that everyone is level-headed and not emotional about what had happened when we had such high expectations," he explained to reporters. Privately, he needed the break as much as anyone after seeing his plans crumble so rapidly in one five-game stretch. He was as exhausted and discouraged by the results as was his owner. "Watching your team lose is like watching your dog die every night," Gillis liked to say. Yet he was determined to present a confident face to the world. Mike Gillis without self-confidence was not Mike Gillis, in the public's opinion.

Despite heated media speculation about the futures of Vigneault, Roberto Luongo, and Ryan Kesler (who would need major off-season surgery for a second straight summer), the cooling-off period served its purpose. On May 8, two weeks after his season-ending presser, Gillis emerged from the hiatus with his contract as president and general manager renewed by the Aquilini family. Said Francesco Aquilini in a release, "These past four years have been the most successful in Canucks history. Mike and his management team have done an excellent job to position us for long-term success on and off of the ice. We believe Mike's presence in this organization is important to the long-term success of this hockey club and we are confident that we will continue to compete at the highest level under his leadership."

In a telephone conference call, Gillis expressed satisfaction at being able to continue his plan for turning the team into a perennial contender. But he also reflected on the stress of the previous four years for him and his privacy.

"The meeting today was more about me," Gillis told the conference call. "I have worked very closely with the Aquilinis for the last four years, and that's the way it has to be for us to be successful. The meeting today was very much on point about how we all work together and the success we have had, and how to continue that success and build upon it ... It was a quick end to the season that we didn't anticipate. It just took a little while, which is not uncommon, for everybody to get together.

"We have a number of situations that we need to resolve," continued Gillis. "I'm eager to get started on them, and I will get started on them as quickly as possible." Namely, trying to satisfy Luongo, who had agreed to a move at season's end if it would help the team; signing Schneider to a new restricted free-agent contract; dabbling in the market for free agents such as Shea Weber and NCAA star Justin Schultz; and shoring up the confidence of his entire organization after its first real setback in four years of steady growth. Oh, and keeping the whole thing under budget.

Not everyone greeted the news of Gillis's contract extension with enthusiasm. Sun Media columnist Steve Simmons, long a critic of Gillis, sneered at the Canucks' progressive policies. "Oh joy, Mike Gillis, who didn't acquire the Sedins, Roberto Luongo, Ryan Kesler or just about anyone of significance in Vancouver, has signed on for five more years as GM of the Canucks. But the team is sleeping better since he got there." Others, without Simmons's agenda, were more sanguine. "Gillis has taken a good team assembled by Nonis and made it better," wrote Iain MacIntyre of the *Vancouver Sun.* "The organization has greater depth, at the NHL level and in the minors, than when Gillis arrived. And the manager has succeeded in creating a playing environment so appealing that key players accept less than market value to stay in Vancouver. The Canucks have never had a period of sustained excellence like the last four years, when the Vigneault–Gillis tandem produced an average of 50 wins and 108 points per season."

With his own future determined, Gillis announced in short order that Vigneault, too, would be back for his sixth year as the head coach, making him the fourth-longest-serving current NHL coach behind Lindy Ruff of the Buffalo Sabres (since 1997, though fired in 2013), Barry Trotz of the Nashville Predators (1998), and Mike Babcock of the Detroit Red Wings (2005). (Tellingly, Vigneault did not receive a contract extension.) Vigneault, too, was mystified by the Canucks' early dismissal in the postseason. "This year, for me, was challenging," he told the media. "That emotional awareness that's needed, it was a challenge to get us to the level probably needed in the playoffs to have success. We got every team's best game. Throughout that whole eighty-two-game process, we finished first in the NHL. I believe we did a lot more good than what was perceived out there."

Vigneault was grateful for the chance to continue in the Canucks family. "There are only thirty of these jobs available," he reflected during the summer. "I know how hard they are to get, and when you've got one, you do everything you can to keep it, especially in a great market like we have in Vancouver, where everybody is so passionate about the game. I wouldn't want to be anywhere else. I think I've got a great vote of confidence from our ownership and management, and I don't intend to let anybody down."

TSN analyst and former NHLer Ray Ferraro didn't underestimate the pressure to get rid of Vigneault in Vancouver. "There was no shortage of guys going after Vigneault's head," says Ferraro, who lives in Vancouver. "The whole city wanted him fired. It was the easy thing to do. But Mike didn't. If you're a marginal player, as Mike was, and you have the stuff to go after Alan Eagleson, then you've got character. For those of us who remember, that was no easy thing. There's no way to make people today understand that. Eagleson was my agent, and he didn't use his one phone call at the jail to call me. So Mike has the stuff to retain Alain no matter how the fans felt, because he thought it was right."

The intense spotlight of the Canadian media was also wearing down other Canadian GMs. Even as Gillis battled to keep a steady hand on the Canucks' tiller, Brian Burke was losing hold of the Maple Leafs' direction after just four tumultuous years running the organization. The media-saturated town was awash with salacious stories about Burke's behaviour. He was given some slack over the tragic loss of his son Brendan in a car accident (just months after Brendan had come out as gay). But the Maple Leafs being out of the playoffs for seven consecutive years—four under Burke—was removing Burke's wiggle room.

163

There was nothing remotely controversial about Gillis—unless a penchant for bone fishing is suspect—but Vancouver wanted its first Stanley Cup, so the pressure ratcheted up on the fifty-one-year-old as he entered year five of his leadership. The principal concern for nervous Canucks fans was whether Gillis had built the wrong style of team to beat the physical, down-low smothering of the Kings and, the year before, the Bruins. But that second-guessing has come with the job for over a century.

THE JOB OF an NHL general manager has evolved from humble player purveyor to a combination of shrink for a city's hockey fans, target for the local media, juggler of salary caps, and convenient scapegoat for ownership when it all goes sideways. If the GM is in a Canadian city, you can increase the pressure to the power of ten.

In the early days of the league, the role was simply called "manager" (as it still is in soccer). The "general" part came later. The task for early managers such as Tommy Gorman, Lester Patrick, Jack Adams, and Art Ross in the 1920s and '30s was to keep the budget low, drum up ticket sales, and find the next great prospect playing in some mining or timber town far out of sight. The notion of organized farm systems, psychological testing, and detailed scouting still lay far in the future.

Bird dogs and friends kept managers in the loop on prospects. When Howie Morenz, a speedy product of Stratford, Ontario, scored nine goals in a game in 1922, it was the referee who tipped off Montreal Canadiens owner/manager Leo Dandurand. With a virtual lock on Canada's most populous province, Toronto's Conn Smythe was in a position to obtain the choicest products of the Ontario hockey system. Smythe channelled his best Protestant prospects to the Marlboros junior team, where they competed against St. Michael's College School, where the virulently anti-Catholic Smythe stowed his "dogan" prospects (as he called them). "With St. Mike's in

Toronto, you had every priest in Eastern Canada being a scout for the Maple Leafs," laughs former NHL general manager Cliff Fletcher. "He wanted them to have papal infallibility, I guess." Thus, Bob Nevin would play for the Marlies against future teammate Dave Keon on St. Mike's. On occasion, Smythe would dabble in Prairie players (such as the Metz brothers) to complete his roster. Needless to say, French-speaking players wouldn't grace the blue and white till Smythe was retired and Marcel Pronovost joined Punch Imlach's over-the-hill gang in the 1960s.

But as the league geared up again following V-E and V-J Days, a powerful new entrant into the managerial sweepstakes emerged in the form of Frank Selke, who had been fired by Smythe upon the Major's return from World War II (where Smythe had been seriously wounded). Despite the fact that Selke had obtained future Leafs icon Ted Kennedy for the team, Smythe cast Selke aside for disloyalty in not seeking Smythe's approval of the deal. It was probably the worst personnel decision of Smythe's storied career, one he came to regret as Selke built the NHL's greatest winning machine over the next twenty years in Montreal. Selke would also create the template of the first modern NHL general manager. Under Selke and his disciples, Montreal would win seventeen Cups in the years between 1946 and 1980.

Selke hammered home the development formula that served Montreal so well on ice and at the box office by making sure the Canadiens always had a French superstar ready when the previous one retired. Thus, Maurice Richard was succeeded by Jean Beliveau, who was followed by Guy Lafleur, who was followed by Patrick Roy. Selke always had an English-speaking counterpart, as well. Richard had Doug Harvey, Beliveau had Dickie Moore, and Lafleur had Larry Robinson and Ken Dryden. In the days before the NHL introduced the universal amateur draft, the Habs' dynasty, controlled (formally or informally)

165

hundreds of players within Quebec and outside the province. In one year, 1966, they brought 110 players to training camp.

Selke's development model was so successful that, in 1958, two Montreal farm teams, Hull-Ottawa and Regina, played for the Memorial Cup, while the Habs themselves won the third of five consecutive Stanley Cups. "Canadiens were able to expand into Ontario and out west though the Regina Pats, a very strong junior team in Western Canada," notes Fletcher, who worked in the Habs system under Selke. "Montreal was more national than all the other teams. Their chances of success were weighted in their favour."

The Canadiens were known as the Flying Frenchmen, a dashing, bold, and aggressive team on the ice. The modest Selke managed in a very different fashion. In contrast to the mercurial Jack Adams or temperamental Smythe, Selke was a patient, deliberate manager not given to rash decisions. The foibles of key players such as Harvey or Jacques Plante were tolerated till they could be replaced by younger talent. Then the veterans were dispatched to a lowly franchise such as the New York Rangers. In this methodical manner, Selke transformed the job description from flamboyance and high-handed despotism to a more sober and analytical approach. "I learned you never, ever trade a young player until you're absolutely sure," recalls Fletcher. "Canadiens were ultraconservative in that respect. Look at Lafleur, who took three years to finally emerge. If you don't know how good he is, you'd better find out, because it may come back to bite you in the ass big time."

Selke's championship legacy is stunning, but that of his disciples might be just as impressive. Selke begat a virtual who's who of general managers who followed him and dominated the competition for the Cup. Sam Pollock, Cliff Fletcher, Bill Torrey, Scotty Bowman, and his own son Frank Selke Jr. were among the men who studied under and drew inspiration from Selke's methods. A third generation of GMs also was spawned by the

Montreal model, including former Habs players Serge Savard, Larry Pleau, Doug Risebrough, and Bob Gainey.

As proteges of Selke, young executives would be dispatched to a Canadiens farm team or junior club in Hull-Ottawa, Winnipeg, Rochester, or the Montreal Royals to learn the basics of managing. Thus, Pollock was schooled in the Canadiens' business model in the minors before emerging in Montreal as Selke's player personnel manager. After his Montreal Junior Canadiens won the 1950 Memorial Cup, Pollock was brought in by Selke at a time when former players usually got the jobs as general managers. Accountants and clerks were rarely groomed for the role.

If possible, Pollock had an even greater impact on the role of NHL general manager than his predecessor. The nine Stanley Cups his teams won from 1964 till his retirement in 1978 (his name is on the Cup a record total of twelve times) were produced at a time when the NHL status quo was shattered by rival leagues, expansion to twenty-one teams, and the universal draft. Even as the ground shifted beneath him, Pollock found a way to turn the changes to the Habs' advantage. When the league decided in the mid-1960s to adopt a universal draft of eligible young players, doing away with the old C forms and bidding contests, it was Pollock who was allowed to devise the rules for the expansion draft. Typically, Pollock got most of his players safely through the draft, losing only role players he could afford to give up. He also got the NHL to allow the Canadiens the top two picks from the available French-Canadian talent between 1963 and 1969 (a loophole the league prudently closed after Pollock snaffled Marc Tardif and Rejean Houle in one notable draft in 1969).

"In '72, they had four first-round picks," says former Hab player Doug Risebrough, latterly a GM in Calgary and Minnesota. "In '73, they had one; in '74, they had five; and in '75, they had three. They were patient, and they believed in development. And they had the most coaches. They had quality people in Cliff Fletcher and Bill Torrey."

Pollock's philosophy was straightforward: "Once we started winning, we worked even harder to continue winning; too many organizations relax at this point." Pollock's modus operandi—healthy doses of research, hard work, and suspicion—became the accepted model of a modern GM that continues to this day. Never a player himself and decidedly unathletic-looking, Pollock took advantage of his unassuming profile to move the GM from former NHLer looking to stay in the hockey culture to businessman applying analysis to the untamed beast of the hockey business. "His biggest impact was how he parlayed his fringe assets into tremendous futures far more efficiently than other teams in the NHL," says Fletcher.

By the time Pollock, in one of his few missteps, handed off the general manager's reins to Irving Grundman in 1978, his success was not unlike a skilful stock picker on Wall Street who stays ahead of the market through individual genius and diligent research. But like any stock genius, Pollock eventually inspired too many admirers to copy his methods. Because of Pollock's utter mastery of the idiom, other organizations began to emulate and adapt his models. Bill Torrey, the GM of the newly founded New York Islanders, was one of Pollock's greatest proteges and admirers. But when the Montreal maestro called him up to discuss Torrey's first-overall pick in the 1973 draft, Denis Potvin, Torrey was sufficiently in awe of Pollock to know that if Sam wanted Potvin, then Torrey should want him even more.

The years between Pollock's retirement in 1979 and the era of free agency and salary caps was dominated by a series of managers such as Torrey, Fletcher, Sather, Savard, and (to a lesser extent) Scotty Bowman, who owed their success to the player-acquisition model of the Montreal GM.

It was also a time when GMs were kings of the sport. "When the wages weren't very high, guys like Harry Sinden or Bob

168

Pulford controlled things a lot more," says Mike Keenan. "When I came into Philadelphia, the entire payroll was only about $2 million. Owners let the managers control the team in every aspect, from paying bills to negotiating the contracts. When the money started to escalate, however, the owners became very involved. My first experience was with Chris Chelios who I picked up in a trade with Montreal for Denis Savard. The history of [Chicago owner] Mr. [Bill] Wirtz was that not even Bobby Hull could get a million-dollar contract out of him. But Chris was going to be the first million-dollar contract—five years at a million a year. That was a tough negotiation and a big transition in the Blackhawks' history. And Mr. Wirtz was involved in that at almost every step."

This new sophistication of the general manager's role pushed the model from Selke's absolute despotism to what Gillis represented; a manager of silos ranging from player personnel to salary cap management to communications strategy. "What a manager now has to do is manage up—manage the owner or manage the CEO or the president of the club," says Mike Keenan. "The owners are quite active now, especially when it comes to big contracts. There are a lot of layers there that weren't part of the process in the early days. In Sinden's day, he just picked up the phone and told the owner what he was going to do. Now there's the process of dealing with presidents, owners. It's quite labour-intensive in terms of what you might be about to do or pay to a player."

ONE OF MANAGEMENT'S first responders in the salary cap era had been Laurence Gilman, a local Winnipegger hired by the Jets in the 1990s to bring rigour to negotiations their hockey people were disinclined or unable to perform. "I remember one time," said Tom Laidlaw, a former player turned agent, in my 2004 book *Money Players,* "I had Dallas Drake as a client in Winnipeg. They'd hired a young guy named Laurence

169

Gilman... He got on the phone and said, 'I'm the new lawyer of the team.' I just went, 'Oh God, this is going to be different.' Before, I was dealing with hockey guys—no disrespect to anybody when I say this, but I felt I could deal a lot more easily with a hockey guy. Now the emotions are taken out of it in most cases. Basically, it's 'Here's the numbers, here's the players' rights.' Both sides fight hard using the CBA. It's not an easier process, but it's a much more professional one."

Gilman's timing in coming into the league—at just the point where salary disclosure among players had sent compensation soaring—was perfect. "Laurence won't talk to you till he's ready to," Gillis told me for *Money Players*. "Some guys just answer the phone and let the agents start the process before they're prepared. Laurence only talks when he's ready to talk. You don't end up with a hasty deal that both sides are uncomfortable with."

And so it came to pass that Gilman moved to Vancouver to join his former adversary in the business of making the Canucks a champion. Organizations seeking to be successful and compete all fell into line with the concept of a "capologist" like Gilman, a person dedicated to helping the GM manage the ramifications of the cap and the ever more Byzantine implications of the collective bargaining agreement with the players. "I guess it came as a surprise to some of the agents," says Gilman. "It was hockey, but I was just following generally accepted business principles about supply and demand."

What was the use of gaining advantages in the CBA if you couldn't exploit them—as the players' side consistently managed to do? Teams now needed to control their salary obligations a decade or more into the future to avoid running themselves into a squeeze when the demands of the players on hand exceeded the ability to pay.

Projecting a player's value over the course of eight-, ten-, twelve-, and fifteen-year contracts and anticipating fluctuations in the salary cap became as vital to a winning organization as discovering playing talent. "With extended contracts, you had to project payrolls almost a decade ahead," says Gilman. "You had to project a player's production and value that far out. Plus, there is no guarantee from year to year exactly what the cap will be. When the lockout ended in 2005, it was $39.5 million. As 2012–13 starts, it's $70.1 million. Under the new CBA [signed in 2013], it's down to $64.3 million [in 2013–14]."

The whipsaw of trying to reward a player without hurting his team's chances at being competitive was a conundrum Gillis understood from his years negotiating contracts as a player agent. In trying to extract maximum value for his clients, he'd also had to respect the ability of those clubs to compete going forward. "What was the point of having your client sign somewhere at a healthy salary if the team he was joining now couldn't win?" he'd said while an agent. A player's value was derived from winning during the playoffs, the most visible time of the year; being a scorer on a perennial non-playoff team could only hurt the market for a player.

Looking at the situation from the other end of the equation in the summer of 2012, Gillis and Gilman were trying to get hometown discounts from free agents while also keeping them happy in Vancouver. It was frustrating not being able to use the financial advantages that came from running a successful hockey business. "It's getting so hard to get good players under the salary cap system," Gillis lamented as he looked towards the 2012 draft in Pittsburgh. "There's only so much talent to go around, and teams are locking up those players on very rich contracts. In this league right now, you're one injury away from being a .500 hockey team if you think you're a good team... You have to develop your own players, and that's tough to do when you draft at the back of the first round."

12

The Meat Market

"They are well prepared long before they sit down with teams at the combine. Our main objective is to gain as much insight into their personality as possible. To that end, we tend to ask them questions that are outside their scope of comfort."

LAURENCE GILMAN, VANCOUVER ASSISTANT GENERAL MANAGER

THE EARLY-SUMMER heat radiated from the pavement on Fifth Avenue in Pittsburgh as fans leaving the Consol Center spilled out into the June afternoon sunshine. After the air-conditioned chill of the hockey arena, this warm bath of heat and humidity went right into the bones of the hockey people leaving day two of the 2012 NHL Entry Draft. One small group making its way down the hill to the William Penn Hotel was oblivious to heat and the other vagaries of the Penguins' hometown. Wearing short pants, open-necked polo shirts, and beaming, satisfied smiles, Brendan Gaunce, his father, Stephen, and brother Cameron were joined by close friends and family just eighteen hours after the Belleville Bulls centre was selected in the first round, twenty-sixth overall, by the Canucks. Today was a day for basking in the excitement of being a No. 1 pick, the thrill of being selected by a team as successful as the

Canucks, and for watching Vancouver use its remaining four draft picks on day two.

In 2008, Cameron Gaunce had been chosen in the second round by the Colorado Avalanche, and by 2012 the defenceman had already played in the American Hockey League (as well as eleven games in the NHL). For younger brother Brendan, there was a template for success. "I've seen guys go through it, like my brother, who has played in the AHL for two years," says Brendan, who grew up playing with, ahem, Cody Hodgson. "I see the work he puts in every day. I'm just trying to follow those kind of footsteps."

But Brendan was now a high-profile first-rounder, and the choice of a Canadian-based team to boot. Heady stuff for a player who, the Canucks hoped, had poise and maturity beyond his years. "A lot of it is because he was used to watching his brother," Stephen Gaunce observed of his sons. "They get along very well. They're very close and work out together. I hear from some of the instructors that they chirp each other, pushing each other. They stay in touch every day, but they usually don't talk hockey, because they get enough of that." As they waited for the crosswalk light to change, the Gaunces and their friends looked like teenage boys always do, playfully roughhousing and joking on a hot early summer's day. It's great to be young and alive and a hockey player. Or, to be specific, a Vancouver Canuck.

It is now accepted in the NHL that drafting in the elite positions—first through fifth—will not guarantee success (see the Edmonton Oilers), but it's almost impossible to win Stanley Cups unless you do draft that high. Once again in 2012, the Canucks' success was working against them on draft day (the order is a reverse-standings format where worst go first). After getting Hodgson with the tenth pick in 2008, they waited till twenty-second to select Jordan Schroeder in 2009. They had no first-rounder in 2010 as a result of the Keith Ballard deal, while they waited till twenty-ninth to pluck Nicklas Jensen in

2011. For the 2012 draft, their first selection came twenty-sixth overall. Winning the Presidents' Trophy for a second year running ensured that the Canucks would be spectators for the first three hours of the seemingly endless first round, drawn out for the Friday night prime-time TV extravaganza on TSN and the NHL Network. Long waits on draft day were nothing new for Gillis. After taking Cody Hodgson in the tenth slot in 2008, he had the twenty-second pick in 2009 and the twenty-ninth in 2011. In 2010, he didn't make a trip to the podium until the fourth round, 115th overall.

In the aftermath of the Hodgson trade and the jarring first-round loss to the Kings, Gillis had begun taking flak for not having a bona fide star in his development system. Critics suddenly began to ask: If Canucktivity was so perfect, where were the stars in the making? Canucks fans and media were impatient for a phenom, even though there was little room for one to play meaningful minutes in the Canucks' lineup. As Gillis strolled the floor of the Consol Center, chatting with fellow GMs, he knew it would be a sweet to produce an instant star in Sidney Crosby's home arena. However, drafting in the final five picks of the first round is an exercise in patience, not pizzazz.

To be ready for the permutations engendered by the twenty-five picks ahead of them, Vancouver needed to have Plans A, B, C, *and* D ready for when NHL executive Jim Gregory called out their turn in the draft. Off-the-board selections like Calgary's reach for unheralded Quebec high schooler Mark Jankowski in the twenty-first spot could allow a prospect to slide to the Canucks. Or a trade might vault another team ahead of Vancouver, snagging one of Vancouver's top-priority players.

Periodically, Gillis strolled restlessly to the back of the floor to shoot the breeze with reporters assembled along the fence at the north end of the arena. He'd have liked to conclude something for Luongo here in Pittsburgh, and he pumped journalists for the scuttlebutt in their cities. He had vowed he must get value in the form of a top prospect or players and draft picks for his goalie, so his GM colleagues were waiting him out, confident he couldn't start another season with Luongo and Cory Schneider tying up $9.3 million in cap space. Even as his mind churned over the possibilities, Gillis affected the bored look of a businessman waiting for a commuter train.

Slowly, the first round unwound, with commissioner Gary Bettman—part MC, part social convener—trying to make himself heard over the steady rumble of boos from the Pittsburgh crowd. (To reduce the booing of Bettman, the league has done away with introducing the commissioner. He just appears, like Secret Santa, from the wings.) Delirious pods of parents and friends screamed in excitement when a prospect was chosen, their hockey and perhaps financial dreams answered. Beaming agents patted their new millionaire clients on the back, and photo ops began. In the TV booth, analysts Pierre McGuire and Bob McKenzie gave thumbnail sketches of each young man's ability and sterling character. To outsiders, it might appear that none of the young men selected this day could fail. But as the Hodgson–Kassian saga shows, there's a long way between this convocation in June and winning steady employment in the world's best hockey league.

THE ENTRY DRAFT is now one of the seminal days on the NHL calendar, a far cry from its first years in the 1960s, when team representatives congregated at the Queen Elizabeth Hotel in Montreal to make their choices in private. The draft was the NHL's attempt to avoid letting the Montreal Canadiens or Toronto Maple Leafs snap up all the best Canadian talent in the sport. By emulating an idea the NFL had long used, the draft supposedly gave everyone a fair shot, with elite young talent distributed more equitably to teams at the bottom of the standings. When it was started, as the NHL Amateur Draft, teams such as Boston and New York were perennial doormats thought to be incapable of competing for the best talent with Montreal, Detroit, or Toronto.

"You had the 'have' teams in Montreal, Toronto, and Detroit, and then you had the three teams who really struggled," recalls former NHL GM Cliff Fletcher, who joined the Montreal organization in 1956. "That's because the strong teams had far greater access to the best talent of the time. You had Montreal's grip on Quebec, and Toronto was strong in Ontario. Detroit had very strong influence out in Saskatchewan, Alberta, and Manitoba."

Prior to the initial draft in 1963, the recruitment of prospects involved a Byzantine world of A, B, and C forms, scouts inducing parents to sign over their kids for pocket change, and bird dogs working the crevices and corners of the sport in search of the next star. (Ironically, as the league was looking to create parity for Boston, the truly awful Bruins of the early 1960s were signing the man many consider the greatest player ever, Bobby Orr, to a C form in Parry Sound, Ontario.) "It was like recruiting college kids in the NCAA today," says Fletcher. "You went into families and homes. I can remember driving with Sam [Pollock] up to Lac St. Jean, a place called Port Alfred, to recruit J.C. Tremblay. I thought I was going into a school. He had twelve brothers and sisters living with him when I was signing him there."

Before the draft, it all seemed a little messy and covert, with entire leagues sometimes being sponsored to get the rights to a player such as Frank Mahovlich, Jean Beliveau, or Bobby Rousseau. But with neither the media nor the fans complaining, there seemed little reason to change things.

General managers and coaches rarely saw the prospects their scouts had signed until they showed up at the team's training camp. Word of mouth and the opinions of *The Hockey News*, advertised as the bible of hockey, constituted the sum total of knowledge about the incoming juniors. And with predictable results.

The end of the sixties brought expansion to twelve teams and the demise of the previous exemptions and protected territories. The league did away with directly sponsored junior teams in 1969, ending the control the Canadiens and the Maple Leafs had exercised over legions of players for years.

It was not until the 1970 draft, however, when Quebec superstar Gilbert Perreault and Toronto Marlboro Dale Tallon topped the prospect list, that the draft seemed to take off as a key fact of hockey life. When the expansion Sabres, under coach/GM Punch Imlach, won a coin flip to draft Perreault from the Montreal Junior Canadiens, they selected the first player to make the Hockey Hall of Fame after being drafted first overall. (Three of the four first-overall picks between 1970 and 1973 were enshrined. The others were Guy Lafleur and Denis Potvin.) It also marked the first time a pre-eminent French-Canadian prospect was denied the Habs, a bracing change for the *Tricouleur.* Perreault led the Sabres to the Stanley Cup final within five seasons. Tallon, meanwhile, never caught on in Vancouver, which had taken him second. But the message was clear: a fortuitous pick in the draft could heal your roster in a hurry.

Despite the high calibre of talent that frequently topped the draft board, there could be enormous flops, too. Such No. 1 selections as Greg Joly, Mel Bridgman, Doug Wickenheiser, Joe Murphy, Alexandre Daigle, and Patrik Stefan were either complete flops or mediocre NHL players despite the glowing opinions of the scouts and GMs who selected them. In part, this reflected the wildly varying competencies of the organizations. The inept Ottawa Senators, just a year into their second life as an NHL team, actually coasted to the end of the 1992–93 season for the honour of drafting Daigle, who wanted to be a Hollywood star more than a hockey hero. As a result of Ottawa's non-effort, the NHL adopted a system in which the bottom teams were placed in a lottery for the top pick (with the worst teams having better odds).

Stories of managerial incompetence in personnel matters are legend. When the Esposito brothers, Phil and Tony, ran the Tampa Bay Lightning, the frugal club had the No. 1 selection in the draft. It was believed Vincent Lecavalier would take the top spot. GM Phil sent brother Tony to scout Lecavalier at the World Junior Championship, where the former star goalie approached Lecavalier's father, Rene, and asked, "Who are you?"

"He didn't know who I am," the stunned father of the team's next superstar told author Gare Joyce in his definitive book on scouting, *Future Greats and Heartbreaks.* "And I'm not sure that he knows Vince."

The Espositos' Lecavalier madness did have its method. Because scouting director Don Murdoch had a minimal travel budget, he tried to get the most out of it by camping out for extended periods with Lecavalier's team, the Rimouski Oceanic. There, he became impressed with a young centre most clubs had discounted after some nominal scouting. But extended viewing showed Murdoch that the scrawny kid from PEI had something special. So despite the peer pressure, Murdoch got his young man in the third round: Brad Richards. Richards is now an NHL superstar.

Four successive dynasties—the Canadiens of 1976-79, the Islanders of 1980-83, the Edmonton Oilers of 1984-90, and the Detroit Red Wings since 1997—were all built on diligent work at the draft table over a specific time. Each had its own particular path to the top. While the Wings did not reel off four or five Cups in quick succession like the Habs, Isles, or Oilers, they are the closest thing to a dynasty in the NHL since salary caps and free agency distorted the model that had been in existence since World War II. In winning four Cups between 1997 and 2008, while rarely selecting at the top of the draft, the Red Wings defied the odds that had remorselessly stalked the Habs, Islanders, and Oilers. More importantly, the Red Wings completely revolutionized the draft in the late 1980s by being the first team to exploit the former Soviet bloc for players as those nations' systems collapsed. Not bad for a team that hasn't drafted in the top ten since 1991.

Swedes, Finns, and a few defectors from the Soviet bloc had made their way to the NHL since the advent of international play in 1972's Summit Series between Canada and the USSR. Stars such as the Stastny brothers, Borje Salming, Kent Nilsson, and Jari Kurri had given the league an international look, even if they only represented single digits in the overall composition of teams. Despite their success, there remained a bias within the NHL's Canada-centric culture against Europeans as soft and uncompetitive players. In the immortal words of former Toronto owner Harold Ballard, his Swedish player Inge Hammarstrom could "go into the corner with eggs in his pockets and none of them would get broken." So the top of the NHL entry draft was largely reserved for the products of the Canadian junior hockey system. Russian players were believed out of reach, both financially and philosophically, for NHL general managers and scouts.

The Red Wings' brain trust under GM Jimmy Devellano, scouting director Neil Smith, and scouts such as Ken Holland and Christer Rockstrom, had a different idea. The key to the Cups came in two seminal drafts in 1989 and 1990, when the Red Wings became the first team to mine the stars of the former Soviet Union via the draft. In doing so, they stocked their roster for the next two decades.

With the breakup of the communist regime in Moscow, the cash-strapped Russians were looking for Western currency. If you made inquiries, you learned that the former commissars were selling off their stars. The Red Wings had heard the siren song and entered Boston's FleetCenter on June 26, 1989, prepared to execute their stealth plan. After the obligatory Canadian prospects in the early rounds (Mike Sillinger and Bob Boughner), Detroit got to work in the third round. They selected a Swede, Nicklas Lidstrom, arguably the greatest defenceman of all time outside of Bobby Orr, in Round 3. In Round 4, it was future Hart Trophy winner Sergei Fedorov. In Round 11, it was stalwart defenceman Vladimir Konstantinov, whose brilliant career ended in a car crash following Detroit's 1997 Cup triumph. The Red Wings also acquired Dallas Drake in the sixth round.

The players Detroit selected in the 1989 draft combined to play 5,721 NHL games, making it arguably the greatest team draft ever by a single team. In 1990, Detroit added winger Slava Kozlov, a key member of Detroit's "Russian Five" in the 1997 and '98 Cup wins. Outside the draft, Detroit also brought in former Soviet stars such as Igor Larionov and Slava Fetisov and Swedes like Mikael Samuelsson and Tomas Holmstrom to fill out their international content. The Detroit teams that won four Cups in eleven years were dominated by non-Canadians and forever destroyed the NHL's bias against players from outside North America.

Soon after Detroit showed its hand, every scouting director was combing Russia for prospects, hoping to emulate the Red Wings' success, but Detroit had gotten there first with the most. Perhaps even more impressive than the 1989 and 1990 drafts were the steals later in the decade that guaranteed a second generation of Red Wings would carry the team past the Yzerman years. Where the Habs, Islanders, and Oilers couldn't overcome drafting later due to their success, the Red Wings' scouting genius brought them franchise players Pavel Datsyuk in the sixth round in 1998 and Henrik Zetterberg in the seventh round in 1999, players who were key to the Detroit Stanley Cups in 2002 and 2008. In 2013-14, they unveiled another European, Gustav Nyquist, who blossomed as a scorer. "The Red Wings want to get at least two players who work out from each draft," says Craig Button, now an analyst on TSN. "They don't care if they come in the first or the sixth round. So long as they turn out. Other teams obsess over their top picks while discounting their lower picks. Detroit doesn't."

DETROIT'S SUCCESS IN those drafts of 1989 and 1990 will likely never be matched. For NHL scouts, due diligence became crucial, and the business of the draft went analytical as the twenty-first century arrived. At the same time, the margins narrowed. The checking and cross-checking that go on around the world mean there are fewer secrets out there. The scouting world is fuelled by gossip, and bad news about any prospect travels fast.

That's how unknown Mark Jankowski went from an anonymous player at Stanstead College to Calgary's 2012 first-round pick within months during his draft year. In the past, he'd have slipped to the middle rounds or free agency as a project. Now he was a known commodity who caused a guessing game on how high he would go. Knowing other clubs were interested in Jankowski's potential, Calgary jumped in, using their first-round pick on him, shocking everyone but the scouts.

Anticipating the analytical direction in which Gillis would later take his team in Vancouver, the NHL instituted combine testing for all its top prospects prior to the draft. A key component of the combine is psychological testing, where teams can meet players off the ice in a controlled atmosphere. Delving beyond play on the ice, psychological inquiry has meant that teams can probe the makeup of controversial prospective players whose desire or personal habits send up a red flag. Many agents think they can coach a suspect client in all the right answers, and some old-timers still like to depend on their guts. (At one time, a high-profile agent had me give his clients rough interviews before the combine so they might be better prepared for the ordeal of so many interviews. Unlike one team's scout, we didn't demand that a goalie prospect take off his pants so we could see how his legs worked in the butterfly position.)

Laurence Gilman concedes that draft-eligible players are thoroughly coached in all aspects of the game, including the interview process. "They are well prepared long before they sit down with teams at the combine. Our main objective is to gain as much insight into their personality as possible. To that end, we tend to ask them questions that are outside their scope of comfort. Basically, we use the interview as a means to supplement the fieldwork that has been conducted by our scouts over the course of the season. It [the interview] gives us a three-dimensional understanding of the player."

One of the Canucks' 2012 farmhands, forward Bill Sweatt, probably gave more information than necessary during his draft interviews in 2007. He showed up with his arm in a sling. Had Sweatt, who played for Colorado College, been hurt in a game or in training? No, he casually explained, he'd been pushed through a glass window by a coed at school. Gilman, then working for Phoenix, heard about Sweatt's candour afterward. "It is clearly an opportunity for a player to audition, and, like any audition, some go well and some don't." The Canucks were Sweatt's second team, after Chicago, which drafted him in Round 2 of the 2007 draft but didn't sign him. A former roller hockey player from Illinois, he was typical of the overlooked projects the Canucks hoped they could mould into something productive.

One of the more notorious recent draft interviewees was Toronto winger Phil Kessel, who was selected by Boston in 2006. Everyone in scouting acknowledged the American-born Kessel was an extraordinary scoring prospect. Reportedly, half the scouting staffs in the league favoured him over Sidney Crosby at one time. The problem was, he was less than loved by teammates and those who'd dealt with him in the development ranks. Organizations posted red flags about Kessel's maturity and ability to find harmony in the dressing room. He'd also been caught drinking underage in a sting run by a TV station.

As Gare Joyce revealed in *Future Greats and Heartbreaks,* Kessel seemed well aware of his reputation as he sat down to be interviewed by Columbus's scouting team. The Blue Jackets' then scouting director, Don Boyd, prompted Kessel with one word: "Teammates." Pause. "Do you know what I'm talking about?" Kessel responded with a terse no. After some shuffling of feet, Kessel offered, "I don't have a problem with my teammates." Joyce then shows how Kessel stopped answering and began offering "Explanations. And rationalizations. And excuses." In a brief exchange, the Blue Jackets heard all they needed to know about Kessel's people skills. Boston selected Kessel fifth in the draft, just ahead of Columbus, relieving the Blue Jackets of having to make the painful choice between talent and character. (Kessel has become a top scorer in the NHL in Toronto after Boston dumped him for two first-round choices—that became Tyler Seguin and Dougie Hamilton. But leadership issues still dog him, along with the heavy price the Maple Leafs paid for him.)

People in hockey believe that fellow teammates and opponents are often the best judges of talent. They know who competes and who will "throw snow." Sometimes, they don't need words to express their emotions about teammates eligible for the draft. According to Joyce, one star defence prospect left his Team USA garb from the World Junior Championship hanging in his locker for his teammates to see; after a time, his resentful teammates burned the clothing in the middle of the dressing room.

One aspect of hockey testing that most agree upon is the more respectful attitude hockey kids bring to the combine. In other sports, athletes are known to turn the interviews into shouting sessions. It's not unusual for basketball or football prospects to show up covered in bling and fashionable running shoes. As Don Cherry continually insists, hockey players, in their conservative suits and ties, are (cosmetically, at least) the best citizens in pro sports.

183

WITH SUCH A level playing field, teams have come to understand that the most important part of breaking the NHL's parity occurs after players are under team control. As such, development was the buzzword at the 2012 draft in Pittsburgh. The ideal, Gillis believed, was to leave players out of the NHL long enough that they matured and developed their full potential. "It's a man's game at this level," he said as he stood in the lobby of the Canucks' hotel in Pittsburgh. "Very few players are ready as eighteen-year-olds. You look at what Detroit did with Zetterberg and Datsyuk. They kept them in Europe to play until they were ready. The temptation is always there to rush a player who has an NHL[-calibre] skill. But it's hard to learn in the NHL when you're only getting eight or ten minutes a game. In the minors, they can play in all situations and learn their craft. If it was up to me, I'd start them all in the ECHL and let them have fun playing the game. If they get put in above their heads, it becomes a business."

How much of this philosophy reflected his own experience as a highly touted first-rounder with Colorado in 1978? Bounced back and forth between the NHL and the minors, Gillis never got a foothold as an NHLer. Devastating injuries from which he attempted to return finally led to his retirement from Boston in 1984. "Of course it would have helped to not be put in that situation," he said as NHL folk in the lobby came by to shake his hand and get a hint as to whether he might trade Luongo that day. "But that's how things were done in those days. I needed more time to develop, and there wasn't any time for a prospect in those days. They replaced you when you failed to meet their expectations. You were done at twenty-two. I don't think a player who hasn't made the NHL by twenty-two is a failure by any means."

So far, only Cody Hodgson had been put on an accelerated timetable by the Canucks—and that was largely to trade him when he balked at the Canucks' way of doing things. Gillis pointed out the long climb of his former client, goalie Mike

Smith, who finally established himself at age thirty as a front-line goalie in Phoenix in 2011–12. After starring in junior at Kingston, Smith was taken in the fifth round by the Dallas Stars in 2001. After bouncing from Utah to Lexington to Houston to Iowa, Smith got his shot in Dallas. But with Marty Turco in front of him, Smith was a backup. Still highly touted, he went to Tampa in the 2008 Brad Richards deal. He got a shot at the top spot with the Lightning over the next four seasons, but with Tampa a dumpster fire on and off the ice, Smith was deemed not good enough to be a No. 1 NHL goalie.

At the nadir of his frustration in 2010–11, Smith was sent to Norfolk. The hockey world, it seemed, had decided he was, at best, a backup goalie. It took the bankrupt Phoenix Coyotes, who had seen their starter, Ilya Bryzgalov, depart for Philadelphia in free agency, to give the six-foot, three-inch Smith a last shot at starting. In coach Dave Tippett's system, Smith was a revelation for Phoenix, leading them to the third round of the playoffs. His league-leading .930 save percentage had him mentioned in the Vezina Trophy talk. Gillis knew the dark moments along the way, so Smith's success brought a smile to his face in Pittsburgh. "He just needed time to develop and to find the right spot for him," he said.

As he talked about Smith, Gillis faced a classic development dilemma with his 2011 No. 1 pick, Nick Jensen, who played the previous season in Oshawa of the Ontario Hockey League and finished impressively with the AHL Chicago Wolves, scoring six goals in eight regular-season and playoff games. The Danish prospect had gotten all he was likely to get out of playing junior, but as a nineteen-year-old, rules said he could not play in the AHL full time. There was an outside chance that, with a great training camp, Jensen would prove to be advanced enough to play in Vancouver in 2012–13. The temptation to vindicate Gillis's draft record by plunking a No. 1 pick into the NHL just fourteen months after being selected was great.

The decision was made before the Canucks came to the draft: Jensen would leave the OHL to play in the Swedish Elite League. "He needs to play against better competition this year," said Gillis, keeping an eye on the lobby for familiar faces who might want to talk trade. "We support Nick in this decision. As I always say, the NHL is a men's league. Playing for AIK will let him see where he stands against older players before he joins us." With that, Gillis's cell phone buzzed and he was off to talk shop with a fellow GM.

AT THE CONSOL Center, the moment was finally arriving for the Canucks in the 2012 draft. Almost four hours into the process, they were getting to select a piece of their future, a player who would help define the success or failure of Canucktivity. There were no Nail Yakupovs at this end of the NHL's draft, no sure things. There were only strong hunches and calculated gambles and the memory of successful players selected well past this point. It was cold comfort for the general manager of a veteran team ("aging" is the pejorative term used by critics) looking to transition into the future. Leaning on the rail next to the media enclosure, Gillis had sighed prosaically an hour earlier as he looked over the scene of the thirty team tables. There were new general managers, like Montreal's Marc Bergevin, energetic and motivated, with the bearing of a man who has not yet made any mistakes or seen losing streaks. Then there was Brian Burke, the flamboyant Toronto GM, trying futilely to redeem four years of losing. Gillis now understood both sides of the equation. "We like what we think we can get at that spot," he said. "Maybe someone will make us an offer, but we are happy to stay there. What are you hearing?"

As Vancouver awaited, many fans had already fled the stands to follow the Yakupovs, Ryan Murrays, Morgan Riellys, and Mark Jankowskis into a night of celebration (well, not that much celebrating—Pennsylvania doesn't allow eighteen-year-olds to drink legally). Through mock drafts, sleuthing, and sheer guess-work, the Canucks figured approximately a half-dozen players might be available when Gary Bettman called out selection number twenty-six from the dais. There was also the possibil-ity that a prospect they liked might start to slide, opening up a trade-up to grab them. Or, by the same token, a chance to trade back, pick up an extra selection, and still get a player on their preferred list. As the picks were made, the Canucks' brain trust around their draft table, next to the Phoenix Coyotes, came to see Brendan Gaunce as their best scenario. He had size at six foot two and 205 pounds, and he had scored well in leadership, according to the team's cognitive testing and interviews done before the draft.

As the picks hit the twenties, the tension started to rise at the Canucks' table. By necessity, Vancouver had a few different jersey nameplates ready, just in case one of the teams before them went off the farm on a pick. The phone rang, and Gillis got up to walk to the corner of the floor to answer it where he could hear above the din in the Consol Center. He then ducked underneath the stands to meet with another general manager, far from the prying eyes of TV. "We were very nervous watching the last five picks," Gillis admitted afterward. "This is the guy we wanted all along... We tried to move up, and then we just held our breath. We had some offers to move it for this guy. But we weren't going to do it."

At number twenty-four, Boston took Malcolm Subban, whose brother P.K. was the Montreal Canadiens' young star on defence. (The Canucks would take their younger brother Jordan, a defenceman, in the 2013 draft.) At number twenty-five, St. Louis had the last chance to mess up Vancouver's plans. The Blues selected defenceman Jordan Schmaltz from Green Bay of the USHL. As the Canucks' turn came up, Gillis picked up the famous blue-and-green sweater, the decision made. At the podium, Laurence Gilman announced that the lucky

187

first-rounder in 2012 would wear the Canucks' iconic number 12 worn by Stan Smyl. Standing nearby on the stage, Smyl was both surprised and pleased at the honour. His craggy face broke into a shy smile.

The Pittsburgh crowd before Gilman was a less hostile audience than the one the previous year in St. Paul, Minnesota, where the Canucks were fresh off losing in the final to Boston. Every mention of the rival Canucks or Roberto Luongo in the 2011 draft was jeered by fans of their Northwest Division rivals. "Draft a goalie," bellowed one fan each time the Canucks stepped up to select a player. With so many of the glamour names gone and the Canucks just another team in Pittsburgh, Gilman made the 2012 selection free of harassment. In the stands, the extended family stood to celebrate as the name Brendan Gaunce was announced by Gilman.

"He's got to get a little quicker, especially in confined areas," intoned Pierre McGuire on the TSN telecast. Gaunce walked up the stairs of the stylish new NHL Draft set, where Bettman, like a wedding planner, got all the Canuck management types and their No. 1 pick arrayed for photographs. TSN analyst Craig Button agreed with the need for speed, adding that, in his international experience, Gaunce got better as the games got bigger. "Jensen [the No. 1 pick from 2011] is the same sort of player," Gillis noted. "He's a little further along, obviously, but they're close." As the final Canadian team drafting, the Canucks were the last point of interest in the mix zone under the stands as Gaunce and Gillis were quizzed. It was a happy moment for everyone.

With the last interviews done, Gillis looked around to the media microphones and notepads. "Okay, guys?" Tape machines snapped off, notepads were shut. Business was over with. With that, the Canucks staff retreated to their hotel for more planning for day two and a glass of 2007 Lewis Cabernet.

On day one, the NHL takes about four hours to draft a single round. On the Saturday, without the prime-time TV crowd, the teams whip through six more rounds in about five hours. In the blur of names and trades that jockey for position, a club must have a firm plan or else get snowed under. At the 2012 draft, the Canucks reprised a theme they had developed in previous drafts, going either for older players who had developed later or for younger players headed to U.S. colleges for extended development.

When Gilman approached the microphone at pick number fifty-seven, he announced that the Canucks were selecting centre Alexandre Mallet of Rimouski, an overage junior whom the Canucks saw as a late bloomer. (Many other clubs had him as a late-round selection, a depth guy for their minor-league teams.) Until his final year, Mallet had been a feisty grinder who hadn't put up many points. In 135 games spread over three QMJHL seasons, he had scored just twenty goals. In his final junior year, however, he shot up to eighty-one points, including thirty-four goals. In the playoffs, he added ten more goals and twenty-five points in twenty-one games. "Kids grow up," Gillis said later. "You look at Chris Tanev [who was an undrafted free-agent signing], he's an NHL player. So in my mind, Chris is a first-round pick."

A solid body at six feet and 195 pounds, the twenty-year-old was pencilled in to play with the AHL Chicago Wolves, accelerating his progress as a centre. Eventually he was sent to the ECHL to keep alive his dream of being a late bloomer. (Metrics developed by researcher Tyler Dellow suggests that this is a long shot; unless a player is dominating his league by twenty, he's unlikely to do so when he's in his NHL prime between twenty-five and thirty-two.)

Fifth-round pick Ben Hutton was destined for the University of Maine (where he became a promising scorer nominated for the Hobey Baker Award as the NCAA's top hockey player). Sixth-round pick Wesley Myron was committed to Boston University (he would jump to Kalamazoo of the ECHL in midseason), while seventh-rounder Matthew Beattie was going to Yale. The collegiate bias in 2012 was not haphazard. In *Moneyball,* author Michael Lewis writes about the research of sabermetricians like Bill James, which showed that college-trained kids have a far greater probability of succeeding than those who come directly from high school. Gillis has read *Moneyball* and absorbed its lessons for hockey, too. As a former agent, he knew what could happen to the development of young prospects who end up in unfavourable junior programs, where development is given a lower priority than winning now.

"If you look at baseball, historically high schoolers never pan out. College kids almost always do," Gillis told reporters at his post-draft scrum. "I apply a philosophy from the fourth round onward that we're going to select players who are going to go to big programs in the U.S. and develop their skills at a pace that is much easier to watch." One example of the approach was defenceman Patrick McNally. The Milton Academy product, drafted in the fourth round in 2010, had a breakout year with Harvard in 2011–12, notching twenty-eight points in thirty-four games for the Crimson. Unfortunately, McNally got caught up in an academic cheating allegation in the fall of 2012, resulting in his being removed from the team, effectively leaving McNally, a six-foot, two-inch puck distributor, without a place to continue his development. He returned in the fall of 2013 and picked up where he left off.

13

Selling Canucktivity

"We have a covenant with our players. We're going to pay
them the absolute most that we can, provided that we are going to
spend to the cap every year. But there is a point in the continuum
whereby, for every dollar we pay them over a certain amount,
[it] inhibits our ability to surround them with players that will allow
us to build a Stanley Cup–contending team."

LAURENCE GILMAN

THE DRAFT IS the linchpin of every organization, and the
Canucks are no exception. But even as they celebrated the
selection of Brendan Gaunce and the other players they
picked on the two days in the frigid Pittsburgh arena, there
was another prize on their minds. In a few days, Gillis and Gilman would make an offer for a free-agent defenceman out of
the University of Wisconsin named Justin Schultz. The lanky
Kelowna product was precisely the kind of player Gillis had tar-
geted in the past. Drafted in the second round by Anaheim in
2008, Schultz did not sign with the Ducks. Instead, he went to
Wisconsin. As he blossomed over his years with the Badgers,
Schultz saw his leverage increase in tandem. Using a clause in
the 2005 collective bargaining agreement that allowed four-
year players to file for free agency if they hadn't signed with the

club that drafted them, Schultz's agents began to see an opportunity. Anaheim suddenly discovered it had waited too long to sign him. By the midpoint of the 2011–12 season, it was clear that if Schultz were a free agent, he'd have almost every NHL club at his door. Naturally, the Ducks were livid that they might lose a player they'd waited so long to sign.

Anaheim GM Bob Murray claimed he had been bushwhacked. "We received no phone call from Justin Schultz," Murray told a conference call. "I'm confused, because if he had it in his mind that he wanted to play in Canada, then okay, I get that. I'm a Canadian too. But Eric Lindros, when he didn't want to play in Quebec, he went to his team that drafted him and said, 'No, I'm not going to play there.' He allowed that team to make a move to get something for him. He told us numerous times he wanted to play with us. He needed to just tell us the truth." (Hands up anyone who thought they'd ever hear an NHL executive say that Eric Lindros handled his rejection of Quebec City the proper way.)

As a B.C. product, Schultz was believed to be well disposed towards the Canucks. If the team could land him, it would be like having an extra first-round pick, maybe even a top-five draft pick. A talented puck mover with a fine shot in college, Schultz would be a natural fit on the Canucks' power play if, as eventually happened, Sami Salo left Vancouver. But the rest of the NHL had scouted Schultz, too, and knew that he could probably play right away in the NHL in 2012–13.

While most agreed on Schultz's talent, four-year free agents out of the NCAA offer no guarantee of success. "We've done some studies and find that the chance of hitting a home run with this category of player is overestimated," says CAA agent J.P. Barry. "They're usually a little older, about twenty-two or twenty-three, and they have to be able to move into place fairly quickly. There isn't a long development window for most of them. Outside of a couple of guys, it's not a shortcut to success."

Agent Rich Evans calls the spring rush to sign college players "a minor 'free-agent frenzy.' Most of these college guys are in [their] early twenties, so scouts feel they have a better read on them than an eighteen-year-old drafted at the NHL draft. Basically, they take a flyer, and because the rookie signing-bonus cap is so low, the financial risk is not significant."

With Schultz as the prize, Gillis and Gilman diverted to Toronto instead of heading back home to Vancouver after the draft. As he left Pittsburgh, Gillis was uncertain about the Schultz auction. As a former agent, how did he view this power play by Schultz, who eschewed the Ducks and triggered this auction? "We don't know yet if we're even going to be invited to bid," said Gillis. "He has the right to find his value in the market. He's been respectful of the process, and so will we."

Schultz's agency was preparing to audition suitors for its client at its Mississauga office. Making the beauty pageant more interesting was the fact that, because of the NHL's salary cap on entry-level contracts, none of the teams could use extra money to lure him. His salary expectation for the deal was set at $925,000 a year, with bonuses taking it to a maximum of $2.8 million. The player's decision would therefore be based on non-monetary factors.

In the days after the draft, the Canucks learned they were one of five or six teams that Schultz was seriously considering out of what was thought to be a pool of twenty-six applications. Further, Schultz was thought to be leaning towards a Canadian team, and the presence of Vancouver, Edmonton, and Ottawa among his final six confirmed that theory. That was about all the eager teams learned in advance. The process was cloaked in secrecy, and, because teams didn't want Anaheim suing them afterward for collusion, neither Schultz nor teams like the Canucks were uttering an opinion about which way it might go until Schultz was officially a free agent.

The Canucks certainly had a strong hand to play. A winning organization that Schultz could grow into. A team he'd grown up following in Kelowna. The chance to mentor with veterans such as Kevin Bieksa, Dan Hamhuis, and Alex Edler. The opportunity to play on the power play with the Sedins. But the Canucks also understood that Schultz would like to play as soon as possible as one of an NHL club's top four defencemen and be featured on their first power-play unit, and he was in a position to demand commitments from teams that he would be a significant contributor. Within the culture developed by Gillis, where everyone earns their way to the top, that might prove difficult.

After meeting with the most serious suitors on Wednesday, Schultz was expected to make a decision within twenty-four hours. But then it was discovered that another cull of teams would occur. When the field had been pared to three teams, Vancouver was still alive, along with Edmonton and, surprisingly, Ottawa. Usually, a player who goes through the lengthy process of getting himself to free agency does so to get to New York, Toronto, Detroit, L.A., or another big, successful market. Of the remaining trio, only the Canucks would be considered anything like a rich market.

The week stretched on in the baking heat of an early-summer heat wave in the East. Thursday and Friday passed without announcement of the lucky suitor. Rumour had it that Edmonton called in both Wayne Gretzky and Paul Coffey to help their old teammate Kevin Lowe (Edmonton's president) by calling Schultz to pitch him on joining the young Oilers. A new arena was in the works for Edmonton, which had just used its first-overall pick (drafting from that position for the third consecutive year) to select Russian Nail Yakupov, who played in the Ontario Hockey League in 2011–12. He would join Ryan Nugent-Hopkins, Taylor Hall, and Jordan Eberle on their phenom row.

Gillis remained stoic when he heard that the Canucks were finalists in the Schultz sweepstakes. "We made our best pitch to him, and he seemed pleased with our presentation. It's out of our hands now." Adding Schultz after Brendan Gaunce and a potential unrestricted free agent on July 1 would make a nice comeback from the disappointment of losing in the first round and go a long way towards placating the fan base and his owner.

The Saturday morning before free agency, the phone rang at Gillis's home. The choice had come down to two teams; the Canucks were not one of them. In the end, Edmonton won the beauty pageant over Ottawa. Schultz would tell the Edmonton media he wanted to grow with the talented young core of the Oilers—all of whom were, like him, in their early twenties.

It was also rumoured that Schultz had some wariness of the Vancouver media fishbowl. Edmonton's media frenzy is nothing compared to that of Vancouver, where the hunger for a Stanley Cup also takes on epic proportions in both the mainstream and social media. There was also the burden of being a B.C. kid playing in front of friends and neighbours all the time. Playing under a little less scrutiny appeared to be part of the equation for the Kelowna product. Which might also explain why Ottawa, another quieter media town, made the final two.

Schultz's decision was very disappointing, but not fatal to the Canucks in the immediate future. Long term? It was going to sting as Schultz's rookie year—eight goals and twenty-seven points in forty-eight games—proved his exceptional skill. (Sadly for Schultz, the Oilers remained a floundering team in his first two NHL seasons.)

As free agency arrived on July 1, the Canucks had fundamental issues to resolve. The void on the power play left by Christian Ehrhoff's signing with Buffalo the summer before had still not been filled. With the announcement that Sami Salo, the only other hard-shooting defenceman, was taking a two-year deal in Tampa (after the Canucks declined to give the thirty-seven-year-old more than one year at a time), there was real urgency to find a replacement.

The Canucks had aspirations to obtain Ryan Suter, one of Nashville's two star defencemen (along with B.C. native Shea Weber), but the price on the Predators' keystone UFA quickly got out of hand. It was also clear that Suter had a pact with his Team USA pal Zach Parise to sign in a tandem deal. Old-timers could only be reminded of the summer when Teemu Selanne and Paul Kariya (both clients of the late Don Baizley and friends from their days together in Anaheim) signed with Colorado in a comparable stunt. Four days after becoming free agents, both Suter and Parise signed identical deals worth $98 million over thirteen years with the previously lacklustre Minnesota Wild. While the Wild celebrated this massive commitment, the rest of the league wondered how to square the spending of Minnesota owner Craig Leipold, a professed hawk on the board of governors, with his concerns about runaway salaries.

The Suter move then produced an unintended chain reaction, one that hurt the Canucks. When he saw his pal Suter leave Nashville, Weber decided he might want out of Tennessee, too. Gillis had secretly been hoping the hometown boy would be free a year from this time, and that his old teammate Dan Hamhuis could woo Weber to the Canucks. He had structured his salary grid to leave money for a run at Weber in 2013. Now the calendar had been compacted for the restricted free agent, who wanted to take advantage of the current CBA market before it changed. He had a short list of teams he wanted to play for, including the Canucks, and was trying to influence one of them to trade for him or sign him to an RFA offer sheet—a little-used ploy that allows a team to make an offer to a restricted free agent at the cost of draft picks. He put the Canucks in a tight situation. The standards of money and term set by Suter's stunning deal were expected to be surpassed by Weber's next contract.

While Gillis was on a trip (in a fundraiser for autism research, the trip with the Vancouver GM had been offered as a prize), the Weber sweepstakes reached a crisis point. The numbers it would take to sign Weber—double-digit term, at a minimum of $7 million a year—were staggering and would seriously distort the grid Gillis and Laurence Gilman had constructed. According to Weber's agent, there was again the concern that a B.C. boy was uncomfortable with the fishbowl of Vancouver. Plus, there was the assumption that, no matter what kind of offer sheet Weber signed, the Predators would match it. The only option, then, was a trade with Preds GM David Poile, who was ill disposed to losing yet another star player. He wanted the moon, stars, and several planets in return for Weber.

Complicating the matter even further was news that broke the same week about the NHL's proposal for a new CBA. The league proposed a possible reduction of the salary cap from $70 million to $46 million for 2012–13. While no one was sure the cap would drop that low, teams like Vancouver, who stayed close to the ceiling, had to leave wiggle room in case. The Canucks reluctantly passed on Weber, a franchise defenceman who might have instantly given them status as a Stanley Cup favourite in 2013.

In the end, Philadelphia dropped the bomb on Nashville with a fourteen-year, $110 million restricted free-agent offer sheet for Weber. To make it even harder for the Preds, the Flyers' proposal called for up-front payments totalling $24 million in just the first year of Weber wearing orange and black. It was a poison chalice, but a reluctant Poile matched the offer, leaving many to wonder how a marginal franchise such as Nashville could pay such a price and still remain competitive. But as Gillis observed, there is such a shortage of talent that teams will do almost anything to hang onto their stars.

While it appeared that the demands of the Vancouver market were scaring off some, the Canucks did manage to attract one of the other sought-after free-agent defencemen, Jason Garrison of the Florida Panthers. Garrison, a B.C. product, apparently had no qualms about the Vancouver media heat.

197

At $4.25 million a year for four years, he took less than market value to play for his hometown team. Garrison had the heavy shot on the power play—as witnessed by his sixteen goals in 2011–12—that the Canucks had missed the previous season. The question about him was whether the breakout season was a mirage or a sign of growing confidence in the NHL. The media were quick to remind Gillis that the result had been less than impressive when he last acquired a Panthers UFA defenceman, Keith Ballard. Coach Alain Vigneault soon appeared to lose confidence in Ballard, a heavy hitter with a proclivity for getting out of position. At $4.2 million a year, Ballard was an expensive sixth defenceman. Would Garrison avoid the same fate? Could Ballard regain his mojo? The success of the Gillis regime could rest on the answers to these questions.

Just as the Suter and Weber dramas were resolved, the Canucks were suddenly offered one more tantalizing summertime prospect. Phoenix captain Shane Doan announced he would consider Vancouver (among five other teams) as a possible next stop. A rugged leader on and off the ice, the thirty-five-year-old had allowed himself to become an unrestricted free agent to protect himself against the possibility of the financially troubled Coyotes moving or even folding. Staying in Phoenix, where he had been since the Winnipeg Jets moved there in 1996, was Doan's preferred option. The never-ending saga of who was willing to underwrite the Coyotes' tens of millions in annual losses had been going on since 2009, when the previous owner, trucking magnate Jerry Moyes, threw the keys on the table and declared bankruptcy. A $270 million bid by Research in Motion founder Jim Balsillie to buy the team out of bankruptcy with an eye towards transferring it to southern Ontario was blocked by the league in an acrimonious negotiation that featured court challenges and intense media coverage.

Subsequent white knights, such as Chicago White Sox owner Jerry Reinsdorf and Chicago-based businessman Matthew

Hulsizer, promoted by the NHL, could never close the deal, requiring the NHL itself to begin underwriting the sea of red ink. Despite the turmoil and the fact that the Coyotes had lost money since their arrival in Arizona, NHL deputy commissioner Bill Daly still proclaimed the franchise "not a failure" in September of 2012.

Through it all, Doan's Coyotes remained a feisty team under coach Dave Tippett (who had succeeded Wayne Gretzky), squeezing into the playoffs and even reaching the Western Conference final against Los Angeles in 2012. In the euphoria of that win, former San Jose president Greg Jamison was announced by commissioner Gary Bettman as the next owner of the Coyotes. In fact, Jamison had simply been given the option to negotiate a deal with the Glendale city council, which had built and owned the Jobing.com Arena, the Coyotes' home rink. Despite positive noises from Bettman that the deal was imminent, the entire summer passed without a successful conclusion to negotiations. Extensions were granted and unnamed investors cited, delaying Doan's decision. With his Phoenix window seemingly narrowing, Doan exercised his No. 2 option, a tour of prospective new teams. They included the usual suspects—the New York Rangers and Philadelphia Flyers, who were said to be offering four years and $24 million. While Doan did not visit Buffalo, it was reported that the Sabres were prepared to offer the Coyotes captain four years at $30 million. Then there were the Canucks. After seemingly avoiding Vancouver, Doan eventually sat down on July 31 for dinner at the Italian Kitchen with Gillis, Gilman, and owner Francesco Aquilini to hear them pitch the team and the market. Gilman knew and respected Doan from their days together in Winnipeg and Phoenix, and he took the lead. "I articulated our position, explained why we thought Shane would be a good fit for us, and why we'd be a good fit for him," Gilman told Matt Sekeres on The Team 1040. "It was an opportunity for Francesco and Mike to open their hearts and souls and convey what we're about—what's the soul of our organization. In terms of the structure of the deal and the financial component—you'd be surprised—but that actually takes care of itself."

The most difficult issue raised by Vancouver's interest in signing Doan was that it would force them to diverge from the team's financial blueprint. The master plan took a dim view of spending big bucks to sign older players who could fall off the physical cliff at any moment. The expiring CBA also had a clause that mandates all contracts signed by players thirty-five or older be guaranteed whether the player retired or not. With his rough style, Doan was a candidate for diminishing returns as he headed for forty. For a team whose window of opportunity was closing, however, Doan's toughness and leadership were tempting commodities. Gilman told Team 1040, "We have a covenant with our players. We're going to pay them the absolute most that we can, provided that we are going to spend to the cap every year. But there is a point in the continuum whereby, for every dollar we pay them over a certain amount, [it] inhibits our ability to surround them with players that will allow us to build a Stanley Cup–contending team."

Even if Gillis and Gilman could get Doan to sign for less than the Sedins or Kesler, they would almost definitely need to jettison salary to accommodate him once Kesler returned from his off-season surgery. And there was no escaping the financial impact of Doan calling it quits before the contract expired. Because Doan stood to lose bargaining power under a new CBA, his agent made it clear that, loyalty or not, Doan would have to make a call on his next stop before September 15, the expiry date of the CBA. In the weeks leading up to the decision, there were frequent stories hinting that Jamison's deal might close any day. To show where his heart lay, Doan kept skating with his Coyotes teammates during the summer.

But as the clock ticked down on the final hours in which to file a new contract before the NHL lockout, the prospects of Jamison's purchase of the Coyotes remained as murky as ever. It emerged that, as was the case with Schultz and others, the Canucks were finalists for Doan. Canuck fans tried not to get their hopes up as Gilman told Vancouver media, "It's very simple: Shane Doan—and I'm not saying anything that hasn't come out of Shane's mouth—his No. 1 priority is to stay in Phoenix and play for the Coyotes."

In the end, Gilman's instinct proved correct. Despite not getting the confirmation he wanted from Jamison, Doan signed a four-year deal with a salary-cap hit of $5.3 million a year to stay with the Coyotes. The contract also included a no-move clause. Once again, through no fault of their own, a valuable asset had slipped through the Canucks' fingers. The positive spin is that almost all the desirable players had Vancouver on their short lists, something the mighty teams of the Eastern Conference could not claim.

While the Doan pursuit fizzled, the Canucks signed one of their own pending UFAs. Forward Alex Burrows had epitomized the Gillis Doctrine. An undrafted player who had worked his way up from the low minors, Burrows had signed a four-year contract in 2009 worth $2 million a year. For a player coming off his first big year, Burrows nonetheless took a hometown haircut to remain as the winger on the Sedin line. As his crucial goals in the 2011 playoffs demonstrated, his earlier deal had been great for both player and team. And now, even as teams such as Edmonton, Carolina, and Winnipeg handed out $6 million salaries to players with virtually no UFA leverage, the Canucks bought out four years of Burrows's unrestricted free agency for an average of $4.5 million a year. While players such as Taylor Hall, Jordan Eberle, and Jeff Skinner promised great things, Burrows, in his prime, had already been delivering them. Whether he'd continue to produce at an elite level was a gamble the Canucks were taking.

Reckless spending elsewhere did not help the Canucks with another impending UFA: Alex Edler, considered their No. 1

defenceman. Coming off a pedestrian season in 2011–12, Edler was in line to sign in the vicinity of the $4.5 million earned by fellow blueliners Kevin Bieksa, Jason Garrison, and Keith Ballard. Then Calgary blew the blueline template to bits, signing UFA Dennis Wideman, a No. 5 or 6 defenceman, for a cap hit of $5.25 million. This despite the fact the Flames were only paying their best defenceman, Mark Giordano, an average of $4 million a year. Wideman's tide raised all boats in the free-agent defenceman category. Despite efforts to come to an agreement before the CBA expired, Edler remained in line for free agency in the summer of 2013.

With the accumulated dramas of Doan, Weber, Schultz, and Edler almost all resolved by Labour Day 2013, it was time to see how the Canucks would rebound from the shock loss to the Kings. There was just one problem: Gary Bettman had other ideas.

Dream Deferred

"Where would we find another Rhodes scholar, graduate lawyer, decorated war hero, and former prosecutor at the Nuremberg trials, who will do what he's told?"

STAFFORD SMYTHE ON FORMER NHL PRESIDENT
CLARENCE CAMPBELL

INSTEAD OF WATCHING his team's 2012 training camp from a perch in the stands of Rogers Arena, Mike Gillis sat amongst the NHL Board of Governors at the Crowne Plaza Hotel in New York City on September 13, 2012. Arrayed at the rectangular desks were the owners, presidents, and other governors poised to vote on the drama known as NHL Lockout, Part III. For the third time since 1994, the owners had decided to lock out a number of Gillis's former clients and current players. On the desk before Gillis sat a red light and a microphone, should he choose to opine on the topic *du jour* for the men who run and own the NHL. Resistance, as they say, is futile in the face of commissioner Gary Bettman, who sat at the table like a well-heeled pasha.

Gillis's presence in this company is comparable to Cesar Chavez suddenly sitting on the board of the United Fruit

Company as they voted to lock out their field workers. Despite other former agents on the owners' side, the strategy would be run by Bettman according to a hardline script drawn up by his former law firm, New York–based Proskauer Rose, well known for its work on behalf of sports leagues. This time, there was no salary cap, the bone of contention in 2004–05. Instead, owners, many of them still losing money on Bettman's watch, would be seeking to roll back the contracts they had willingly granted the players in the flush of their 2005 triumph at the bargaining table.

Gillis could imagine what labour-for-life men like Donald Fehr, the new executive director of the NHL Players' Association, must have thought of his predicament, stuck amidst the union-busting zeal of owners such as Boston's Jeremy Jacobs and Calgary's Murray Edwards. But if he was worried about the slings and arrows cast against him for his transition to the dark side, Gillis appeared largely unconcerned. As the owners voted one after the other to follow Bettman's call to the bargaining barricades, Gillis's ultimate loyalty was now to Francesco Aquilini and his family, the ones who owned the Canucks, had hired him, and generously supplied him with the money needed to succeed. Everything else was secondary.

Profitable, responsible, competitive, the Canucks were poised for another good year of business under Gillis and chief operating officer Victor de Bonis. In the Gillis years, the Canucks would vault to the second-most profitable team in the NHL while their estimated value shot up into the top five. If everyone operated like the Canucks and a few other clubs, this attempt to cow the help would be unnecessary. "They're a very good club," said Brian Cooper, CEO and president of S&E Marketing Group, at the time. "Players want to play there. The way they use their players in the marketplace is perfect. They're also a very stable brand, and you need that stability when marketing to your community. I'd say they and Maple Leaf Sports & Entertainment are the best in Canada."

The Canucks would still pull together with the others, despite the fact that a lockout would be a monumentally awful idea for them. Nor would they complain; there was Bettman's fabled million-dollar fine to anyone publicly dissenting from the script to focus the mind. The Crowne Plaza meeting was stage-managed in the finest politburo tradition to keep the owners primed for another battle with their labour/product and to get everyone out of the meeting hall for a nice meal in Manhattan or a flight home that night.

Gillis was, understandably, not offering public comment on how it felt as the governors unanimously raised their hands to give Bettman another blank cheque to bring them a big cheque. By this point, most league people had forgotten Gillis's past as an agent and accepted him more as an alternate governor for the Vancouver Canucks, a franchise that was the envy of many in the sport. And with a veteran team whose competitive window was currently open, another season lost to labour strife represented a missed opportunity for his club. Would the club be ready to play if or when the lockout ended? Crucially, would a new CBA threaten the salary grid established by the Canucks management?

To keep them sharp, young players Chris Tanev, Zack Kassian, and Jordan Schroeder were assigned to the Chicago Wolves, Vancouver's AHL affiliate, to continue their development. Dale Weise destroyed the Dutch hockey league, averaging almost two points a game. One of the more visible Canucks in CBA negotiations, Cory Schneider, would eventually head off to play in Switzerland. Most of the Canucks' locked-out veterans remained in Vancouver to work out amongst themselves. Defenceman Kevin Bieksa organized an October charity game called Bieksa's Buddies that featured a few of the Canucks and their families against the UBC Thunderbirds at Thunderbird Arena. It raised $200,000 for charity. Due to league rules, the Canucks would be able to treat (and

205

pay) players injured in the spring, such as Ryan Kesler, Jason Garrison, and the soon-to-be UFA Alex Edler. (Coincidence or not, Edler would sign a new contract extension as soon as the lockout ended.)

If the history since the NHLPA decided to bargain as a proper union in 1991 was any guide, player–management relations were going to get worse before they got better. The script authored by Bettman and his handlers was too far advanced to pull back now. Fans could be excused for being confused, in light of Bettman's persistent boast—till now—that his business had a billion dollars in new revenues since 2005. (As the old joke goes, "Telling *you?* He's been telling everyone.") Many could remember Bettman spiking the ball upon curb-stomping the players in 2005. "I know the league's future is bright, and this [CBA] will be to the benefit of the game." In the face of such buoyant numbers, reviving calls for a reworking of the league's business plan to head off an alleged financial Armageddon seemed counterintuitive.

Some of the new revenue had come via the 35 per cent escalation in the value of the Canadian dollar since 2005. More still had come via increased ticket prices, improved merchandising, and the skyrocketing TV and digital rights fees being reaped by pro sports everywhere. The public had been led to believe that the salary-cap regime designed by the league after going a full year without play had solved the NHL's long-term problems on ticket prices and franchise stability.

Apparently not. But no one at the Crowne Plaza mentioned that at the meeting. No one does brazen like Gary Bettman backed into a corner of his own construction. Wielding a blizzard of arcane statistics; ad hominem jabs at his adversary, Donald Fehr; and condescending remarks to the press corps, Bettman proved to be a master of the duck and cover in a PR campaign that would be, in part, orchestrated by Frank Luntz—who, coincidentally, was running Mitt Romney's doomed 2012

Republican presidential campaign. Having whipped the vote at the board of governors, Bettman dealt with the media in his usual manner when they raised impertinent points. Asked by reporters after the meeting to explain his rationale for shutting down a successful business, Bettman pointed out that a lot had changed since he had given himself and his CBA an unqualified pat on the back in 2005. Yes, the league had willingly signed off on that deal, but the players' 57 per cent share of hockey-related revenues had proved too great a piece of the frozen pie. Jet fuel cost more. So did insurance, and ... other stuff. To help its have-nots, the NHL needed to rework the equation, and it "was not going to apologize for it." What Bettman didn't say was that fellow sports leagues had made better deals in the interim, and now his owners wanted the same.

If Bettman felt any pangs of shame over this public about-face from 2005, he had seven and a half million reasons to tough it out—the dollars he was paid by the NHL to be their public face. (Owners have always appreciated a docile front man. Stafford Smythe once said of NHL president Clarence Campbell, "Where would we find another Rhodes scholar, graduate lawyer, decorated war hero, and former prosecutor at the Nuremberg trials, who will do what he's told?")

Beneath the orchestrated agenda in New York, there was some discomfort at the prospect of facing Fehr, whose legendary battles as leader of the Major League Baseball Players' Association included a cancelled World Series in 1994. The phlegmatic Fehr had then presided over labour tranquility till his retirement in 2009. Yet he remained a very different adversary from the combustible Bob Goodenow. Since taking over the helm of the NHL Players' Association in 2010, Fehr had been playing hide-and-seek with Bettman, declining to be lured into negotiations. However they felt about Fehr's reputation, most owners believed his clientele would buckle under stress as they had done in 2005. And they had Gary Bettman and the

207

sports union–busting lawyers at Proskauer Rose, fresh from successful NBA and NFL lockouts, on their side.

None of this came as a surprise to the president and general manager of the Vancouver Canucks. As a quasi-hawk on the players' side in 2004, Gillis had accepted the strategy of executive director Bob Goodenow, a disciple of Fehr and his baseball predecessor, Marvin Miller. Goodenow's position was that players might need to stay out for eighteen months or even two years to show Bettman and the owners who paid him that they were united against a salary cap.

While he was still an agent, in 2004, Gillis appeared on TSN's *Off the Record,* where he had a sharp exchange with deputy commissioner Bill Daly about the inflationary impact of the $45 million contract he'd won two years earlier for Bobby Holik. Gillis's repeated refrain then was that, if the NHL's general managers had driven the bus into the ditch, why were none of them being fired?

Gillis had bitten his lip when fellow agents and NHLPA president Trevor Linden went behind Goodenow's back to arrange a surrender to the league on salary caps in February of 2005, well aware that, in their haste for a settlement, they were simply inviting the owners to do it all again in the next round of collective bargaining. Gillis kept his distance and lit out for the owners' side, which, while not perfect, at least had a sense of order under Bettman.

The players were far from blameless as the lockout of 2012 arrived. Having disposed of Goodenow in 2005, they had a chance to build a new approach to their relationship with the league via a new leader. But instead of establishing a path that would prevent future lockouts, the NHLPA instead wasted the seven years with an internecine war for control. Ted Saskin, who had succeeded Goodenow, drew criticism from players such as Chris Chelios and Eric Lindros for his rich contract and the fact that he had been selected by Trevor Linden with no hiring process. Saskin finally did himself in when it was found he'd been reading players' emails without permission.

Next up in the executive director's chair was Paul Kelly, the former U.S. attorney who had prosecuted Alan Eagleson in Boston. Kelly, supported at first by Lindros, promised a less confrontational approach to the league. But soon it was felt that he had grown too comfortable with the NHL, attending meetings of the Board of Governors alone. Others began citing his lack of experience negotiating labour deals, as if something had changed from the time he was hired.

Thwarted in his efforts to control Kelly, Lindros turned on him, calling in former Canadian Auto Workers president Buzz Hargrove to engineer Kelly's dismissal. In August of 2010, a hastily convened meeting in Chicago dismissed Kelly and sent his supporters, such as former goalie Glenn Healy and Mark Recchi, out of the union. With less than two years till the CBA expired, players realized they needed to act quickly to get an experienced leader who could match wits with Bettman.

Enter Don Fehr, who admitted he knew little about hockey or hockey players. He quickly embarked on a whirlwind campaign to replicate his MLBPA formula with the fractured membership of the NHLPA. Those who thought that restoring the union's bargaining power would be little problem should have considered the impact of previous changes wrought by the NHL owners' tinkering with the payment model. By the time play resumed after the 2005 lockout, 215 players who had worn an NHL jersey in 2003–04 were out of the league, because of either the financial squeeze or the rules changes that put a premium speed and skill. The fears of the members were real, and the prospect of another schism sent shivers through dressing rooms.

That won no sympathy from the owners, who complained that Fehr was dragging his heels, trying to promote an eleventh-hour negotiating strategy. Even as Gillis pursued Shane Doan,

Jason Garrison, and Shea Weber, the league issued a prelimi-
nary bargaining offer on July 13, 2012, to finally bring Fehr
to the table. It was a scorched-earth demand that the players' share of hockey-related revenue shrink from 57 per cent
to 46 per cent. Contracts would be capped at five years and
players would have to wait ten years for free agency. They
wanted a five-year term for the CBA. Salary arbitration would
be cancelled and entry-level deals stretched to five years from
three. And, of concern to the Canucks, they wanted an end to
"back-diving" provisions that allowed for heavily front-loaded
contracts with very little paid in the final years, when players
were in their late thirties or even in their forties, thus reducing
the salary-cap hit.

There were other demands, but the message was clear. It
was a "Declaration of War," said the *New York Post*. The league
wanted to test the resolve of the NHLPA early, letting players
know they'd lose millions if they chose to fight. "It will cost
them some now or more later," said one management figure.

The gambit had the opposite effect, however. The aggressive
offer politicized players. Instead of scattering the moderates
and players who had lost millions in 2004 or even 1994, it
instead sent them into the arms of Fehr's classic trade-union
stance. The move guaranteed more cancelled games and lost
billions as players adopted Fehr's hardline messages, rooted
in his MLB experience. Famously, Fehr had prevented baseball
from adopting a salary cap.

The NHL had a cap, but the miracle 2005 CBA cure proved
neither a cure nor a miracle in the years after 2005. Ticket
prices, especially in hockey-mad Canada, zoomed ever upward
as the supply/demand equation destroyed Bettman's assurances about savings for fans. The same structural flaws in the
league's franchise model re-emerged, pitting large markets
against small ones and Canadian markets against those in
the U.S.

Scarcity of superstars and granting even limited free agency to younger players had resulted in twentysomethings such as Taylor Hall, Jeff Skinner, and Jordan Eberle receiving lucrative extended contracts upon completing their entry-level deals and being paid the same as recognized superstars. Contracts of ten, twelve, or even fifteen years—effectively, lifetime deals—were used to circumvent how much players counted against the cap.

Brian Burke, then the Toronto GM, railed against his colleagues' disregard for the spirit of the CBA. He was ignored by other GMs who kept using front-loaded, long-term contracts to lower their franchise players' salary cap hits. Barely halfway into the seven-year term of the CBA, it became clear that Bettman's salary-capped ship was springing leaks, and the commissioner was determined to do something drastic so that the NHL could continue in its current rickety thirty-team iteration.

Two days after the fateful board of governors meeting on September 15, 2012, Commissioner Bettman announced the commencement of the lockout. "We are nowhere close," he said after turning down three proposals from the NHLPA, adding that he felt "terrible" about having to shut down the NHL yet again. "I view the proposal made by the Players Association in many ways [as] a step backward," he said. "I don't know what the next step is. I'm obviously very discouraged."

The NHL's hair-shirt argument had been undercut by the teams in the final days before the meeting at the Crowne Plaza in New York. With just days left for players to take advantage of what would certainly be a more lenient system after the new CBA, clubs had unburdened themselves of hundreds of millions in commitments to players who were entering the final years of entry-level contracts. Teams rationalized that deals for their young players were simply making nice with the guys who represented the future of their franchises. But as one Twitter wag observed, Lou Lamoriello was mean to his players in negotiations and had three Stanley Cups to show for it; the Edmonton

Oilers and Columbus Blue Jackets were nice to their key players and could barely make the playoffs the past twenty years.

So there were entry-level money grabs and overpayments for fringe players. The classic case of "do as I say, not as I do" was thirty-five-year-old Shane Doan of Phoenix, among the veterans who beat the rush by re-signing with the Coyotes. As the NHL owned his team, the commissioner himself signed off on paying Doan $5.3 million a year till he was forty. This would be the same commissioner who had routinely flayed general managers for their profligacy in the past.

As opposed to 2004–05, when the sides held no talks till December, there was almost continuous contact throughout the 113-day process. Rarely did more than a week or two go by before contact would resume. Fehr told his membership that the league was following the blueprint of the NBA lockout the prior year, when the sides went into December before settling on a new CBA. It would take a similar amount of time—probably through late December to early January, Fehr warned players—before NHL players would see the owners' best offer.

The problem, from the NHL's point of view, was trying to get the NHLPA to negotiate off the league's offers. Fehr continued to offer the NHLPA's own proposals, frustrating Bettman and his tight council of owners, which included Jeremy Jacobs of Boston and Murray Edwards of Calgary. These counteroffers impertinently (from the NHL's perspective) made suggestions about restructuring the macroeconomics of the NHL's business plan in small or weak markets, galling the league's heavy thinkers—who were, after all, responsible for the plan. The feinting and jabbing continued into November, with the league cancelling games in chunks. The NHL tried to leverage the prospect of cancelling the Winter Classic, planned for New Year's Day at the 115,000-seat University of Michigan Stadium. The game was expected to produce very healthy revenue and, even more, a media spotlight as Detroit and Toronto played before

NBC's cameras. That, too, failed to produce a settlement after Bettman's announcement that the Winter Classic had been scrubbed. With the sides about $380 million apart on the issues, the 2013 All-Star Game followed soon on the cancellation list.

Beneath it all lay the NHL's conviction that it could win players away from Fehr and what it alleged were his dirty or unprofessional negotiating ploys of delay, missed meetings, and failure to negotiate off the NHL's position. (As if, having provoked the fight, the league could complain about its opponent's tactics.) To assuage the NHL's Fehr factor, a meeting was arranged in early December of 2012 between six "moderate" owners, led by Pittsburgh's Ron Burkle, and eighteen players, headed by Penguins star Sidney Crosby. The purported idea was to get the "pros" out of the room and let the sides speak mano-a-mano. Expectations were raised when NHL deputy commissioner Bill Daly and NHLPA special counsel Steve Fehr (Donald's brother) made a joint media statement after the first day of these talks. Hopes for a settlement brightened when Fehr met the media after some promising talks to say that a deal was in sight. The monetary gap was "certainly not unbridgeable," he said.

No sooner had Fehr spoken than an agitated Bettman returned serve at his own press briefing. Calling Fehr's characterization of events "almost incomprehensible," Bettman said owners were "beside themselves" that Fehr was still negotiating at this late hour. The players had been given a strict all-in offer, yet Fehr was trying to counter it. Deputy commissioner Daly ratcheted up the rhetoric, saying the PA's offer was "insulting" and that a five-year limit on player contracts was "a hill we will die on." From seeming elation for hockey fans, players, and management figures, the air went out of the balloon. "It looks like this is not going to be resolved in the near future," Fehr said.

It took exactly a month of recrimination, compromise, and the involvement of federal mediator Scot Beckenbaugh to get the deal to salvage a forty-eight-game season. In one sense, players had won a victory from the NHL's first offer in July. It was now a ten-year CBA with a seven-year limit on individual contracts (eight for a player who re-signs with his home club). The players' share of hockey-related revenue fell from 57 per cent to 50 per cent effective in 2013, but every dollar of existing contracts would be paid. In addition, clubs could now buy out the contracts of two additional players before the 2013–14 or 2014–15 seasons. Re-entry waivers were eliminated.

The escrow payments so loathed by players largely disappeared, as the NHLPA was no longer required to guarantee payment out of union funds. If overages occurred, the money would come out of the players' share the following season. By the time the CBA expired in 2022, the NHL's minimum salary would be $750,000. Random drug testing would take place during training camp, regular season, playoffs, and in the off-season.

On the other hand, prosperous NHL owners were able to pocket millions more dollars, and smaller markets could qualify for $200 million in revenue sharing to lessen (but not eliminate) their losses. There was debate about how much that might help the league. "You're taking seven percentage points of hockey-related revenue [and adding them to the owners' side] and that will help the low-revenue franchises," sports economist Andrew Zimbalist told *The Globe and Mail*. "The increase in revenue sharing, from $150 million to $200 million, will help, too… But instead of losing $15 million to $20 million, some teams will lose $10 million to $15 million. The situation is not resolved."

No, it was not. For all its artificial levelling devices, the NHL still remains a *Downton Abbey* league. In the top floors live up to a dozen successful hockey operations (including the Canucks) that make money. Lots of it. In 2011–12, the Toronto Maple Leafs, who hadn't made the postseason since the 2004 lockout, had revenues estimated at $193 million by *Forbes* magazine. The New York Rangers garnered $169 million, said *Forbes*. The Canucks' estimated revenues in 2010–11 were $147 million. Montreal pulled in $163 million. The Calgary Flames, out of the postseason for a third consecutive year, were reported to have $105 million in revenues that same season. For these clubs, life was grand even if the teams' play stunk. The only irritant came when they couldn't just strip-mine their less fortunate partners of their best players. They resented being asked to pony up for owners who couldn't manage their teams or sell them to their public.

Then there were the owners lurking downstairs, almost all of them lured into the NHL since 1993 by Bettman's persuasive pitch on the virtues of grabbing a ride on the NHL's money machine. Unfortunately, with only one Stanley Cup to give out each year and fourteen teams deprived of playoff revenue every season, living the dream was proving to be something less than it sounded in Bettman's breathless prospectus to buyers. At the bottom end in 2001, according to *Forbes,* were the bankrupt Phoenix Coyotes, with $70 million in revenues; the New York Islanders at $63 million; and the St. Louis Blues at $78 million. The downstairs teams felt treated like second-class citizens, watching as their established partners made money by the handful—and, they felt, shared too little of it.

In a classic franchising operation such as KFC or McDonald's, underperforming franchisees would be closed down and new markets given the chance to open a store. But the NHL was a franchise operation with a catch: it couldn't or wouldn't practise tough love on the Phoenix Coyotes, Nashville Predators, or Florida Panthers. Instead of boarding up the windows and moving to hockey-friendly locations such as southern Ontario or Quebec City, the league performed financial and mental gymnastics to try to right the floundering franchisees. In part, the NHL believed that winning a Cup had made teams like the

215

Carolina Hurricanes or Tampa Bay Lightning viable for a time; if only the other poor devils could get a Cup, all would work out.

Under this strategy, the NHL wants to emulate the success of the NFL model, particularly when it comes to revenue sharing and maintaining parity. But the bulk of the NFL's revenues are league-generated, from its massive TV contracts—worth more than $5 billion a year starting in 2014—which allow the league's head office to control the sharing of wealth among teams. As a result, maximizing revenues in the strongest markets is less crucial to the NFL. It's one reason the NFL has prospered since 1995 with no team in Los Angeles, the second-largest U.S. media market.

The NHL's revenues, however, are predominantly generated at the team level by a handful of the upstairs teams—such as Aquilini's Canucks, who were prospering under Mike Gillis's Canucktivity. Still, the NHL mirrored the NFL redistributive system (salary cap cuts, universal draft, redistributing skill players), hoping to reap similar financial rewards and to assure that the Stanley Cup dream is evenly spread across the thirty teams. But the NHL needs its larger markets to drive revenues. Having small markets win a proportionate share of Cups actually depresses hockey-related revenues. What the NHL needs for financial success is for smaller markets to win two of every ten titles, not five or six. You can't get there using the NFL's model.

That was not the Canucks' biggest concern coming out of the lockout. It was hard to see how the CBA hammered out by Gary Bettman and Don Fehr would help the Vancouver Canucks. While they were able to keep their payroll intact at $70 million for 2012-13, Mike Gillis and Laurence Gilman, his capologist, had challenges ahead of them when the cap went down to $63.4 million in 2013-14. The team was being forced to pare its payroll by almost $7 million before the 2013-14 season.

As well, limits were imposed on the length of contracts such as Roberto Luongo's. Trading Luongo's ten-year contract, with its $5.3 million cap hit, would be next to impossible after a new provision against "back-diving" contracts. Simply put, should Luongo retire before age forty-two, the Canucks—or any team that acquired him—would not be forgiven the remaining dollars on his contract (as would have happened before the lockout). Under the mellifluously named Cap Advantage Recovery Penalty, if a player under a front-loaded contract retires early, his team is docked the amount of the salary cap benefit it derived by paying him a salary higher than the cap hit.

Wrote Stu Hackel in the *New York Times,* "It applies in the case of Luongo, who for the next several seasons will make at least $1.3 million per year more in real dollars than his average salary... The thorniest part of the recapture provision for Luongo is that if he is traded, the team that acquires him shares in the salary cap charges if he retires early." Teams that had signed similar deals—Philadelphia (Chris Pronger), New York (Brad Richards), Detroit (Henrik Zetterberg), and Chicago (Marion Hossa)—argued that, having signed off on these deals, the league could not now punish them retroactively. In the rush to get a deal, their pleas were ignored. While the Cap Advantage Recovery Penalty was simply a technical possibility in January of 2013, it would become a major crisis for the Canucks as they resumed play that month.

15

Louie Louie

"I'm human and sometimes it gets to you ... I'm going to
gather myself the rest of the day, make sure when I come to work
tomorrow, I'm 100 per cent dedicated to this team."

ROBERTO LUONGO

THE HUSH IN the Norm Jewison Media Room at Rogers Arena
was palpable on trade deadline day 2013. Looking haggard,
veteran Vancouver goalie Roberto Luongo stood before the
writers and broadcasters who had pestered him incessantly
about his status over the past year. Eyes red, shoulders hunched,
attitude resigned, the Canucks goalie held nothing back after
learning he would not be traded away in this lockout-shortened
NHL season. "My contract sucks," he said in a mocking tone.
"I'd scrap it if I could right now." That would be the twelve-year,
$64 million contract Luongo had signed with the Canucks in
2009. It was originally seen as a creative way to get Luongo
the money he deserved while reducing his salary cap hit from
$6.7 million to $5.3 million. Now, thanks to the accounting
of the new NHL collective bargaining agreement, Luongo's
lengthy contract was seemingly a prison that held him in Vancouver behind the new starter, Cory Schneider. ("At the time it

was done, it was very favourable for this organization and very favourable for Roberto," Vancouver GM Mike Gillis later said.) Clearly, the drama had been crushing for the otherwise free-spirited thirty-four-year-old who goes by the Twitter *nom de plume* Strombone1.

Minutes earlier, Luongo had been pulled from practice at Rogers Arena by a Canucks official in case a last-minute deal with the Toronto Maple Leafs could be struck. Immediately, Twitter went ballistic. "Roberto Luongo pulled off ice early at practice," tweeted the staff of *Hockey Central* on Sportsnet. After months of speculation and controversy over a trade for his former starting goalie, had Mike Gillis finally granted a hall pass to his erstwhile star? Or was Luongo punking the army of critics and second-guessers among the social media? Some, like *Hockey News* columnist Adam Proteau, smelled a rat: "This is what's known among expert Twitter pranksters as being Strom-boned." Despite urgent efforts to make a hockey deal with the Toronto Maple Leafs, who had been inquiring about Luongo for a year, the Canucks declined to budge on what they believed to be good value for their goalie. So Luongo remained in Vancouver to face the press, his feelings raw.

"It's been an emotional ride the last year," Luongo told the overflowing media horde. "I'm human and sometimes it gets to you ... I'm going to gather myself the rest of the day, make sure when I come to work tomorrow, I'm 100 per cent dedicated to this team."

When asked if his insistence on returning to Florida had scuppered trades the previous summer, Luongo suggested he had never been asked to drop his no-trade clause to facilitate any trades in the past year, and if he had been asked, he'd have agreed. "I was never approached about a trade and said no," Luongo said. "Nothing ever materialized to the point where I had to make a decision whether or not I was going to waive [his no-trade clause]."

That was soon tempered by Gillis, who suggested Luongo was a tad upset and that his goalie had been presented with potential trades. "I think he was very emotional, and I think these days are emotional for everybody," Gillis told the press corps. "When you have a day like this, when your whole life could be turned upside down and you speak to you guys right after, I think there's an opportunity for things to be said that, in the clear light of day, might not be reflective of how he really feels."

As for Luongo's onerous deal, which was flayed the entire day on TV by panelists and pundits, "I've never been told there was a stumbling block [with his contract]," Gillis said in the measured tones that either reassured or infuriated Vancouver's emotionally fragile hockey culture. "The discussions we've had didn't surround a stumbling block, they surrounded players, draft picks, places where he might go. Those were bigger hurdles than discussions about his contract." What Gillis didn't say was the difficulty of Luongo's no-trade clause, a hangup that allowed the goalie to dictate his next destination. Which, in this case, was only one destination for much of the time: Florida.

The media, at least, were unimpressed by the draft day dramatics. LUONGO, CANUCKS MIRED IN LOSE-LOSE SITUATION, opined the *Vancouver Sun*. GILLIS'S PRICE TOO HIGH; WILL THE CANUCKS END UP PAYING FOR IT? wondered the *Province*. Suddenly, critics who'd seen the deal as creative when it was signed now called it a mistake. Several local columnists suggested that Gillis had erred in not trading Schneider after re-signing Luongo in 2009. Tying up so much cap space in goal was a waste of resources, they said, and Schneider might have returned even more in a trade. The episode had some asking whether Gillis's vaunted Canucktivity had run out of gas.

Where the lockout had dominated the first half of the Canucks' 2012–13 season, the disposition of Luongo's contract took hold of the remainder of Vancouver's regular-season business. Worse, it threatened to scuttle the progress Gillis had made since becoming the Canucks general manager in 2008. Rarely did a day go by without some reference to the who, what, where, when, and why of Luongo being traded. With the injury-racked Canucks struggling for first place in the Northwest Division against a charging Minnesota Wild, a Luongo trade had been touted as the engine to restock the lineup—his $5.3 million cap hit could have been used on other players. There were those who felt the alleged "tension" between Luongo and Schneider (spoofed by TSN in a droll video) was going to wreck the room. The clamour for a deal, any deal, involving Luongo had reached a fever pitch in Vancouver, a city not disposed to calm when panic was called for.

MIKE GILLIS SIGHED wearily as he looked down from his perch in the stands of Rogers Arena. It was practice time before the start of the 2013 playoffs and Gillis had been asked to describe the forty-eight-game season produced by the labour lockout. "It's been challenging," he conceded as the Canucks practised below him in preparation for their first-round series with San Jose. "Having no training camp, no real practice days during the season. We couldn't try things out or experiment. And then the injuries . . ." His voice trailed off. The noise from the players below reverberated in the emptiness of the rink. For the research analyst in Gillis, this was dismaying.

For all the challenges Gillis enumerated, the Canucks still managed to clinch a fifth straight Northwest Division title with a week to spare at season's end. Despite the local angst over the Canucks' season just past, they had surpassed many traditional powers in the league, such as Philadelphia, Detroit, and the New York Rangers, who either missed the postseason or barely qualified. Not that the problems of other teams mattered much in anxious Vancouver, where every setback on Gillis's watch registered on the Richter scale.

The forty-eight-game sprint after the CBA was settled was like an improv exercise. The Canucks never got the chance to play with their roster intact at any point between mid-January and late April. Centre Manny Malhotra, who had returned from a devastating eye injury in 2012, was forced to retire just nine games into the season, when the Canucks determined that the faceoff specialist was in danger on the ice because of his eye issues. (He later came back to the NHL, with Carolina.) From the moment Malhotra left the ice, faceoffs became a liability for the Canucks. It got worse. Such was the decimation on the blue line that ten different defencemen played for the Canucks during the season, including marginal NHLers Derek Joslin and Cam Barker. As a result, the back end was a fire drill many nights, with the team unable to escape its own defensive zone.

One position wasn't a liability in the regular season: starting goalie Cory Schneider missed games, too, but the combination of the Boston product and his backup, Luongo, was the prime reason that Gillis's Northwest Division champions were awaiting the Sharks in the playoffs. When injuries stripped the lineup of key players, Vancouver resorted to a defence-first posture. Out went the blitzing, attack-first Canucks; in came a team that, relying on its two outstanding goalies, could be outshot and out-chanced (often by a considerable margin), yet still win games. It was the antithesis of the hockey Gillis envisioned for his club in 2008, but necessity makes for strange bedfellows— sort of like the $9.3 million tandem of twenty-five-year-old Schneider and the thirty-three-year-old Luongo still sharing the net for the Canucks months after a decision had been made to send Luongo elsewhere.

222 **AS GILLIS ENTERED** his fifth year with the Canucks, Roberto Luongo, not Canucktivity, had become the defining issue surrounding his stewardship of the franchise. From Gillis's first day as GM, the Montreal product had been advertised as a core

piece of the Canucks. "That's why we made him our captain," Gillis replied in 2009 to questions about Luongo's importance to the team. Even as fans faulted him for their playoff disappointments and the media skewered him for his intemperate comments, the Canucks stood by their erstwhile No. 1 goalie. When Schneider made it patently clear in 2011 that he was ready to be a starting goalie in the league, Gillis still proclaimed that Luongo was the team's starter. Loyalty to key players had been a major plank in Gillis's platform since 2008, and he was damned if he would jettison Luongo to soothe the media or the nervous nellies among his team's fan base.

With the Canucks' core group aging (the Sedins turned thirty-two that winter) or injury-prone (Kesler had had yet more off-season surgery, while David Booth was hurt on the first day of training camp), using Luongo to extract a young player had become the accepted way to turn a veteran asset into younger ones. That narrative had worked until the final moments of green-garbage-bag day in the Canucks dressing room following the 2012 playoff loss. With reporters swirling around his locker in the Canucks room, Luongo denied that he would invoke his no-trade clause should Gillis find a trading partner. "Yeah, of course, if they ask me to," Luongo replied when asked about waiving his right to refuse a trade. "I don't want to be one of those guys who is going to stand in the way of anything. I always want to put the team ahead of me. I don't want to be one of those selfish guys. Obviously, they have a guy here who is going to be a superstar in this league for the next ten, twelve, fifteen years, so I'm okay with it. It is a business, and that's the way it goes. I've loved being here the last six years. If I'm here in the future, then great. If I'm not, that's good also."

Luongo's willingness to cede the starting job to Schnei- 223
der sent Vancouver media and fans into a speculative frenzy. Deadlines were suggested by which Luongo would be dealt. Prospective teams were lined up as likely targets for Luongo's

affections. TSN's respected Bob McKenzie didn't think there would be "[as] much of [a] market for Luongo as originally thought."

Damien Cox of the *Toronto Star* led the scribes in criticizing Vancouver's position. After suggesting that Toronto sign Schneider to an RFA offer sheet, Cox wrote, "If there were a plethora of teams anxious to upgrade in goal, that would create a nice situation for Canucks GM Mike Gillis in his efforts to move veteran goaler Roberto Luongo and his ridiculous contract, which still has 10 years left to run. Except there aren't many teams looking to upgrade... this is a doable deal as long as Vancouver doesn't overestimate what it should get and the Leafs don't squeeze the Canucks overly because there's no market for Luongo."

But anyone thinking that Gillis was going to rush into any deal by the NHL draft clearly was not paying attention. Presented with a challenge during his four-year tenure, Gillis had always played for time. No season was bigger than others. No panic would be allowed. The Canucks GM remained convinced that the pressure was on the other guy, who could use a top-ten NHL goalie, not on him. Time would bring requisite value.

And so the reported drop-dead dates came and went heading into the summer of 2012. The first certain deadline was going to be the NHL draft in Pittsburgh. Nothing. The next certain drop-dead date passed on June 28 when Schneider signed a three-year, ten-million-dollar deal with Vancouver. The Canucks couldn't carry $9.3 million in goalie salaries, could they? Still there was no trade. The machinations around the July 1 free-agent frenzy were then supposed to germinate a deal that would let Gillis escape with his honour intact and a valuable return for his goalie. But still, nothing could shake Gillis's contention that offers had to improve before he would give up Luongo.

Finally, when Luongo—discovered playing in the 2012 World Series of Poker in Las Vegas during the summer—told Vancouver reporters that "it's time to move on" from the Canucks, it was deemed undeniable that Gillis would have to relent and send Louie to a new home. Where was Gillis's leverage anymore?

Yet none of these purported deadlines swayed Gillis. "We talk to teams every day," Gillis told the club's radio broadcast partner, The Team 1040. "There's lots of teams that are interested in an all-star goalie, even though some people refuse to believe that, which is stunning to me because great players are so difficult to get."

At the Canucks' Jake Milford charity golf event in September, Gillis told reporters the Canucks were an elite financial team in the league and would have "no fire sales" to please the media demanding a trade. What Gillis didn't say was that Luongo had expressed a desire to be dealt to either of the teams in his wife's home state of Florida, where he planned to settle after retirement. Having been told that the bankrupt Panthers might still find a way to handle his contract, Luongo privately told Gillis to go slow on other teams until Florida had a chance to put together a deal. Then came the back-diving provisions of the new CBA, which added more complexity to moving his contract.

The brief, mad post-lockout scramble in January of 2013, in which teams had just a week to assemble a roster, saw no thawing of the Luongo market. Gillis bristled at suggestions that he now had to make a hasty deal for Luongo. "If you start giving all-star players away you'll be at the bottom of this league in a hurry," he told The Team 1040. "As it sits today, we need to get something in return that is going to help our team, and we're not in the business of just helping other teams so... I'm comfortable with both these guys starting the season here, I'll be comfortable if we finish the season with them. If something happens and comes our way that allows us to improve, then we're going to do it. And it's all subject to Luongo wanting to go to that city. So it is a little bit more complicated than people like to think."

Finding himself still a Canuck, the Twitter presence known as Strombone1 reported for action with the Canucks on January 15, expecting to be the backup to Schneider. He amused himself by playing a cat-and-mouse game in the social media. On January 8, he tweeted, "Thinking about making an Internet video: 2 guys 1 crease." The next day, "If this keeps up I'm pretty sure I'm gonna have to go on meds..." At NFL playoff time, he teased himself. "[Colin] Kaepernick looking fantastic proving you could never go wrong in going with the youngster over the old vet..."

Luongo's supposedly genial acceptance of the No. 2 spot did something else: it changed the perception many had of Luongo as a diva or a head case. Suddenly, Luongo was a sympathetic figure with the Canuck fans and media members who had ripped him liberally in the 2011 playoffs. And, in the eyes of fans, Gillis was (unfairly) becoming the man holding him in bondage. Luongo's rep was not hurt when Schneider was bombed by Anaheim 7–3 on opening night, requiring the former starter to come into the game. As the team made an early winning run, Luongo was suddenly the No. 1A goalie, turning in vintage performances and winning four of six starts (including a shutout). Coach Alain Vigneault began a long-running joke, saying he was flipping a coin to determine whether Luongo or Schneider started the next game.

It was fun while it lasted. Then, in a key February home game against Detroit (who had ventilated him for eight goals in an earlier game), Luongo stumbled in a pivotal match, losing 5–2. Something seemed to change in the goalie rotation. With the trade deadline nearing and the Canucks' power play—and offence in general—nonexistent, the pressure on the goalies became immense. Worse, the Minnesota Wild was mounting a furious charge for the lead in the Northwest Division, something everyone in Vancouver (including the Canucks) seemed to feel was Vancouver's exclusive property. At that point,

226

Schneider reeled off six straight wins, all but one by a margin of a single goal. The jokes about the coin flip grew stale, as did Luongo sitting at the end if the bench with a baseball cap on his head. Something had to give by the trade deadline, proclaimed the talking heads.

Luongo was far from Gillis's only problem. His decimated team arrived at the April 3 trade deadline on the heels of two desultory efforts, being shut out by upstart Edmonton and out-classed by San Jose. Kesler was back on the injured list with a broken foot, having played just seven games. David Booth, who'd returned after missing the first fifteen games because of his training camp injury, joined Kesler on the sidelines—this time for the season—with a high ankle sprain. Further injuries to Dale Weise, Keith Ballard, Chris Higgins, Mason Raymond, and Zack Kassian meant that Vigneault was giving serious ice time to players such as Tom Sestito, Steve Pinizzotto, Cam Barker, Andrew Ebbett, Andrew Gordon, and rookie Jordan Schroeder. Coveted prospect Nick Jensen was even summoned for two games. The team that had overwhelmed opponents with its speed was now reduced to a plodding, dump-it-out squad counting on Schneider for miracles in the net. The Canucks won twelve of nineteen such games by a single goal. The power play was at the bottom of the table.

It might have been the lowest point for a Gillis team since the eight-game losing streak in early 2009. Hockey publications were rating the prospects in Vancouver's development system twenty-ninth out of thirty. Hometown scribes watching the scene were assessing the "window of opportunity" for the Canucks to win the Cup in terms of days and weeks.

The day before the trade deadline, Gillis took action on his stated top priority, picking up centre Derek Roy, a future unre- 227 stricted free agent, from Dallas for a second-round pick and Kevin Connauton. That would give Vancouver Henrik Sedin, Ryan Kesler (when healthy), Max Lapierre, and the veteran playmaking centre Roy down the middle, seemingly a strong equation heading into the playoffs. There was a sigh of relief that maybe now, with Roy and with Kesler returning, Vancouver could play up-tempo offence again. But Roy came with a deserved reputation as a player who could disappear for periods of time on-ice.

Addressing the gap at centre a day in advance also meant that the entire focus of the networks' TV coverage of trade deadline day now coalesced around Luongo. Making it more inviting for the Toronto-based networks, Maple Leafs GM Dave Nonis talked openly about getting a veteran goalie to help his young starter, James Reimer. Luongo fit that bill; Nonis had once traded for Luongo in Vancouver. You figure it out. But Nonis was still bearing the scars of his dismissal by Francesco Aquilini. To say there was tension between the organizations would be to understate things. Nonis pinned his hopes on getting Miikka Kiprusoff out of Calgary.

Once Nonis learned, in the days shortly before the deadline, that Kiprusoff was staying put, the reluctant sides were forced together for one final effort to get Luongo to Toronto. It took a meeting in Phoenix between subordinates (Toronto's former GM Cliff Fletcher and Vancouver assistant GM Laurence Gilman) to precipitate talks between the battling clubs as the deadline neared. In the pressure-packed final hours, it seemed the outline of a deal might be emerging, with Toronto taking on Luongo while Vancouver acquired two second-round picks and young goalie Ben Scrivens. Then Nonis floated the notion of the Canucks taking on a chunk of Luongo's salary. The Canucks' ownership was not interested in the notion, particularly since it was introduced at the last moment. Nonis, meanwhile, didn't have so great a need that he would swallow the Byzantine aspects of Luongo's deal. He'd wait till the summer, if then, to revisit a trade for a goalie (he ended up with Jonathan Bernier of Los Angeles). Deal over.

228

Management informed Luongo as he left the practice ice that he was staying put. Having spent a sleepless night before, his reaction was equal measures of exhaustion and disappointment. He'd finally accepted that he wasn't going to Florida, and yet that hadn't thawed the market. Which helped explain Luongo's memorable media availability. "If I'd taken a different approach as to the way I conducted myself, things might be different. I'm not disappointed in the way I handled myself, I didn't create negative energy around the team. I don't regret the way I handled this... I'm 100 per cent dedicated to this team the rest of the year. I love this team, and I love this city. The goal is the Stanley Cup, and I will give myself 100 per cent to that."

Making matters more difficult for Gillis was the inability to add anyone besides Roy after saying the Canucks were all in to win in 2013. The team had hoped to use draft picks obtained in any Luongo deal to do more business—specifically, picking up former Canuck Raffi Torres from Phoenix (he wound up in San Jose). They were also finalists for another rugged forward, Ryane Clowe, who opted to head to the east coast with the Rangers to be closer to his girlfriend there. But the Leafs' dithering till the end over getting Kiprusoff from Calgary had left no time to pursue other deals.

There was also the exorbitant cost of making trades under the current CBA. Typical was Minnesota's acquisition of winger Jason Pominville from Buffalo. The Sabres captain at the time of the trade, Pominville was a character player and a top-six forward, though he had not been included in TSN's ranking of the top fifty NHL players at the start of the season (nor would he be considered for the Canadian Olympic team). On deadline day, he fetched two excellent prospects, goalie Matt Hackett and forward Johan Larsson, as well as a first-round pick in 2013 and a second-rounder in 2014. (Minny also got a fourth-round pick in 2014.) The paltry seventeen trades (few with players, and not

229

draft picks, going both ways) demonstrated that the Wild were the only ones willing or able to pay such a price on deadline day.

"We were in every deal we could possibly get in," a weary Gillis told the media at Rogers Arena. "They often don't work out, so you just have to keep staying in them." Privately, Gillis conceded that the extreme pressure and usurious prices of trade deadline day make it a terrible way to do business. It certainly felt terrible, especially when the fickle fans began to turn against the management team that had brought them so close to a Stanley Cup. It became accepted to mock the Canucks as the NHL's drama queens.

THERE'S ANOTHER REASON Gillis felt put upon that spring. "People complain about our goal production, but it's hard to score if you're not getting any power plays," he told bystanders on the eve of the opening-round series with San Jose. After a positive start by NHL referees in the 2013 season, calling games strictly, the standard had fallen off remarkably of late—just as it had the year before. The numbers supported Gillis's contention that, in terms of offence, the NHL was returning to the "dead-puck" era between the first two lockouts. In 2005–06, the first season after the 2004–05 stoppage, NHL teams averaged 5.86 power plays a game as the league clamped down on obstruction fouls. The Canucks' power play prospered as a result. But by the 2012 playoffs, the average team got 3.3 power plays per game. While it was true that players had learned to work around the new rules, the drop was also attributable to referees "managing" games. If a team led a game, it took a capital crime by the opponents to draw a penalty. Likewise, teams that were trailing or already playing shorthanded could be assured that the referees would ignore all but the most outrageous penalties. (Oddly, Canucks forward Alex Burrows, who had criticized NHL refs, was still penalized at a prodigious rate. Despite never getting a fighting or misconduct penalty, Burrows was the most penalized player in the NHL. The Canucks, who had spent much time calming Burrows's on-ice persona, took note of the · pattern.)

There was evidence that the league wasn't overly concerned with scoring. The NFL has a certain minimum number of points per game that it wants scored. When the average drops below that, it changes the rules to keep scoring in the game. The same with the NBA when it instituted the twenty-four-second clock into the game. Baseball lowers its mound or moves in its fence. But hockey didn't seem overly interested in encouraging goal-scoring.

For Gillis, who had supported the fight to crack down on fouls at the GM meetings the previous summer, the regression was discouraging. The lax standard had allowed the bigger L.A. Kings to dominate Vancouver's skill players in 2012 while also negating the Canucks' potent power play. The Kings didn't so much hit teams as they steamrolled over them. Conference foes St. Louis and Minnesota had followed their example, getting bigger and tougher. For the NHL, where everyone seemed to decry the number of overtime games with their three-point formula (two points to the winner, one to the loser), no one linked the dearth of power plays to the inability of games to be resolved in regulation time. While the media bleated about the defensive posture of games and the challenges facing scorers, no one wanted to do anything to upset owners of unskilled teams.

For Gillis's team, a reluctance to call the rule book strictly meant that they would face a steady diet of what the Kings had delivered the previous spring. He had started bulking up his system with young players like young Zack Kassian, but that was not going to help a roster dominated by the Sedins, Mason Raymond, Derek Roy, Alex Burrows, and Jordan Schroeder if referees put the whistle away. 231

The Canucks certainly could have used some power-play scoring when they (briefly) faced the San Jose Sharks in Round 1 of the 2013 playoffs. In a series that most predicted would cost the losing coach his job, San Jose's Todd McLellan earned job security as the Sharks swept Vancouver in four straight. Despite starting the first two games at home, Vancouver never scored more than three goals in any one game, blew leads twice late in the third period, and was decimated by San Jose's power play in a series that saw the Sharks with a 24–10 edge in man-advantage situations.

For those following the Canucks' issues closely in the mini-season, Alain Vigneault's swan song contained a splash of low comedy, a bitter dose of irony, and enough heartache to match a George Jones country ballad. The low comedy was a mysterious injury to Cory Schneider in the days just before the playoffs. Having posted brilliant wins over Detroit and Chicago in the final week of the season, Schneider suddenly disappeared with a "body injury," in the felicitous phrase of Vigneault. It was widely believed the young American was being rested for the playoffs and that his mysterious condition would clear up like adolescent acne. But when Game 1 started in Vancouver on May 1, Canuck fans were presented with the forgotten man, Roberto Luongo, standing between the pipes. The collective gulp could be heard as far away as Haida Gwaii. For a second straight season, the Canucks entered Game 1 denied one of their core players (in 2012 it was Daniel Sedin). For those still thinking coherently, the reluctance to trade Luongo was now looking quasi-prescient. The impression was only reinforced by Luongo's stalwart play on home ice in both Games 1 and 2. While he surrendered three goals in Game 1, it was Vancouver's failure to score more than a single goal (an own goal by the Sharks, at that) that cost them the game.

Game 2 saw a positive explosion of offence from the Canucks as Ryan Kesler notched two goals and Vancouver took a 2–1 lead into the final minute of play. But after Jannik Hansen missed an open net, the Sharks mounted a furious rally to tie the game on a goal by Patrick Marleau (set up by the Sedins' failure to clear the zone). For irony, it was ex-Canuck Raffi Torres, whom the Sharks had obtained in a trade-deadline deal, converting a two-on-one to win it in overtime. That, plus a phantom hand-on-the-puck call against Henrik Sedin, cast a mighty pall over the Canucks faithful, who rarely need help in summoning gloom.

Back in San Jose, Vigneault played his final card, starting Schneider for the first time in two weeks. But with the game tied at two, a rusty Schneider gave up a pair of goals nine seconds apart early in the third to seal a 5-2 Sharks win. "When you score goals that quick, it's tough on the bench, it's tough on the goalie," said Sharks scorer Logan Couture after the game. "It ruins his confidence a little bit. They were big goals."

The fourth and final game outdid the George Jones factor of Game 2 by an order of magnitude. While it wasn't a last-minute goal this time (Joe Pavelski scored with 4:27 left to send it to OT), the outcome couldn't have been more bitter in overtime. Noted goon Daniel Sedin was penalized for a shoulder-to-shoulder check that sent Daniel Wingels spinning like a deflating balloon. "It's the playoffs, it's shoulder to shoulder," Sedin explained after earning a misconduct for directing some choice language at the referee. "I didn't talk to the ref, I screamed. I apologized to him later. But it was a bad call." On the ensuing power play, Marleau jammed home a rebound and, despite forty-three saves from Schneider, another season was done. "This is the most frustrating team I've been a part of," Daniel Sedin said in a hushed dressing room. "We have a good team, and what cost us? Little mistakes, taking penalties. We have ourselves to blame." Brother Henrik was no less cranky. "This year, this is not the way we wanted to end," the captain said. "It was almost like we were a first-time playoff team going to the box too many times. A lot of guys have been together for a long time. It's very disappointing because you only have so many chances."

Gillis's annual state of the union a few days later at Rogers Arena was no less grim-faced as he announced a reset of the plan. "From my perspective ... it's been a terrible season for us," Gillis told the media. "Five years ago, we came in here and reset this organization, and it's time to do it again.

"We're going to have to reinvent ourselves and do things differently in order to be successful. The macro look at this team is that changes have to be made ... but I'm not going to commit today to what those changes will be. It's difficult when things end so quickly and they end so negatively for all of us. It's pretty emotional to go through. We went through so much stuff this season. It was just really a difficult year on everybody here. We've got to overcome it, forget about it, and move on ... But this has been the most challenging season in my tenure here."

Had the skill and dash of Canucktivity been discredited? The man whose philosophy and practices had been pilloried finally cried uncle. "When I took this job, we decided on a style of play that resulted in great success. And clearly, the landscape has changed and we have to address those changes. We don't have a choice. It's not something I necessarily agree with. But that's what we face, and that's what you have to do."

Gillis was asked if Vigneault would return. As usual, he asked for a pause to breathe before decisions were made about anyone. "We're going to treat people fairly, like we always do, and honourably. That's not going to end because we lost four hockey games.

"We have to make the changes and adjustments necessary to compete for a Stanley Cup. It's my intention to do it and recognize what's going on and make sure we have a team that's better equipped." One change that was not going to made was to use a compliance buyout (a device introduced in the new CBA, whereby a team could bury an unwanted contract at two-thirds of the remaining value) to get out from under Luongo's contract. The concept of paying Luongo more than $27 million

234

over eighteen years for not performing was a nonstarter for the Aquilinis. The goalie jam would be solved in more conventional ways. So would Roberto Luongo still be a Canuck come September? "I think it's unlikely," Gillis responded.

16

==

They Call Me Torts

"I made my own bed with this, with this stuff that is on me. But you know what? I think I'm a pretty good coach, too. This is the mess I put myself into, and this is the mess I need to get myself out of."

JOHN TORTORELLA, MAY 2013

NHL COMMISSIONER Gary Bettman strolled to centre stage at the Prudential Center in Newark, New Jersey, on draft day, June 29, 2013, to announce the ninth pick of the draft. Waiting out the swell of boos that inevitably greet his every public appearance, Bettman smiled wickedly. (At his most excited, the public Bettman looks like a man about to tell you a lien has been put on your house.) The hometown New Jersey Devils were supposed to be on the clock—or were they?

"We have a trade to announce..." Bettman's eyebrows arched in mischievous glee. "I think you're going to want to hear this one," he said. Suddenly, the building went quiet. Devils general manager Lou Lamoriello sat stoically at the New Jersey table, his face betraying none of the frantic dealing that had just concluded. At the Vancouver table, where they were not scheduled to draft till pick number twenty-four, Canucks general manager Mike Gillis looked straight ahead, his concentration on a phone call he was making. To keen observers, a folded blue Canucks jersey could be seen at his elbow.

Bettman then supplied the punch line to Vancouver's never-ending Who's On First? goalie drama. The Devils, he proclaimed, had traded the ninth pick in the draft to Vancouver in exchange for—wait for it—goalie Cory Schneider. If timing is the secret to comedy, then Bettman brought the house down with one sentence. The arena exploded at the MacGuffin-like twist to the story, drowning out the rest of Bettman's brief speech. A breathless Pierre McGuire of NBC announced that Lamoriello, the veteran New Jersey GM, had "pulled a major heist" on Gillis, a man who'd sought to emulate the success of the Devils organization. His TSN colleague Ray Ferraro, a Vancouver resident, drew a line from *Rounders,* a poker movie, to describe the Canucks' situation as they tried to leverage two elite, well-paid goalies. In poker, you have to leave yourself some outs, said Ferraro. "And the Vancouver Canucks didn't have any outs." As the news circled the stands, a TSN floor reporter broke in abruptly to announce that Vancouver had turned down an offer from Edmonton of a first- and a second-round draft pick, plus a prospect, for Schneider. There was immediate disbelief in hockey circles. How could Gillis turn that bounty down for a shot at a single draft pick? (He hadn't, in fact. It turns out that that was Gillis's ask, not the Oilers' offer.)

To escape the din, Gillis retreated beneath the stands of the rink. But within minutes, impassive as ever, he was on the stage, watching Laurence Gilman announce that the Canucks were using the pick to select highly regarded centre Bo Horvat from the London Knights. But no one, for the moment, wanted to talk about Horvat. The issue *du jour* became the disposition of Luongo, the goalie the Canucks had seemingly thrown away the year before. Was he onside with all this? Gillis soon made it clear to TSN's James Duthie that the team, despite earlier statements, once again considered Luongo to be their No. 1 man.

What Gillis didn't say was that moves were already being made to placate the goalie. Even as the Canucks GM was being interviewed on TV in Newark, a scene from a spy thriller was unfolding far to the south. Canucks owner Francesco Aquilini was clandestinely calling at Luongo's Florida home just as the trade news went down. He was there to welcome Luongo back into the good graces of his organization and request a little forbearance as they tried to rewrite the narrative of the previous eighteen months. The idea was to make sure the player heard it from the team first. A stunned Luongo asked for time—which summed up the reaction of almost anyone who'd watched the game of chicken that had unfolded over the previous year and a half.

For a man whose reputation in the hockey business is "steady as she goes," Mike Gillis had just set off a nuclear device. In fact, the last-minute trade of Schneider, the supposed untouchable, was only one of a series of detonations triggered since the loss to San Jose. The first rumble came fifteen days after the season's end, with the firing of head coach Alain Vigneault after five consecutive division titles (six in total) and 313 wins since 2006. "When I took this job, the assumption was five years ago that Alain would be fired," Gillis told a press conference. "We found a way that we could work together, were successful together. I believe it's been the best five years in the history of this franchise. But the last two years, we haven't done the job... and we're in a results-oriented business and we have to look at the results.

"We're at a point now in the evolution of this team... where a change is required. There's no other motivation other than that. We didn't get the result that we wanted to get... You have to keep evolving and keep moving because it's a very fluid business. Alain has been a great coach here. He's a terrific person. But in our evolution, it's time." Gillis declined to get too specific about a description for Vigneault's replacement.

Vigneault, the third-longest-serving NHL head coach at the time of his firing, took the news in stride, thanking the Aquilinis, the city, and the organization for seven great years as head coach. The man who had helped clean up the riot the day after his team lost the Stanley Cup in 2011 was being the good soldier again. (Any pain he felt was quickly soothed when the New York Rangers hired him to replace the fired John Tortorella as head coach. The Rangers then made it to the Stanley Cup final in Vigneault's first season behind the bench.)

As when Gillis himself had come from nowhere to become the general manager in Vancouver, the Canucks' next head coach would be the man seemingly the farthest off anyone's radar on the day Gillis cashiered Vigneault. Favourites in the media had been former Philadelphia coach John Stevens or Toronto Marlies head coach Dallas Eakins (who wound up in Edmonton). Likewise, recently fired Lindy Ruff (hired in Dallas) and Guy Boucher saw their names bandied about. Chicago Wolves coach Scott Arniel, who had guided the Canucks' top farm team, was also thought to get an interview. It was believed that the successful candidate would have to dovetail with the cerebral, patient Gillis philosophy in place since he assumed the helm in 2008.

That would seem to eliminate available coaches in the old-fashioned, fire-breathing, media-loathing mould. Guys like John Tortorella.

So imagine the seismic rumble that passed through Vancouver on June 25, when Gillis stood before yet another media conclave at Rogers Arena to welcome the fifty-five-year-old American as the seventeenth head coach of the team. Sulphuric in his dealings with the New York press, emotive behind the bench when scolding players, impatient with the NHL's rule of law, Tortorella was seen as exactly the kind of coach the Canucks had been trying to get away from. But Gillis reminded everyone that Tortorella had won a Stanley Cup as head coach in Tampa Bay and had been a successful assistant coach in Buffalo and Phoenix, and that young players had developed in the Ranger uniform under Tortorella's guidance.

"You have a shelf life as a coach in the National Hockey League," Gillis said. "Occasionally, a different voice is necessary. I think John just has a different voice than Alain. Alain is a very good hockey coach. John is a very good hockey coach. But they approach it from different places, and they approach it in different ways, and I felt it was necessary to make a change."

The Aquilinis and Gillis had a message they wanted to send to a veteran team that seemed unprepared in the playoffs in the past two years, and it wanted that message delivered in the inimitable style of Torts, as he preferred to be known. Loud and clear. A vow to employ the Sedins on the penalty kill was one clear change; under Vigneault's model, the twins had sat out the PK. The Sedins said they were ready for added duties. "It doesn't matter if you have a type that comes in that yells and screams," Henrik told reporters. "It has to make sense. As a player, you have to sit there, and say, 'Well, he's right, this is the way it should be.' There's nothing wrong with doing that."

Still, the native of Massachusetts was going to have to change some things to fit in on the mellow West Coast (he chose to live in Point Roberts, Washington, commuting to Vancouver for his duties). That meant reforming his fractious approach to the media, a lowlight reel that included exchanging F-bombs with *New York Post* reporter Larry Brooks. The Vancouver charm offensive started at his introductory press day. "I made my own bed with this, with this stuff that is on me," Tortorella said. "But you know what? I think I'm a pretty good coach, too. This is the mess I put myself into, and this is the mess I need to get myself out of." Asked how he'd gotten his reputation, Torts said it was his deep loathing of losing. "That's a big part of it. I can't stand losing. Everybody says, 'Be a good loser.' I think if you're a good loser, you're a loser." Another volatile American, Ryan Kesler, liked what he heard about the hard-driving coach. "We need to be tougher to play against."

The short-term effect was encouraging. Media stories in Vancouver were talking about a rescue-dog lover who was really just a softy. Not all media reports were as glowing, suggesting that the decision on a new coach had been taken out of the hands of the GM. "Tortorella is the kind of knee-jerk decision that other organizations make, not the Canucks," wrote Ed Willes in the *Province*. "Yes, he represents a personality type diametrically opposed from his predecessor Alain Vigneault. But he also represents a personality type diametrically opposed to Gillis's core values. He is loud and profane; narcissistic and temperamental. He is emotional to the point of irrationality. Tortorella, in fact, is so far removed from Gillis and his methods that this hire had to originate from somewhere else; somewhere, and we're just spitballing here, like Canucks ownership." It would not be the last time that culpability for hiring Torts was tossed around the front office like a hand grenade. Willes later backtracked from the insinuation that the Aquilinis were now calling the shots at Rogers Arena. But the theory persisted in Vancouver's hockey-fever swamps that Gillis might be losing control. Or that Canucktivity might soon go the way of the old Electric Kool-Aid Acid Test jerseys from the 1970s. (Torts was known not to be a fan of Gillis's mind room and some other progressive wrinkles, which quietly disappeared.)

With the Vancouver fan base starting to bay at his heels (and ownership growing increasingly restive), Gillis needed to reassert himself as the Canucks arrived in New Jersey for the 2013 NHL Draft. The media pack that arrived to see Nathan Mackinnon go first overall to Colorado also was waiting eagerly to see just how the Canucks GM planned to extricate himself from the two-headed goalie pretzel he'd twisted in Vancouver. Gillis was also saddled with stories about his team's relative lack of high-profile prospects or success at the draft. He was haunted by the

241

concept that his team's window of opportunity was closing. Just how much more could Torts whip from the aging Sedins? went the narrative. Who would he have as his goalie?

Gillis moved quickly to take charge of the narrative. It was clear that there was little market for Luongo after the NHL got its revenge on the goalie's lengthy, front-loaded contract. Likewise, ownership had no continued appetite for the two-headed goalie costing $9.3 million or for a compliance buyout. Interested teams knew Gillis was very short on Luongo options. It had been conventional wisdom the past two years that, had Gillis been peddling Schneider instead of Luongo, he would have received a hefty return and avoided the heartache of the last eighteen months. (For the same reasons that Schneider was an attractive bauble to other teams, the Canucks had tried to hold on to the well-spoken man from Marblehead.) Suddenly, Schneider's name was in play, perhaps available for a reasonable price. The bidding began. In a forty-eight-hour auction, Gillis had to extract maximum value for the man he had anointed as his starting goalie just a year before. The hours before the draft produced a sequence of phone calls and bartering (plus getting Francesco Aquilini to Florida on the sly). Then there was the tension of the long hours as the draft wound its way to New Jersey's number nine spot, earned by a thoroughly mediocre season capped by missing the playoffs.

Three years of trying to stage-manage their goalie glut was ended by the commissioner's dramatic announcement that Schneider was headed east and Luongo was again on his way from Florida to the Lower Mainland of B.C.

The reviews of Gillis's handiwork were not kind. "So, it's about-face time," wrote the *Province*. "Wonder how that kiss-and-make-up session [with Luongo] is going to go? Can they even reach each other over the burned bridges? All of it, of course, could have been avoided. If the Canucks had set a deadline to deal Luongo last summer, he either would have been gone or they could have moved on to trying to get the most out of a Schneider deal. The two goalies also could have been labelled co-No. 1's this past year, avoiding the bad feelings which developed by the end of the season." In *Grantland,* Sean McIndoe noted, "The bottom line is that Luongo's contract turned out to be untradeable, and that left Gillis with only two options: Spend $27 million of his boss's money to buy out Luongo's deal, or trade Schneider for whatever he could get. In the end, he didn't even get as much as he was asking for Schneider. So yes, Gillis and the Canucks wound up getting stuck with a deeply unsatisfying outcome here. But it was still better than any of his other options."

Wrote Harrison Mooney in the *Pass It to Bulis* blog: "The Canucks were over a barrel. They waited too long to trade Luongo and when the new CBA turned Funny Bob's contract into a Gordian knot—a petty act from the NHL designed to make those that made them look foolish for the loophole look even more foolish for exploiting it—they were done for, and Luongo wound up hard done by."

As the reviews flowed in, Gillis mused about how Schneider's rapid ascent had brought the organization's long-term plan 360 degrees back to him. "Our plan three years ago was to develop Cory and move him for a high pick," he told reporters with a bemused smile. "And that's what we ultimately did." Just not quite the way he had foreseen. One thing his critics had never done was to accuse Gillis of not being thorough in exploring his options. "For the last year, we've explored every option that we could possibly have. Things were heating up this week, and we just felt we couldn't wait any longer with the situation we were in. We felt for our organization . . . we had to do something to get the situation resolved, and this was the best opportunity we had. It was a very difficult decision. At the end of the day, we didn't feel there was drop-off in either one's play and felt they were both excellent, super players, and it really came down to where we could get the most value."

One thing Gillis might have done better was to explain how Luongo's Florida obsession had tied his hands. With the no-trade clause, the GM did not have full latitude to move Luongo. Here, with the national media assembled, he might have suggested that his goalie had trolled him, wanting to escape to low-pressure Florida, where he'd make more money under the state's no-income-tax policy. Gillis passed, even as he knew the Vancouver media and fan base would blame him for incompetence or worse.

The Schneider deal also partly obscured what had become, in fact, a good day for Gillis in his efforts to replenish the Canucks' assets. In the midst of the trade noise, Gillis pointed out that Horvat was the kind of prospect the Canucks hadn't been able to draft since picking Cody Hodgson tenth overall in 2008. "We have been drafting twenty-fourth or twenty-sixth, and you can't find this type of player there." Described as "the real McCoy," Horvat was one of the most complete forwards in junior hockey, drawing comparisons to Patrice Bergeron of Boston and Ryan O'Reilly of Colorado.

Draft analyst Corey Pronman was bullish on Horvat: "He is a strong, physical center who will lay the body, displaying the two-way work ethic NHL teams want to see. He is an aware penalty killer, good at faceoffs, and overall projects as a center who will start his shift in the defensive zone more often than not. His creativity progressed throughout this season, and his puck skills, hand-eye coordination, and playmaking vision all rank as above average; he can flash high-end offensive skill. It is difficult to find a weakness in his game."

Tyler Dellow of mc79hockey said that getting Horvat high in the draft augured well. "The players acquired with those [number nine] picks have, generally speaking, turned out to be really good players to great players too. This is where I think that the people complaining about the return are kind of missing the point. The thing about a pick in the top ten is that you're talking about a player who has a non-marginal chance of being an honest to god star in the NHL. That potential, which may or may not be realized, has real value."

The skill upgrade didn't end there. In their regular twenty-fourth spot, a more traditional perch for the Canucks in recent years, they were able to find another skilled scorer from the Canadian Hockey League, Hunter Shinkaruk of the Medicine Hat Tigers. The shifty forward had projected as high as sixth overall, with most assuming he would never get by Calgary, his hometown team, in the twenty-second spot. (Shinkaruk's father had worked as team dentist with the Calgary Hitmen of the Western Hockey League, among others.) So when the Flames opted for QMJHL player Emile Poirier at number twenty-two, the Canucks happily scooped the darting sniper from their rivals. The slight Shinkaruk's game was predicated on pure offence and it was judged that he might take a while to fill in.

Seeing the Canucks go for skill with Shinkaruk, a pick in tune with Gillis's philosophy, some asked why he had passed over the huge Russian winger Valeri Nichushkin at number nine for Horvat, a two-way player still not assured of being an NHL scorer. (Dallas chose Nichushkin tenth overall.) Gillis remained bullish on his picks. "I think they're really highly skilled players and they bring a lot to the table," Gillis said. "We're very enthused about both of them... They're both two-hundred-foot players, play in every situation. Hunter is a more offensive player, a more dynamic player, a really fast skater. So we got two complementary players in the first round."

The rest of the draft was peppered with some familiar names. Diverting from their tendency towards college prospects and overage players in recent years, the Canucks also plucked the son of former Canuck Andrew Cassels when they snared Oshawa Generals centre Cole Cassels in the third round. Undersized Jordan Subban, brother of 2013 Norris Trophy winner P.K. Subban, followed in the fourth round. Swedish defenceman Anton Cederholm (destined for Portland of the WHL), jumbo Albertan defenceman Mike Williamson (headed to Penn State), and OHL defenceman Miles Liberati completed the haul. It was instantly rated the best draft Gillis had orchestrated since getting the GM's job.

Added to the backlog of prospects now approaching the NHL level, it created the chance for the Canucks' maligned farm system to have as many as six first-round picks—Kassian (via Buffalo), Jordan Schroeder, Nicklas Jensen, Brendan Gaunce, Horvat, and Shinkaruk—at the NHL level within the next two years. Added to Frank Corrado and Chris Tanev, it could produce the evolution of the team's core. The question was: Could it happen soon enough to keep Gillis ahead of the building wave of dissent?

17

The King of Torts

"I just can't go off the rails as I did. Off the rails?
I was off the country."

JOHN TORTORELLA

FOR CANUCKS FANS, promised by John Tortorella the previous summer that his brawling days were done, the sight of their coach assailing the Calgary Flames dressing room in January of 2014 was a jolt, to put it mildly. For players who'd experienced Alain Vigneault's droll worldview, the guerrilla mission was mind-bending. Inflamed by Flames coach Bob Hartley's decision to start a lineup of fighters against his team at Rogers Arena, Tortorella had blown like Vesuvius. After meeting Hartley's challenge head-on with a line brawl on the game's opening faceoff, Torts then made his solo dash to the Calgary dressing room after the first period. While he didn't get anywhere near Hartley, his foray still earned him a fifteen-day suspension from the league. (The Flames were fined $25,000 by the NHL for their provocation. Their GM, Brian Burke, always good for a chuckle, growled, "I'm not happy with the fine that coach Hartley received, especially since we all know the Canucks started it.")

With his assault on both the dressing room and good sense, the King of Torts had repositioned the Canucks to something closer to his temperament. This was no longer a club defined by Vigneault's wry smiles and sarcasm or Gillis's dyspeptic style. The first-year Canucks coach was now establishing his bond with the 1982 Canucks, Roger Neilson's grinding guys with the chips on their shoulders. Under Tortorella, the team that had Daniel Sedin turn the other cheek in the 2011 Stanley Cup final was now a throwback to the wild days of the NHL, when coaches went after fans and line brawls were a regular occurrence. Under the urbane Vigneault, the Canucks would simply skate away from goading; under Torts, they were suddenly about standing up for each other against the bruising California teams.

The blowup was not happenstance. The seeds of Torts's dressing-room dash had been sown earlier that same week. In a January 13 game in Los Angeles, the Canucks had spent much of the contest taking penalties against the Kings' Dustin Brown and Jordan Nolan, purportedly avenging heavy hits on the Sedins and Luongo in an earlier contest. In emulating the Bertuzzi Canucks of 2004, Torts's boys announced they would strike first and ask questions later. The first period alone featured fifty-three penalty minutes and four power plays, including a man-advantage of eight minutes and thirteen seconds after Tom Sestito was assessed twenty-seven minutes in penalties and ejected for attempting to instigate a fight with Nolan.

Such was their zeal for revenge that Vancouver neglected to do much about scoring; they lost 1–0 on a third-period goal by— guess who—an unrepentant Dustin Brown. Despite the loss, there was much talk in the aftermath about the Kings' game being a turning point in the Canucks' attitude. Under Torts, the Canucks wouldn't be intimidated. The game resulted in a course correction, all right: straight into the rocks. Two nights later, the same Canucks were humiliated 9–1 by the Anaheim Ducks, followed by a 1–0 shutout loss in Phoenix the night after that. Three losses, one goal scored, no points. Followed, two nights later, by Torts's tirade against Calgary.

Those among the team's fan base who longed for the rough-and-tumble Canucks of 1982 still applauded the gritty approach; others who had admired the science and cool professionalism of Canucktivity since Gillis's arrival wondered just what was happening in the Vancouver dressing room. Or what was happening in the Canucks' executive suite. What was happening was a lot of losing. Following a nearly perfect December, the Canucks went a dismaying 4–13–1 between January 1, 2014, and the Olympic break in February. Their once-intimidating offence disappeared with just forty-four goals in twenty-three games. The power play—their competitive advantage between 2009 and 2011—ranked twenty-eighth in the league as Vancouver's coaches juggled different combinations every night. Injury-plagued Alex Burrows, a thirty-five-goal scorer in 2010–11, had not scored in the entire season before the Olympic break (prompting Tortorella to suggest the Canucks buy him out of his new contract at season's end). The Sedins, who didn't score a goal in the month of January, were on pace to produce numbers they hadn't seen in a decade. Ryan Kesler was a shadow of the forty-one-goal scorer from two years before. Many nights, the offence—such as it was—was being carried by Chris Higgins, Zack Kassian, and free-agent bargain Mike Santorelli (till he was lost for the season in January with a shoulder injury).

Only the goaltending tandem of "Reluctant" Roberto Luongo and rookie Eddie Lack resembled anything like the team that had come within a game of the Cup in 2011. To most, it appeared that the window of opportunity for the Canucks core had slammed shut rudely on Mike Gillis's fingers—just as he had re-signed the Sedin twins, Burrows, Alex Edler, Kevin Bieksa, and Luongo to lengthy and expensive deals. Predictably, many who applauded the contract extensions when they were signed now bashed them as wasteful and reckless.

According to the general manager, the league's new premium on goals was also killing the Canucks. "Look at any evening in the NHL and you're seeing multiple 2-1, 3-2 games," Gillis pointed out as his team limped into the seventeen-day Olympic break. "If you look at three, four years ago, we adapted to a more pressing, transitional skating approach and had success. But now that's changed. And if you don't adapt, you're going to be left behind. So you have to shoot from bad angles, get the puck to the net."

Sounding like a convert, Gillis continued, "Scoring in this league has changed dramatically in the past two seasons. Looking for a perfect pass doesn't work. You have to get the puck to the net, hope for a bounce, and jam away. It seems like we've been on the outside too much. You see a lot of goals that are jam plays and scrambles rather than [the result of] playmaking. Teams block shots and you have to get inside. Our team has been reluctant to get inside."

The trend towards the physical, scrumming hockey popularized by the L.A. Kings had Gillis again bemoaning the dearth of scoring in the league. "As goalies become more dominant, we have to find ways to encourage generating offence. Now you see teams' power plays the same, you see penalty kills the same, so you see shots from the goal line that you never saw before. You have to figure out ways to succeed as the league changes . . . We have to find ways to encourage offence. If a goalie stops forty shots and there are ten to twelve great chances, then give him credit. But today, when you have four or five scoring chances in a game and half of them come in a shootout, you've got a problem."

250

Gillis probably also needed to ask: Do our fans think this is a problem? As the losing accelerated, discontent could be seen in the growing number of unoccupied seats in Rogers Arena. The defence-first style promoted by Tortorella drained games of the Canucks' former daring. "I just couldn't believe how slow they'd gotten since 2011," said TSN analyst Ray Ferraro, who worked between the benches. Media that had extolled the virtues of the management team were turning on them, ripping Gillis for not providing enough depth or prospects. Despite thrifty additions of Ryan Stanton, Santorelli, and Brad Richardson the previous off-season, critics railed against the acquisitions of David Booth, Keith Ballard, Derek Roy, and Samuel Pahlsson. Purported trade offers from the past were revived to hammer Gillis and his group. In a city that doesn't need much to have a fainting spell, Vancouver's hockey fans were getting *verklempt* over their one-time darlings.

Outside of the Tortorella sideshow, there were other reasons for the stall. For all their attempts to mitigate the travel handicaps they suffer, the Canucks were battling again to create enough time for rest and practice in a compacted Olympic schedule. With the new NHL rules mandating four off-days a month per team, Vancouver struggled to get practice time around their usual travel challenges (travel days don't count as days off). In spite of their travel experts, fatigue became a factor in the epidemic of injuries that struck the Canucks in midseason. As the team put together a sterling 10–2–2 record in December, an injury plague accelerated. By the time the Olympic break arrived, it had cost the services of Burrows, Edler, Stanton, Bieksa, Santorelli, Jordan Schroeder, Chris Tanev, and, finally, Henrik Sedin for extended stays on the injured list. While the offence had been modest during the winning streak, it completely disappeared in the injury wave. There was no immediate help from the farm system, as Gillis held back his best prospects in the minors or junior to develop more fully.

The injuries and the loss of practice time were not helped by the Canucks head coach being sent home for two weeks. Having hobbled the team's season with his "forlorn hope" attack on Calgary, Tortorella returned from his suspension just before

251

the Olympics, expressing a mix of remorse and retribution. "I just can't go off the rails as I did," he told reporters before coming back in Detroit on February 3. "Off the rails? I was off the country." But he quickly pivoted. "I think our team needs to be pushed. I do. But pushing, everybody takes that sometimes the wrong way. We need a mental push, we need to develop some skin mentally, and we have not done that consistently enough. We have done it during the year. But certainly not consistently enough through the first few months here.

"We have forgotten how to defend, and no matter what is going wrong with your team offensively, to have any chance of competing, you need to defend, and we're not defending. I have seen this team defend and play the right way. I just don't think we have played the right way, I think we will, and that's part of the coaches' responsibility, and I will tell you right now the coaches are in this too with them."

You could have fooled many about Torts's loyalty to his players when the Canucks celebrated the coach's return with another lame effort (a 2-0 loss to a Red Wing team playing its second game in two nights). After the game, Torts acidly remarked, "I thought our best forward was David Booth, which is good for him. That's not good for our team, to have him as our best forward." The invocation of oft-injured Booth was a low blow to the player and further evidence that Torts was ignoring management's requests not to cut players up in the press.

Ominously, Torts then turned his sights on his GM. "We need to change the complexion of our hockey club, either with our play or with different people, because we looked like a slow hockey team tonight," Tortorella said. "We are going to keep banging away to try and get better, but I tell you, it is very frustrating to see the same looks. It worries me—I'll leave it at that. It really worries me."

Gillis tried to squelch any controversy around his coach. "We're absolutely on the same page," he told reporters. "In terms

252

of communicating, we discuss every issue on our team. Every day, the conversations we have are about how the team is performing. But you have to keep things in context, or we'd trade every player who has a bad game."

Every team looked forward to the Olympic break. Having rapidly sunk out of a playoff spot in the Western Conference, the battered Canucks might have greeted the respite with more relief than others. With seven players on five Olympic squads, it wouldn't be a complete rest for the team, but Henrik Sedin, Bieksa, Tanev, and others took a pass to heal injured ribs while others recharged their batteries. A playoff spot was still within view.

Unless it wasn't. The Olympic hiatus proved to be the lull before a much bigger storm, one about to be upgraded by Torts to a Category 5. In the ten days after the Olympic break, the franchise was probably rocked more than at any time since the Bertuzzi incident. The trigger was the long-awaited Heritage Classic game against the Ottawa Senators at B.C. Place Stadium, a showcase before 54,194 fans in the facility across the road from Rogers Arena. The franchise had invested much in the community and charitable aspects of this showpiece event. It was assumed that the glitz, the throwback uniforms, and the modest opponent might spark the Canucks in their run for the final playoff spot in the Western Conference. Once again, no one consulted the unpredictable Tortorella.

Since returning from the Olympics with a gold medal, Roberto Luongo had rested while watching backup Eddie Lack allow just one goal in two games, including a shutout of the dangerous St. Louis Blues. It was assumed these contests were a chance for Luongo to recharge his batteries after Sochi, to re-emerge in the marquee game against Ottawa at B.C. Place. Then Tortorella dropped his bombshell: Eddie Lack, not Luongo, would get the start against the Senators. The young Swede gave the team its best chance to win on this day, declared Torts. The coach's vote of confidence immediately backfired

253

when Lack, booed by elements in a crowd that chanted for Luongo's appearance, was beaten 4–2 by Ottawa.

For Luongo, sitting on the bench for the nationally televised showcase, it was the final straw. Having gone through enough drama with the Canucks in the previous two seasons, he called his new agent, Pat Brisson, and instructed the CAA Hockey executive to extricate him from Vancouver for good. After hearing the agent's plea, Gillis allowed Brisson to assess the market for the man who had been considered untradeable just a year earlier. There was a difference this time, however: the Florida Panthers, the team Luongo had pined for without success, now had a new owner who wanted to make a splash. More than that, he had the money to do so. Knowing his No. 1 goalie was now as good as gone, Gillis went to work on the Monday after the game to make a deal with Panthers GM Dale Tallon, a frequent trading partner. By Tuesday, the deal, two years in the making, was done: Luongo and prospect Steven Anthony for centre Shawn Matthias and goalie Jacob Markstrom, considered the best goaltending prospect in the NHL just eighteen months earlier. The Canucks also agreed to take back $800,000 of Luongo's annual $5.3 million cap hit.

Even Luongo was shocked at the speed of the deal prompted by Brisson's efforts. "We had a brief conversation, and [Pat] kind of took matters into his own hands," Luongo told reporters. "I'm not exactly sure how the whole thing went down, but I was not expecting to get traded." Brisson conceded that while a Luongo trade was probably inevitable, Tortorella's choice of goaltenders in the outdoor game had hastened the process, having ripped open a wound that had been healing over since Schneider's departure.

The howls from the fan base and media were immediate. Within nine months, the Canucks had given up two bona fide No. 1 goalies in exchange for a prospect in Bo Horvat, a project in Markstrom, and a No. 3 centre in Matthias (while

254

also retaining $800,000 of Luongo's annual salary cap burden). "While it's one thing to trade Schneider and argue the Canucks are just as good with Luongo," wrote Iain MacIntyre in the *Vancouver Sun*, "it's impossible to promote the idea of winning now by trading Luongo, too, and giving the No. 1 label to rookie backup Eddie Lack, who had 25 games and nine wins on his resume." Who was now calling the shots: Gillis, Tortorella, or Aquilini? "The message from above has to be major because the clamour for change has gone beyond who's playing," Ben Kuzma warned in the *Province*. "It's who is making those calls, and John Tortorella is clearly in the crosshairs for the lineup. So is general [manager] Mike Gillis for assembling the roster and getting those affordable long-term extensions for unproductive core players, who received no-trade clauses in return."

"It's about the credibility of this organization under this ownership, this general manager and this coach," wrote Ed Willes. "They can send out all the letters they want explaining their plan. The story they're telling on the ice is far more convincing." Only NBC's Pierre McGuire saw a positive for Vancouver. "I don't know what Florida is thinking," he said, pointing to the potential of Markstrom as a No. 1 goalie and the production of Matthias.

Sideswiped by his coach's decision, Gillis finally gave some insight into the limits of his control over Luongo's future. "People out there want to think that we have total control over this," Gillis remarked. "We signed Roberto to a long-term contract that had a no-trade [clause] in it, and he was able to exercise an element of control over how we proceeded. Unfortunately, a team he really wanted to go to ... was Florida, and they didn't have the wherewithal financially to take him on. Would we have done some things differently? Perhaps, but we didn't have complete control of the situation ...

"These are tough decisions. It takes a lot of courage to trade a player like Roberto Luongo and insert younger players into your lineup. We felt strongly that this was the right time frame to think that way, and this was the first opportunity to act on it."

Having declared a pivot point in the Canucks' retooling of their roster, Gillis was then tasked with trying to hit a home run at the trade deadline for centre Ryan Kesler, who had quietly asked Vancouver to explore limited options for him to be traded. Saying he had no particular plan to trade Kesler, Gillis did admit that he had received many inquiries about the rugged centre. As March 4 approached, it was received wisdom in the Vancouver hockey market that Kesler would be dealt for younger players and draft picks. Whetting the appetite of Canucks fans was the potential to acquire a young star. Reports from Pittsburgh hinted at a deal that included first- and third-round picks, centre Brandon Sutter, and elite defensive prospect Derrick Pouliot. The inescapable trade deadline TV extravaganzas did nothing to lessen the heat on the organization, placing Kesler at the top of the list of available trade subjects. But the deadline—noon Pacific time—brought no trade. The predicted bounty for Kesler never materialized. No deal was judged to be better than a bad deal. Kesler would stay and Eddie Lack would now be the No. 1 goalie. But raising the expectations of Canucks fans is a dangerous business. Thus, Gillis was seen as having missed an opportunity that existed mostly in the fans' own minds.

More ominously, sources suggested that Canuck owner Francesco Aquilini (who was in the Canucks' war room in Phoenix on trade deadline day) had turned down deals for Kesler in the hope that his team might revive itself and get into the playoffs. Pittsburgh voices suggested that the Canucks' decision-making was holding back trades. The Canucks quickly sought to stifle the notion that Gillis was not getting the final call on trades. But in the culture of gloom embracing Vancouver, there were ever more in the fickle fan base who embraced that idea and demanded Gillis's dismissal.

Forget Canucktivity, this was now *Survivor* time, with many in Vancouver ready to vote management off the island. The job prospects of Gillis and Tortorella rested on the rookie Lack as their go-to goalie the rest of the season. Which produced the final drama of March and April.

18

FUBAR

"I'm not sure if I'll be back next season."

MIKE GILLIS

THERE IS AN old joke from the Cold War era about an incoming Soviet leader meeting with his predecessor on that man's final day. The newcomer asks what advice the venerable man might offer. The outgoing leader hands him two envelopes. "Open the first when you reach your first crisis. Read the instructions. When you have another crisis, open the second envelope and follow its instructions." The new leader thanks the retiring premier. Sure enough, in time, the new leader encounters trouble. In desperation, he reaches into the drawer containing the envelopes, pulls out the first one, and reads the instructions: "Blame everything on me." Sure enough, the besieged leader does just that, and the crisis passes. When the premier next finds himself in trouble, he wastes no time in reaching into his desk drawer for the second envelope. If it works as well as the first, he reasons, he'll be out of trouble. Then he reads the instructions written in the second note: "Take two envelopes. In the first, put a note that says, 'Blame me for everything' . . ."

You could excuse Mike Gillis if he didn't find the humour in this story as Canucktivity vanished with stunning rapidity in the early spring of 2014. In the second game after he traded Roberto Luongo, the Canucks were bombed 6–1 by Dallas. The new No. 1 goalie, Eddie Lack, gave up five goals on seventeen shots in two periods. Markstrom, brought in to finish, stopped four of five. From Florida, Luongo twisted the knife on Twitter. "If I was still the back up I coulda came in and mopped this game up nicely," he tweeted. After a 2–1 win at home over hapless Calgary, the Canucks took a 3–0 lead into the third period of their next game, against the mediocre New York Islanders. Two wins in a row, and there might still be hope of making a playoff run with many home games left on the schedule. Or not. Lack, who'd looked impeccable till then, was ventilated for six goals in the third (a seventh went into the empty net) before a stunned crowd at Rogers Arena. Even without their star, John Tavares, the Isles pumped four goals past the Canucks in just seven minutes while, behind the Vancouver bench, John Tortorella performed his signature operatic gestures of hair tugging and holding his head in his hands, as if the whole world had conspired against him. (The onslaught tied a club record for most goals allowed in a third period.) The 7–4 loss was the worst possible news for Lack, whose confidence seemed deflated. The carefree quipster was now replaced by a goalie with the weight of the team on his shoulders—or, as Tortorella put it, "It's easy to be Robin. Being Batman is the hard part." On cue, Torts's former No. 1 goalie, Strombone, tweeted from Florida, "#PrayforEddie."

With fan signs and social media burning with calls for Gillis's ouster, the GM sent out a missive to the team's season ticket holders. Calling them "a very important part of the Canucks family," he attempted to put the turbulence of 2013–14 in perspective:

Last summer, we said we had to make some changes to our team. We need to get younger, faster and stronger to succeed. That process is happening now, as we look to retool by surrounding our veteran stars with new, young talent. You can look at Anaheim as a recent example of a team that has retooled successfully.

Trading Roberto was not an easy decision... But the moves we've made go beyond goaltending. We are now younger and we are getting deeper. We've added a big, strong 6-4 centre in Shawn Matthias, who is excited to be here and will help this team now. And we believe in our talented group of prospects, including Bo Horvat, Nicklas Jensen, Frank Corrado, Dane Fox, Brendan Gaunce and Hunter Shinkaruk, who will be part of our short and long-term success. We are also well positioned financially, having created over $5 million in cap room to make the right deals for this team. That's in addition to the $7 million we expect the salary cap to increase next season... We are enduring a challenging period, but your passion makes it possible for us to put our team in a position to compete.

The soothing words placated some, but for the most part, the Vancouver fan base had simply tuned out Gillis's gospel of Canucktivity. Missing the postseason for the first time in his six-year regime was a bitter pill to swallow in a city now spoiled by the greatest run of success ever in franchise history. Where other Canadian cities are fanatical about their hockey teams, Vancouver was ratcheting its expectations a step higher. Witness the two riots and a trail of former executives consumed by an insatiable pack mentality.

"This city can be a poor loser," concedes John Shorthouse. "Maybe because they have little experience of winning. I've seen people I know transform into completely different people in the face of these losses. People doing things on the streets of downtown, doing things they'd never do again. I've seen more debris thrown on the ice either here or at the [Pacific] Coliseum. Seems to be a phenomenon [particular] to Vancouver."

Small groups of attention seekers began showing up on game nights at Rogers Arena, demanding Gillis's dismissal. Signs went up. The initial reports on season ticket renewals showed disenchanted patrons vowing not to renew unless Gillis, Tortorella, or both paid the price for the misbegotten season. The multiple charitable and community outreach efforts fostered under Gillis (he donated $50,000 to the team's annual charity drive in 2014) that had once been hailed were now forgotten. Suddenly, the aloof public manner of the Ontario outsider had become an issue within Vancouver, which seemed to forget that most of the greatest GMs in history—including Sam Pollock, Harry Sinden, Lou Lamoriello, Glen Sather, and, yes, Brian Burke—had never pandered to media or fan demands. Once again, Vancouver fans wanted tuna with good taste, not tuna that tasted good.

Worse, the river of blame in the media was threatening to run upstream to the owner himself, tying the disastrous hiring of Tortorella to Francesco Aquilini. How sensitive was the owner about owning that decision? Aquilini sent cease-and-desist letters to *The Globe and Mail* and the *Province* when they hinted that he or his family might have been involved in the interviewing or hiring. To the *Globe*'s David Ebner, he wrote: "I read your article today. You are a prick." Legal notice followed hours later. To the *Province,* the Aquilinis' lawyer stated that, "by writing [the Aquilinis] had a prominent role in the hiring it was designed to 'incite ridicule for making bad or embarrassing judgments.' " (Giving the subject of the "embarrassing judgment" himself, John Tortorella, an early job review should he desire one.)

So even as Gillis earnestly penned his report to fans, his owner was scrambling to assign blame for the Tortorella disaster to the 2011 *Sporting News* Executive of the Year, the man who'd brought him so much success and money the previous six years. As Aquilini would reveal a week later, he was already talking to former Canucks hero Trevor Linden about parachuting the former Canucks captain into Gillis's job as president, a happy face from the past to placate the madding crowd. Abandoning the meticulous plans laid out by Gillis, Aquilini would now take a flyer on a former player who'd been out of the NHL for six years, who had no comparable management experience, and whose tenure at the NHL Players' Association had ended in a disastrous capitulation for the players during the 2004-05 lockout (the owners' confidence that players would once again break unity led directly to the 2012-13 lockout).

Any doubts in Aquilini's mind about throwing Gillis to the mob probably were lifted on April 2, the date of Gillis's weekly radio appearance on The Team 1040. Gillis had become renowned for the art of saying little in his radio spots, and doing so in a laconic, sometimes irritable, manner. This interview with Brother Jake and David Pratt would be different. It began when Gillis was asked whether Tortorella would be back. "I'm not sure if I'll be back next season," Gillis remarked drily. "The running of this team is my responsibility, and I really feel the last couple of seasons we have chased goalposts that have been moving and got away from our core principles of how I want this team to play and how I want it to perform and the tempo we want to play with.

"People love to pick someone to blame, but the reality is, as an organization, we have deviated from some of the things that made us successful and some of the things that I know will be successful. We're going to get back to those levels, get back to that style of play that we started six years ago. We have the personnel to do it; we just have to be committed and have the guts to be able to carry it out ... I want us to play an upbeat, puck-possession, move-the-puck-quickly, force-teams-into-mistakes, high-transition game," he continued. "And I think we have the personnel to do it, and if we don't have the personnel to do it, they will be changed.

"That's my vision. That's how I believe you are going to win in the Western Conference and the National Hockey League. Look at the top teams in the West. There isn't a lot that separates any of the teams in the West, but the top teams play that way. That's the way we played, and in playing that way we made a lot of enemies, but we had the success that we wanted to have. And that's the style that we are going to get back to and that is the way I want to see our team play."

Gillis then turned his attention to the coach's style. "Six years ago, people thought Alain Vigneault couldn't change from a defensive-style coach to an offensive-style coach," Gillis said. "If given the resources, and if the players are committed to it, I think any coach can coach the team that he has ... If people don't want to get onside with how I view this team and how it is supposed to play, then they won't be here."

It didn't take long for reporters and fans to divine the meaning of the GM's comments. "There has been a power struggle within the Canucks for some time now," wrote Ed Willes in the *Province*, "and while ownership—specifically Francesco Aquilini—goes apoplectic at its mention, Gillis's interview on Thursday revealed much about that inner turmoil. It isn't just the losing this season that's eaten away at Gillis. It's the betrayal of his principles which preceded the losing. We'll leave to you to conclude what that says about the decision to hire John Tortorella to coach the team in the first place." TSN analyst and former NHLer Ray Ferraro saw a line in the sand. "That is as big a distancing from the coach as I've seen. That's pushing you to that side of the room and I'm on this side of the room and whoever is making the decision upstairs, you've got one or the other. I see it as totally unlikely that ... both are back."

The implicit criticism of the team's direction as it descended into a season of ineptitude might have been the first negative

263

comment Gillis ever made about his bosses, the organization. It would also be the last.

On April 8, 2014, as the chants of "Fire Gillis" still rang in the rafters of Rogers Arena after another loss to Anaheim the night before, the axe fell. Even as Linden was on Global TV, publicly denying having ever spoken to Francesco Aquilini about a job, Gillis was exiting a meeting with the owners without his job as president and GM. Despite his protestations, Linden was in fact the new president, charged with finding a new general manager.

Aquilini thanked Gillis for his service at a hastily arranged press conference, but was opaque about why he had fired the most successful general manager in club history. As he had been when hiring Gillis in 2008, Aquilini was long on platitudes about "new directions." He was also short on specifics about how someone with no managerial experience, who had been out of the NHL for six years, was going to avert further erosion of the team's brand in one year. For now, Aquilini had bought some time with his fan base by propping up the local hero. How much time would be a function of Linden's survival skills. Fans hoped he'd work out better than he had during his stint at the NHLPA, when he unilaterally hired a new executive director, Ted Saskin, who had to be fired shortly afterward for spying on players' private emails.

As for Gillis, hockey's chattering classes delivered a mixed verdict. His Toronto critics insisted he had simply coasted with a core inherited from Dave Nonis and had been unable to find the final pieces after 2011 to guarantee a championship. In Vancouver it was his "arrogance" with the media that had poisoned the well and affected the extended drama of the Luongo trade. Because he had come from outside the mainstream of the NHL's management culture, Gillis had few allies to cushion the inevitable criticisms that came his way. Certainly, his former employer had done nothing to still the doubts within the community when the Tortorella hire went sideways. (To illustrate what the Canucks owner had done to his ex-president and coach, *Hockey Night in Canada*'s Glenn Healy showed clips from the movie *Gladiator,* in which the emperor turns thumbs down for the mob howling below him).

Supporters emphasized that Gillis had improved on Nonis's core with clever acquisitions such as Christian Ehrhoff, Maxim Lapierre, Manny Malhotra, Mike Santorelli, and Chris Higgins, and the key contract re-signing of the Sedins, which kept Vancouver under the salary cap. It was observed that the 2011 team that made the Stanley Cup final was ultimately sabotaged by injuries and wonky goaltending. Gillis's innovations on travel and training were on the cutting edge within the league. There was finally a backlog of young talent in the system that would give Linden some organizational depth. Tony Gallagher of the *Province* pointed out that Gillis had been great for business. "While numbers can be manipulated in many ways, you could argue that in fact the Canucks have gone from seventh to second in the NHL in revenues during his time here. Yes, second. You can argue [Gillis] didn't have much to do with it, that much of the credit goes to the coaching of Alain Vigneault, the great work of the players or the marketing department, or even [chief operating officer] Victor de Bonis or ownership, and you would be able to mount an argument... But that's been the case while he's here, and any general manager or president making that kind of progress is not likely to be easily dismissed by any owner without a lot of careful thought."

Ultimately, Canucktivity was doomed by the interminable Roberto Luongo saga and the public perception it created. Without considering the backstory of no-trade clauses and "back-diving" contracts, many in the media condemned the Canucks' front office as dithering and ineffective. Luongo, too, played the role of the hurt party to a sympathetic crowd, even though he was a major architect of the delay surrounding his trade. Finally, Tortorella's inept handling of Luongo's benching at the Heritage Classic game reopened a wound that had been, for the time being, cauterized. From the moment disgruntled fans booed Lack at the B.C. Place game, Gillis was a participant in a narrative he no longer controlled.

Had any of this happened in one of the NHL backwaters in the U.S., Gillis might have ridden out the Luongo storm. Fellow general managers had managed to survive for years despite records that paled in comparison to Gillis's results. But the day-by-day, shift-by-shift mania that gripped Vancouver under his watch magnified every move Gillis made. (As happens in Toronto, Montreal, Ottawa, Edmonton, and, to a lesser degree, Calgary and Winnipeg.) He also had to placate the team's No. 1 fan, its owner, who was the recipient of much advice (wanted or not) from voices in the community.

In the end, Gillis was a victim of the expectations he'd created for himself when the Canucks came so close in the spring of 2011. "I think he just got off the road after Game 7 in 2011," says Ferraro. "He went from leading with his system to chasing the way other teams, like Boston, do it. That's what he was saying in that final radio broadcast. He'd gotten off the road."

As Gillis observed when he took the job and first encountered the cynicism surrounding the team, many of the things that matter in Vancouver don't necessarily matter to winning hockey. Blogger Harrison Mooney had a droll but telling explanation of the culture war that had played out over the previous six seasons. When Canuck fans get stressed out, explained Mooney, they go to the "panic room," a black-and-orange party room festooned with pictures of 1994 heroes Linden and Kirk McLean, where the players are free to talk to fans about the *annus mirabilis* of 1994, while stroking fans' hair gently and "telling tales of Pavel Bure's overtime winner versus Calgary. '2014 was stressful. But you're back now, safe and sound in the year 1994'." Mooney says that nostalgia for the past was threatened by the newfangled ways of the Gillis years. "This is why the Canucks needed to remove Mike Gillis in such short order. He was blocking the door to the panic room," concluded Mooney.

There would be much sniping later about "mind rooms" and "travel consultants," but none of the 20/20 hindsight invalidates the program Gillis and his staff brought to Vancouver and to the NHL. In many respects, Canucktivity was a notable achievement that outran the volatile Vancouver market for longer than many had predicted when the unknown agent was hired. Its tenets—the management of salary caps, travel, nutrition, and player development—still represent a template for a successful operation somewhere else, perhaps a city more open-minded to change than Vancouver. Gillis had said that he's not a serial GM, someone parlaying one hockey job into the next. But should he accept another opportunity, you can assume he has his plan in place for how to act. Next time, he won't be deterred from it.

AFTERWORD

———

TWO THOUSAND, two hundred, and twenty-one days after Mike Gillis was introduced as the president and general manager of the Vancouver Canucks, ushering in a most untraditional era for the sad-sack franchise, media in the B.C. city assembled for a more traditional Canucks ritual: starting over again.

In place of a *Moneyball*-style transformation, this time the 'Nucks were veering towards conventionality in the person of former NHLer Jim Benning, a career hockey-management man in Buffalo and Boston. After years of trying to be different, the Aquilinis had settled on being like everyone else again. In its latest philosophical lurch, the team was rejecting Gillis's lab coat in favour of a man who'd helped defeat the 2011 miracle team. While Benning's supporters said Trevor Linden's former Canuck teammate would bring the "Bruins model" to the Left Coast, the taciturn Alberta native simply said he couldn't define the Bruins model beyond winning. "We're going to be about hard work," Benning told the Vancouver media. "We're going to be a team here. We're going to ask our players to be selfless and play hard for one another. And us, as a management team, are going to be the same way."

For a hockey culture still steeped in the lunch-pail values of its 1982 and 1994 Stanley Cup finalists, the words about hard work and selfless players were soothing after the challenges to convention made over the previous six years (departures from the norm that might ultimately have been accepted had the 2011 team won that seventh game versus Boston). The fifty-one-year-old Benning certainly came by his old-fashioned values honestly. He had earned his chance to manage a team after apprenticing in Buffalo with Darcy Regier and in Boston with GM Peter Chiarelli. His bona fides as a player evaluator were said to be impeccable, and his experience as a player meant that he, like Gillis, understood hockey culture. He was respected in the corridors of the league's arenas, where men sip coffee and exchange opinions before practice. In a backhanded compliment, Benning professed that the problems that brought him west were not long-term issues. "Before last season," he said, "this team had, like, an attitude about them, almost a relentless attitude, that they were going to skate to wear teams down and to score. For whatever reason, that didn't happen last year."

But the job of general manager of the Vancouver Canucks is about more than accurate player evaluations and fine draft picks. The big question about Benning's suitability was not hinted at on his resumé: How would he fare as the focal point of a franchise that routinely consumed club executives? An organization that had handed its presidency to a former player and local legend who'd been selling elliptical machines the previous six years? A fan base that had never forgiven his predecessor for not winning a Game 7 in 2011?

Little in his background suggested how Benning might react when the inevitable media and fan churn in the Lower Mainland come looking for him over alleged poor trades or weak drafts. Early hints showed him to be as plainspoken as Gillis was eloquent. Linden's solution was simple: he would handle the flak. "We weren't looking for a face of the franchise," Linden said. "I wanted an individual who had a real specialized skill, was cut from the cloth of a talent evaluator, has built teams, who had been part of successful organizations and lived in a hockey environment." While hiring former team heroes to fill management posts was all the rage in the NHL in the spring of 2014, nothing suggested this hydra-headed model would survive the reality of daily business. (Assistant GM Laurence Gilman and director of player personnel Lorne Henning were retained for the foreseeable future.)

In hiring his former teammate, Linden then took a veiled swipe at the high-tech Gillis approach. "I think Jim comes from a place where there were no titles and no egos, and he just wants to roll up his sleeves and have a real good dynamic with his group and go to work. At the end of the day, he's going to be able to shape that group and shape the organization."

Part of the shaping included hiring a first-time coach, Willie Desjardins (a successful junior and minor-league coach who'd also coached Canada's national junior men). Benning's first personnel move looked a lot like Gillis's last move: trading Ryan Kesler. Given a freer hand to deal the big centre than Gillis had been allowed at the trade deadline, Benning flipped Kesler to Anaheim for promising forward Nick Bonino, defenceman Luca Sbisa, and a first-round pick in the 2014 draft.

"We don't want somebody who doesn't want to be here," Benning said upon moving Kesler, who had fumed about losing his status as an assistant captain in 2014.

Was the Ducks' deal better than what Pittsburgh had offered at the deadline? Few thought so. "The sad irony of the package they did wind up getting is that they were reportedly being offered a better one from the same team back at the deadline," said the website CanucksArmy.com.

Benning also moved out defenceman Jason Garrison, who'd had a tough time under Tortorella, helping to free more cap space for the summer. With two picks in the first round again, Benning selected impressive prospects Jake Virtanen and Jared McCann, augmenting the base left to him by Gillis.

But impressive draft picks alone would not soothe the beast that is Vancouver's hockey culture. Gillis had consistently tried to defuse those emotions with his low-key public persona. But even his phlegmatic strategy couldn't survive a fan base so tortured and apprehensive that success seemed to be a burden to be endured, not a joy to behold. Having grown up resigned to forty-plus years of mediocrity, handling success is not yet in the Canuck fans' DNA. After turning on the greatest Canucks team ever assembled (rioting when they lost Game 7 in the 2011 final), the fan base knew what it didn't want. What it *does* want from Aquilini, Linden, Benning, and Desjardins is harder to define. But after forsaking the bold tenets of Canucktivity, the future of Aquilini's ownership of the Canucks is counting on predictable and proven being the answer.